ONCE
Through the
HEART

•

Ralph Blumenthal

SIMON & SCHUSTER

NEW YORK LONDON TORONTO SYDNEY TOKYO SINGAPORE

SIMON & SCHUSTER
Simon & Schuster Building
Rockefeller Center
1230 Avenue of the Americas
New York, New York 10020

Copyright © 1992 by Ralph Blumenthal

SIMON & SCHUSTER and colophon are registered trademarks
of Simon & Schuster Inc.

Designed by Karolina Harris
Manufactured in the United States of America

1   3   5   7   9   10   8   6   4   2

Library of Congress Cataloging-in-Publication Data

Blumenthal, Ralph.
Once through the heart / Ralph Blumenthal.
p.   cm.
1. DeGregorio, Pat.   2. Narcotic enforcement agents—New York
(N.Y.)—Biography.   3. Narcotics and crime—New York (N.Y.)—Case
studies.   4. Undercover operations—New York (N.Y.)—Case studies.
I. Title.
HV7911.D437B58   1992
364.1'77'097471—dc20   92-27944
CIP
ISBN: 0-671-70750-7

For Tommy and Joe
who were pulled from the game too soon
and for
Sophie Rose
who was sent in for them

Prologue

THE car was a small lox-colored Chevy Nova, what cops called a shitbox, and it was sitting in the city parking lot on Union Street in Flushing, blocked by a radio car whose driver had disappeared somewhere inside the One Hundred and Ninth precinct station house across the street. Detective Patrick DeGregorio, who had just emerged from the squat beige station house, cursed his luck. He fumbled in his jeans for his keys and opened the door far enough to reach in and pound the horn, four long pathetic bleats that reverberated in the heat of this August afternoon in 1988.

DeGregorio, a bulky man of forty who slouched as if embarrassed by the 195 pounds he carried on his six-foot frame, was in no mood to wait. He wanted to get home. He had already pissed off his sergeant who wanted him to pick up half a dozen homeless from the shelter for a robbery lineup. They'd made a collar, the victim had come in to make an ID, and the lineup needed fillers. DeGregorio had bitched. He had done his eight-to-four and wanted to be out of there.

Not long ago he would have welcomed the overtime, but not now; too much was going on in his life. He wanted to get home. He fobbed off the detail, riling the others, who plainly thought that DeGregorio, having come from narcotics, felt he was too good for robbery. Cops were always sticking it to each other, delighting when they hit a nerve. DeGregorio had settled the matter by muttering a "fuck you" and walking out.

His beeping finally attracted the attention of the radio car driver, a young rookie who now sauntered out of the station house and across the parking lot. DeGregorio gave him a scorching look. "You know, kid," he said, "when I had your time, if I had double-parked this fucking police car, I wouldn't have been allowed inside it for six months."

The rookie seemed unimpressed. "Right, pops," he said, then got in and lurched ahead a few car lengths with the door held open.

Disgustedly, DeGregorio swiped a hand through the thick hair that stuck up like porcupine quills off a center part. The lot was emptying out. Shoppers who had flocked to the busy Main Street stores and Korean markets earlier in the day were drifting home to air conditioning, Oprah, and dinner. DeGregorio squeezed himself into his little Chevy and followed them out.

He was back where he'd started as a cop fifteen years before when his shield was silver and he walked a footpost in the one-oh-nine. Now his badge was the gold of the New York Police Department's detective division and no longer worn for the world to see on his uniform, but secreted in his wallet. His weapon, too, did not hang visibly on his hip but was strapped to his right ankle under his pants. His uniform was jeans and a T-shirt or jacket and tie, whatever he wanted it to be that day. His promotion to plainclothes hadn't been without cost. In between had come three difficult years in narcotics, including a year under cover inside a Mafia-sponsored drug ring, a daring exploit that had won him a citation from the director of the FBI and, ultimately, his detective's shield.

The Clearview Expressway was already bumper to bumper. He drummed the wheel impatiently, hoping the Northern State Parkway was better. At the thought of home he felt a spasm of uneasiness. Things had been so crazy lately, who knew what was waiting for him? Then he remembered the milk. They had run out. He'd pick some up at the 7-Eleven.

Like many New York cops, DeGregorio made his home in the suburbs. Aside from the fact that the better neighborhoods of New York were priced out of reach, there was something about living among the people they were policing that seemed to turn many cops off, especially white cops. Enough was enough. At the end of their tour they liked to leave the carnage behind.

The town of Kings Park was forty miles east, in Suffolk County on Long Island's north shore. In a typical suburban subdivision, in a plain cedar-shingled house with a backyard pool, DeGregorio lived with his slim, red-haired second wife, Barbara, who was also a detective, and Mary Anne, his sixteen-year-old daughter by his first wife. Their street, a tree-lined drive off a town park, was a family affair. Next door to DeGregorio, Barbara, and Mary Anne, in a similar brick-trimmed ranch, also with a pool, lived DeGregorio's parents, Joe and Anne. And on the other side of them, in another cedar-trimmed ranch with a little portico and no pool, lived one of DeGregorio's three younger brothers, Ralph, with his wife and three sons. It seemed to say to the world: Look how close a family we DeGregorios are.

He thought of the milk again, wondering if Barbara might already have picked it up, then realized she wouldn't. Even in normal times he did most of the shopping, so now she didn't remember anything. She'd hardly be worrying about groceries, he thought. They'd been fighting a lot lately about Mary Anne, and he'd be lucky if she came home at all.

The Northern State was clear and he sped through, thankful yet queasy with a dread that had begun to overtake him every day as he approached home. After the Northport exit he noticed, as he did each time, how the forest seemed to rise up and swallow the road. It was a beautiful stretch; the name Northport no longer carried the associations it once had for him, the place where he and his first wife, Mary, had settled right after their marriage. At the green Kings Park sign he peeled off in a wide arcing turn, then exited again at Indian Head Road which, unless you knew it was coming up, you could easily overshoot. Speeding now, he drove past the big church auditorium and a new subdivision rising nakedly out of bulldozed land: Country Woods. The Kings Park Knights of Columbus and the Boy Scouts welcomed him, then Tennis Time and the Superior Ice Rink with its posted skating sessions reminding him of the weekend nights he used to drop Mary Anne off to hang out with her friends. He barely saw the winking lights of the Kings Park Plaza mall off to the left before he clattered over the Long Island Rail Road tracks and turned right at the firehouse in the center of town. Behind him lay the four blocks of Main Street, a toy-scale village receding in his rearview mirror.

A stone marker on the left pointed the way through the woods to the sprawling Kings Park Psychiatric Center, built a century ago to serve what was then the separate city of Brooklyn. The grounds, along with the population, had shrunk dramatically over the decades, chunks having been sold off for a nature preserve, a church, a Jewish center, and the junior high school where Mary Anne had gone after they moved here. He couldn't see the sign without thinking of Mary's brother, Tommy, who had worked there as a groundskeeper. He smiled despite himself, imagining Tommy hiding his bottles in the hospital bushes. Poor Tommy. It wasn't his fault, it was a disease—like Mary's. Only it killed him.

As the car mounted a rise, he caught a sweeping view of the high school's green fields with their white soccer nets and football goalposts, and beyond, the school building with its name scrawled like the logo on a tacky Italian catering hall, he thought. At the traffic light at Popeii's Clam Bar he started to swing right reflexively into the crosshatch of his suburban development when he once again remembered the milk and swerved to continue straight. He skimmed past the little shopping center across the road, a row of stores he had long since memorized: Romeo's Pizzeria, Cleanwell Cleaners, the delicatessen, and Legend Pharmacy with its big blue electric sign, DRUGS. Ahead he could see the 7-Eleven just past the Getty station.

He was about to flip down the left turn signal when his eye caught a gray van stopped halfway down the street. It was Ivy Lane, a dead end. There was something haphazard about the way the van jutted from the side of the road between the pharmacy and Dee's Ceramics, as if it had pulled over abruptly. A bunch of teens clustered around the van. Were they just hanging out? he wondered. Why there of all places on a hot summer afternoon? Had something happened?

Telling himself that cops were paid to be curious, he spun the wheel into a U-turn at the gas station and drove into Ivy Lane. To his surprise the kids scattered, melting into the parking lots and weedy fields at the end of the road. The gray van started up and sped past him. It screeched to the corner, veered right at a stop sign, and disappeared west on 25A.

One figure was left standing there, a girl with teased blond hair, a broad, heart-shaped face, and puckered bow lips. She saw him now too and was staring at him as if in a trance.

He threw the car into park, jerking it to a stop, and leaped out. By her feet was a paper bag. As he picked it up, he tried to tell himself he had expected this, that he knew this would happen, that he had wanted it to happen. He looked inside the bag, quickly closed it again, and let it drop to the ground. In disgust he kicked it away. "Get in the car!" he ordered. He wrenched open the passenger-side door and shoved her, unresisting, inside.

Should he toss her? he asked himself. Pat her down for whatever else she might be carrying? But he wasn't on the job now, he thought; it wasn't his turf. He didn't work there, he lived there.

He lurched the car backward and forward into a tight turn in the narrow street, then sped to the corner, turned right at the stop sign and then left again quickly at the light into the meandering grid of houses and lawns. The hum of traffic receded. The silence of the suburban lanes was broken only by the swish of automatic sprinklers and the distant barking of a dog. This was what his parents and now he had come here for, this encompassing peace, this refuge from a mayhem he was happy to leave behind at the end of his tour. Here he'd resolved to raise his family in their little enclave of front lawns, backyards, nearby kinfolk, and like-thinking neighbors, a life like episodes of "Father Knows Best," one of his all-time favorite TV shows. They were his idols, the engagingly plastic Andersons. Imagine, he'd often marveled, a family that never bellowed or spilled wine over the dinner table, never walked around the house in pajamas, and in the space of half an hour cheerfully resolved every crisis.

The intersections were posted with four-way stop signs, but he barely slowed, hurtling through with only darting sideways glances. Neither of them spoke. Skirting the park he saw a batter popping flies to the outfield, and he thought automatically of Tommy, *his* Tommy. Tommy had loved playing ball. Tommy would be what today? Twelve? No, he calculated quickly, thirteen. What would Tommy say now about this if he knew? And where he was, DeGregorio reassured himself, Tommy would know everything.

He pulled into the asphalt driveway of his house and shut off the engine. As he walked ahead to the front door, he prayed that he was right about Barbara's schedule, that she would not be home. From behind the door came a furious scratching and howling. A hundred-pound ball of tawny fur hurled itself at him the moment he entered the house. Delirious with joy, Buddy, a three-year-old golden Labrador retriever, panted and slobbered for attention, but DeGregorio barked a stern command and pointed inside. Buddy obediently retraced his steps and with a few whimpers of protest resettled himself under the kitchen table.

Buddy was alone. The house was empty, as DeGregorio had hoped. He waited for her to enter, then slammed the door and followed her through the dim hall into the Harvest Gold kitchen. It must have been a big color in the fifties or sixties, DeGregorio often thought.

He paced while she dropped listlessly into one of the blue wooden chairs around the oak table. Through the window he caught a glimpse of the top of the pool slide, glowing turquoise from the water. Wordlessly, he swept aside a pile of paper napkins, a box of Entenmann's cake with icing, and a pair of salt and pepper shakers with wildlife scenes. He reached over and took her black pocketbook from her unresisting grasp. He upended it on the table, spilling out change, some crumpled bills, compact, lipstick, keys, and a tangle of gold necklaces, rings, and bracelets.

He was puffing up with rage now. He knew that was what it did to him, making him look like a cartoon figure, with eyes popping out of his head. Choking with fury, he thought for a moment that he could kill her. He had his gun. He could just shoot her.

She seemed to read his mind. Her eyes widened in terror. Or was she just pretending, playing for sympathy, getting over on him as she had gotten over on all of them for so long?

Only now did he surrender his last illusions and admit the truth of what had been staring him in the face for so long, what Barbara and his brother Ralph had been trying to tell him, what even his partner Mike had intuited. For just a moment his writhing mind grasped for another explanation. She was holding it for someone else. It was some sort of practical joke, a setup by his enemies. But he knew it was futile. Of course it was hers. The signs had been there all along, plenty of them, and he had ignored them. As a cop—a good cop; why bullshit himself, he knew he was good—he would have picked up on the same signals on the street in a flash. But what was he at home? Deaf, dumb, and blind?

The mad fury that had consumed him a moment earlier passed, replaced by a sickening realization. She hadn't betrayed him. He had betrayed himself. Once again his life was in ruins, this time by no hand but his own. He had deluded himself into believing that the curse which had shadowed him for so long had been lifted. Obviously, he had been wrong. Only this time he had done it to himself.

He had seen what was in the paper bag. To someone who had spent years making buys on the street, it was unmistakable: Ziploc bags of brownish dried leaves, tiny purple pills rolled in newspaper, sheets of white paper with strange cartoon decals—marijuana, mescaline, LSD.

Now what? he asked himself. What was he supposed to do, bust his own daughter for drugs?

PART
One
·

1

WHEN he reached back for the good times—and through everything he could remember the good times—Patrick DeGregorio remembered summer nights in Coram when he would scoop her out of bed in her pajamas and bundle her into the backyard to look at the stars. On moonless nights the sky vaulting over the distant ocean was tar-black, dusted with talcum powder. He didn't wait for Mary Anne to ask. He asked her what she thought was up there. They sat in the dewy darkness, faces crooked to the heavens, picking out faint pinpoint images that they turned into stories of saints and monsters and fairies, angels and flowers and cats.

He remembered a precinct football game on a sunny Saturday afternoon. Mary Anne toddled around in a blue T-shirt from the eight-three that hung on her like a dress. He remembered taking her to feed the ducks at a pond in Old Setaucket. They always stopped on the way to buy a loaf of white bread at a market. Mary Anne wadded the bread in her thick little fingers and squealed with delight when the ducks and geese and swans flapped around her, fighting for the scattered offerings. She didn't even seem to mind when they nipped her slow-moving hands. Often, too, he remembered, he took her to the Long Island Animal Park, where he could still see her chasing the fawns, hugging them fiercely as they lunged for the feeding bottles of milk she waved. She was fearless and self-confident, a brash, round-faced urchin with a pug nose, deep-set black beads for eyes, her mother's flaxen hair, and his full lips. Once, he could remember, she found him cleaning some mackerel their neighbor Frank had brought over from his boat. "I want to!" she announced excitedly. DeGregorio carefully placed his hand around hers on the sharp knife and guided her wild slashes through the messy fish guts. Squeamishness was not in her makeup. She scrapped at football and baseball like a boy. But she also loved Barbie dolls, dressing up, and going to parties. "You know, Mary Anne," he used to tell her, "girls can do everything *and* look pretty. Boys can't do that."

DeGregorio doted on Mary Anne, and while for many years he was not able to provide her with what every child needs most, a stable home, he did what many parents instinctively do in such circumstances: He sought to compensate by turning up the flame of his affection, indulging her every fancy to reassure her of his devotion and, perhaps, assuage his own guilt. She, in turn, came to adore him as a giant, shaggy-haired playmate who roared with laughter and sometimes, to her amazement, also cried real tears. It was a mutual adoration, deep and tender, an alliance against a domestic breakdown they were struggling to overcome. They grew closer than father and daughter. They were partners in survival, soulmates, and, to a point, confidants; she came to confide in him things that other girls would tell their mothers. He became her mother as well as her father. And she was his everything.

On the job DeGregorio concealed his sensitive, impressionable nature under an armor of macho gruffness, but his fellow cops, expert at unmasking vulnerabilities, found him out soon enough. He was a "bleeding heart," some kind of *liberal* who felt sorry for people, who was actually against the death penalty. Unashamed, he taunted them back, saying, Sure, you want to kill people, so kill people but it wasn't going to solve the problem. Why not just arrest all the people who couldn't read and write? he asked. Didn't it amount to the same thing? He was hard to make out. He had a large curved nose like a shark's snout that seemed to point him relentlessly in search of prey. But what might have been a savage profile was softened by warm brown eyes, a crinkled smile, and sensuous, finely carved lips.

He had always dreamed of a daughter. Most men wanted sons, or so he assumed, but he had his heart set first of all on a daughter, a little girl he could cuddle and fuss over. It was hard for him to explain. Why should he even have to? Any man who had a daughter would understand, he figured; those who didn't probably wouldn't. It could have had to do with Luisa. His sister had been the only girl among four boys in the DeGregorio household, a particularly treasured and pampered member of the family. As the eldest, Patrick became Luisa's chief protector, glorying in the responsibility and the pride he felt when she looked up to him. Mary Anne, when she arrived, evoked the same rush of proprietary love. Perhaps, he thought, she could even save the marriage. But he soon realized that children, however much they make a good marriage better, only make a bad marriage worse.

For sure, DeGregorio often thought later, there ought to be a law against marrying at twenty. What did anybody know at twenty? What did he know? His university, like his father's before him, was Luke Spano's, the neighborhood soda fountain in Bensonhurst, where learning took place on the red leatherette stools along a chrome-trimmed counter sticky with egg cream and malted slopovers. Down the street was his great-uncle Dominick's Italian-American fruit and vegetable market, and at the end of the block, his home, a two-story redbrick house adjoining a plot of garden land, a property that his grandfather Pasquale had bought in 1939, seven years after immigrating with his family from Italy.

Patrick had spent what seemed like a large part of his youth under Spano's green awning listening to Luke hold forth on the forbidden mysteries of women, while fantasizing about getting Luke's daughter Margaret alone in the stockroom. Luke, however, kept a wary eye out, and if he missed Margaret for even a moment, he would shout out her name, summoning her to reappear, quickly and innocently, to lay her father's suspicions to rest. Thus reassured, Lukie would make sure she was out of earshot, park himself on the stool next to young Patrick, and confide in a hoarse whisper: "The best thing you'll ever get from a woman is this. . . ." Patrick blushed crimson to the tips of his protruding ears, scandalized, yet treasuring the secret and embellishing it luridly later at the Wednesday night confraternity dances in the cavernous Shrine Church of St. Bernadette, where the boys all wore white shirts and red ties and had to dance at least six inches away from the girls, as measured by nuns with rulers. Alas, he was stuck with his hormones and his fantasies. Biology and a stubborn social code were setting him up for a debacle. Intimacy had its price. It was called marriage.

• • •

He had spotted her a few times at St. Joseph's, a massive fortress, intimidating in its neo-Gothic starkness, that rose up not far from the psychiatric hospital grounds a few blocks from the center of Kings Park. His parents attended an early mass. Eighteen-year-old Patrick preferred to sleep later and drive over himself in the 1960 black Impala he was so proud of, a gift from his grandfather Pasquale. He wore clean jeans, a clean shirt, and hair wet-combed into a rolling pompadour.

On this fall Sunday in 1966, Patrick saw her again, standing near him in a rear pew. She was blond and blue-eyed, about sixteen, tall and thin with pale, translucent skin. He sneaked glances at her and thought of a word that took his breath away: *Scandinavian.* She looked *Scandinavian.* He sensed, too, that she was nice in some wholesome, approachable way. After all, she was in church. He had watched her for the last four Sundays, and each time he wanted to talk to her but no opportunity presented itself. This time, though, he waited until mass was over and followed her out through the huge arched doors into the October sunshine.

He blurted a few words, and she turned and smiled. Emboldened, he fell into step beside her, asking her name—it was Mary, she said—and almost before he knew what he was saying, he invited her to lunch. He drove her proudly up Main Street, past the meat market, the pet shop, Carvel, and Cheap John's, to the Longhorn Diner, where he ran around and opened the car door for her.

They chatted a little stiffly about the town, people they knew in common, their families. Her family was Dutch. She was going to become a hairdresser, she told him. He heard a little about her sorrows, her fatherless childhood, and drew the wrong conclusions. She had to be strong, he thought, a survivor.

After lunch he drove her home to a garden apartment close to the church. He took her telephone number and promised to call her soon. He kept his word. They went out on a few Saturday nights, and she invited him to a Halloween party. Then suddenly they were dating regularly.

It was his first deep relationship and nothing like what Lukie had said. Lukie had made it sound dirty and, from what he'd been able to see until he met Mary, it was, kind of. The dark animal urgency, furious groping in the backseat of his Impala. But this was nothing like that. This was magical, pure, intoxicating, and blinding. Mary always stopped him before they went too far. They would have to wait, she insisted primly, heightening his anticipation, his admiration for her purity.

In the vague way teenagers have, Patrick told his parents about Mary and thought of bringing her home. But how, he wondered, would she react to his chaotic houseful of clamorous and possessive DeGregorios? Kids of all ages were constantly underfoot, and relatives were always dropping in for uproarious family feasts. And how would his parents, Joe and Anne, react to her? He crossed his fingers and hoped for the best. To his relief Joe and Anne seemed to accept Mary easily, but how could they not? He had met Mary, after all, at St. Joseph's. What could be more proper? They continued dating through the winter and the following year.

Then on a Saturday morning in 1968, at his suggestion, they drove into the city to the Busch Jewelry Company store on West Fourteenth Street, the Tiffany of the workingman. He invited Mary to scan the showcase and pick out a diamond engagement ring. She settled on a quarter-carat ring for $400. He put down two twenties and took the ring and a bunch of little envelopes to mail in his weekly payments. Only afterward did he tell his parents he was getting married.

Joe was appalled. It was nothing against Mary, he told his son, but Patrick was too young, not yet twenty. Why the girl herself was only eighteen! He had gone through this before with Patrick, in a different way. When Patrick was seventeen he had showed up with a Navy recruiter who just needed a parent's signature and he could be off to see the world. Joe, though torn, was almost ready to agree. He handed Anne the pen, but she went into hysterics and refused to sign. Later Joe thanked her for it. He wasn't going to make the same mistake twice. "I could break your head!" Joe stormed at Patrick. "You got no stability, no future. You're only a machinist!"

The wedding was at the hulking St. Joseph's, where they had met. Afterward the DeGregorios hosted a reception for a hundred and fifty relatives and friends at the Villa Pace in Smithtown. Mary was radiant in a white gown and a lace veil that mysteriously shrouded her delicate features. DeGregorio, in a white dinner jacket, thought she had never looked more beautiful. Guests plied them with the traditional envelopes of cash, and after the party, bride and groom roared off in the Impala for a week's honeymoon at the Mount Airy Lodge in the Poconos.

They came back to a basement apartment they had rented for $130 a month in a two-family house in a poorer section of Kings Park. Mary furnished it with a Formica kitchen set and some colonial pieces. She selected a sofa with gold upholstery and a bright red rug. DeGregorio thought the effect was a bit garish, but he left the decor to her, even after he saw his parents cringe when they came to visit.

Mary, DeGregorio knew, bridled at her in-laws' outspoken ways. She knew nothing of large immigrant Italian families, where privacy fell victim to a raucous communal life and the most personal questions were argued around the dinner table. The DeGregorios loved meetings; there were meetings to decide everything. Mary called it meddling. DeGregorio felt caught in the middle. He was used to his family's ways but could see how they exasperated Mary. He took her side; she was his wife. He told his parents to back off.

But other tensions he barely acknowledged were gnawing at them. Mary had told him a little about her father, an alcoholic who had been thrown out by her mother, also named Mary, and about her brother Tommy and his addiction to drinking. DeGregorio had been awed by her seeming resilience. She had seen and overcome so much. The memories of his happy home, in contrast, almost shamed him. But he told himself she had overcome her adversity. The triumph had to have strengthened her.

At first, she kept away from alcohol—she had seen too much of its abuse, she said. But as they went out to parties and bars, she began ordering drinks. And then she began drinking more and alcohol quickly soured her mood, he saw that. They usually had a cocktail hour in the evening, and she often became angry and argumentative. He shrugged it off. So maybe marriage wasn't all it was cracked up to be. What else was new? He was prepared for a little letdown after the high of the wedding and the move into a new place.

After a year in Kings Park they found a larger apartment in East Northport. It was further away from Joe and Anne, which De-

Gregorio figured would please Mary. Still, he couldn't keep his parents away, although every visit was preceded by an argument.

Joe absorbed the anger and the drinking without comment, but Anne, in her relentless, maternal way, felt compelled to intervene. She told her son that something wasn't right, that Mary needed help. DeGregorio defended Mary, telling his mother things would take care of themselves. But to her son's dismay, Anne sometimes took her daughter-in-law aside and pleaded well-meaningly, "Mary, you're such a lovely child, get some help." That only fed Mary's resentment against her in-laws and sparked conflict between DeGregorio and his mother. DeGregorio patched it up afterward and convinced himself that there was nothing basically wrong.

They tried to have a child early, but Mary suffered two miscarriages. Then, in 1971, after nearly three years of trying, Mary had a healthy pregnancy.

That was what was lacking, DeGregorio told himself, a child to anchor the marriage, to strengthen their bond. It was what children did. In fact, he noticed, Mary's mood did brighten. She seemed to have stopped drinking, and even smoking. As her time grew near, DeGregorio told himself he knew what it would be. It would be a girl. He had always wanted a girl.

They would have to move, that was clear. The apartment would be too cramped for the three of them. He was working in construction now and had met a builder who was putting up homes all over the Island. He picked out a model he liked and scouted an open one-third-acre site on a cul de sac in wooded acreage by a bird sanctuary in Coram. The house and land were reasonable enough, $27,000, but it was still a stretch for them. Joe chipped in some of the $3,000 down payment, and DeGregorio arranged to spend his own time working on the house, which lowered the cost a little. In the end they gulped and signed the papers for a mortgage payment of $265 a month. To save money they gave up their apartment and, a week before the baby was due, moved into Joe and Anne's finished basement. Mary grumbled about being beholden to her in-laws. Anne wanted to run everything, Mary complained. She felt Anne resented her because she wasn't Italian. DeGregorio promised the boarding was just for a few months, until the house was ready.

Patrick drove Mary to St. John's Hospital in Smithtown on a Saturday in May in 1972, the day before Mother's Day, and waited nervously outside the delivery room. It was a long and difficult labor. When the baby had not yet come by the early hours of the morning, he drove, bleary-eyed, to his parents' house where, at nine o'clock, he was awakened with the news. He had a daughter.

He rushed back to the hospital and peered through the nursery window, frantically scanning the rows of swaddled newborns until he spotted a basinette with a cute pink sign, I AM A GIRL, and the scrawled name, DEGREGORIO, MARY ANNE. A nurse saw him waving and making faces and hoisted the baby for him to admire. He stared, enraptured, at the wrinkled little face topped with a fuzz of downy blond hair. His daughter. He felt a stinging in his eyes as they moistened with tears.

They had named her for her two grandmothers, Mary and Anne. As the hospital's first Mother's Day baby of the year, she received a silver cup-and-spoon set. She was a strong, healthy newborn of six pounds, fulfilling every prayer he had had for a daughter. After visiting Mary, who was exhausted and only wanted to sleep, De-Gregorio got to hold Mary Anne. He picked her up delicately, as if afraid she might break, and rocked her gently, humming a tune. Then, feeling there was little else for him to do there, he drove home to join his Kings Park softball team in a big game against Smithtown. He saw nothing strange in that.

Mary suffered severe postpartum depression. As DeGregorio looked on helplessly, she moped around the house, edgy and irritable. She couldn't be touched and wouldn't be consoled. He found it difficult to understand, he was so happy. The doctors explained it was a chemical thing that happened to women.

Mary had decided not to nurse, so DeGregorio and his parents were able to prepare some of the bottles and help with the feedings, particularly the night wakings when Mary sometimes couldn't get up. Anne told her son she suspected there was more to it. There was something wrong with Mary. He resisted the suggestion. She had never liked his wife, DeGregorio told himself, she was exaggerating.

In September, after four difficult months, the house in Coram was finally ready, and DeGregorio moved the family in, glad at last to be out of his parents' house for Mary's sake if nothing else. After months as boarders they were thrilled to be in their own home, simple as it was. The front door opened onto a foyer, the living room was on the right, and the kitchen was straight ahead. Past the kitchen to the right was the dining room, a small den, and down a hallway, a line of three bedrooms. The one-car garage had its own outside entrance. They put down their red carpet and moved in with a new, heavy Spanish oak chest, a Spanish dining set with red velvet chairs and the gold-upholstered sofa, hung a wooden globe chandelier and pronounced themselves home.

DeGregorio felt a great burden lifted. Even Mary seemed sunnier. They reveled in their rediscovered privacy. Mary Anne had her own room and a backyard to crawl and, soon, toddle around in. But once the novelty passed, familiar strains resurfaced. Mary resumed drinking, which DeGregorio could tell from her erratic mood swings. He never actually saw her drink a lot, but even a drink or two of Seagram's, the whiskey she liked best, seemed to affect her. How had he not noticed that before? he wondered. Was it something she'd started after they got married, or had she always had trouble handling alcohol and he had just refused to see it?

Anne told him she'd dropped in unannounced a few times to visit and found Mary Anne in a sopping diaper, while Mary seemed dazed and preoccupied. Anne said she'd tried to draw her out, but Mary irritably shook off her questions.

Anne also said she'd gotten calls from a friend next door to the DeGregorios who was worried for Mary Anne. It impelled Anne, she told her son, to visit Mary's mother and plead with her to seek help for her daughter. "You're the mother, I'm just the mother-in-law," Anne related. "You've got to get her some help." The mother reacted coolly, Anne reported, saying she didn't know about any problem. But she must have talked to her daughter because later Mary unleashed her fury on DeGregorio. Torn between his mother and his wife, he sided with Mary. "What do you mean, talking about my wife like that?" he angrily demanded of his mother.

2

DEGREGORIO joined the police as an afterthought, a whim. No one in his family had ever been on the job, as cops say, as if there were only one job worth mentioning. Not that any DeGregorios had tried. In the Irish-rooted and tradition-bound NYPD of the thirties, when the DeGregorios first settled in Brooklyn, shields were customarily passed down through generations of O'Sullivans, McCarthys, and Boyles, and a DeGregorio in blue would have been a suspect curiosity.

In later years many in Italian Bensonhurst seethed over a sense of victimization that in the world beyond Bensonhurst their names equated them somehow with Mafiosi such as Joe Colombo—in fact, one of the more popular of the local Bath Avenue boys. It was a time of angry griping about discrimination, a time of *The Godfather*, Mafia frenzy in the press, and raucous protest marches against the FBI by Colombo's Italian-American Civil Rights League. Yet at the same time the police emblemized the forces of authority; they were therefore deserving of respect.

Joe had begun instilling it in Patrick the day they were out walking and came across an unruly drunk in the street. The boy was frightened. Joe took him in hand. "I'm going to show you what you do about that," he said, leading Patrick to the precinct house where they reported it. "These are the people you tell," he instructed his son.

If anything, Patrick grew up with too high a regard for the police. They had to be geniuses, he thought. Didn't they have to know all the laws by heart? For an indifferent student who lived to play ball in the schoolyard, not sit imprisoned in a classroom, it seemed like too much to learn. Anyway, parents were the real police of Bensonhurst. Their justice was swifter and harsher than the law's and more terrifying than jail. Grown-ups exercised automatic dominion over all children and were empowered to mete out discipline at will.

A comforting order ruled the familiar streets. The mailboxes read Alba, Battistoni, Cucchiara, Fiannini, Labozetta, Sammartino, Valenentinetti, Zampino, with only an occasional Gallinovitch and Gottesman sprinkled in. Everyone knew everyone. Many hailed from the same towns and villages outside Naples, and life unfolded under the watchful gaze of women in black at second-story windows. At dinnertime the tables were similarly set: *zuppa di fagioli con la pasta, spaghetti alla carbonara, scaloppine al Marsala,* with jelly glasses of red wine from straw-covered gallon jugs or bottles of Manhattan Special, coffee and sugar water with a slight carbonation. Outside the groceries, mozzarella smoked on sidewalk braziers. Green store awnings shaded the streets, the fragrance of burning garlic hung perpetually over the stoops, and each fall the planted fig trees were faithfully wrapped against winter's chill.

As a schoolboy Patrick was tall and ungainly, goofy-looking, with protruding ears, a chipped front tooth, and a rakish pompadour. Mornings, running across Fifteenth Avenue to school, he was sometimes stopped to have his tie straightened by his friend Anthony's father. Sometimes Mister Carraturo—and Patrick needed to remember the *Mister* or risk a slap—caught him sneaking a cigarette and made him stub it out and eat it. And if he was crazy enough to complain to his father, Joe would make him eat *two* cigarettes. On the other hand, his grandmother—Joe's plump, round-faced mother, Angelina—often took Patrick's side. It was like having twenty or thirty fathers and mothers. Mostly, the grown-ups stuck together. Everyone knew the rules, and they were the same for everybody. It was often harsh but was what they expected so nobody noticed, and it kept life simple in a simple time.

By tradition he should have been christened Pasquale, after his grandfather, but Joe had proudly Americanized the name of his firstborn son to Patrick, dumbfounding Pasquale. *"Che Patricka?"* Pasquale demanded, mouthing the harsh Anglo syllables with distaste. *"Io mi chiamo Pasquale!"* What the hell kind of a name was Patrick? Tradition was important to the DeGregorios. One of Joe's younger brothers, Dominick—named after his uncle, a brother of Pasquale—had claimed the right to name his firstborn son after Pasquale. But Joe, the eldest, insisted the honor was his. After all, he had been named Giuseppe after *his* grandfather, Pasquale's father, a peasant farmer from Cervinara, a farming town in the Campania countryside outside Naples. Joe won out. But when it came to actually naming his son, Joe, who had boldly Americanized his own name during the war, pulled a switch. "I'm not going to hang a moniker like Pasquale on him," he told people—but not, of course, his father.

Pasquale DeGregorio was born in the last year of the nineteenth century, one of the generation doomed to be raked like dry leaves into the bonfire of the Great War. The name, it was said in the family, was derived from Gregory, a Greek word for "watchful" and the name chosen by a line of early popes. The family's house, squalid and primitive, lay on a road outside Cervinara, with low windows open to the prying glances of passersby. His father, Giuseppe, a mustachioed red-haired giant standing well over six feet tall, barely eked a living from the unforgiving land. But he was stubborn. When he took ill late in his life, he waved off the doctor's dietary warnings. "If I am going to die, I am going to eat what I want," he insisted, and in fact ate his way to recuperation.

From the age of thirteen, manhood in the countryside, Pasquale had a sweetheart, fourteen-year-old Angelina Mainolfi next door. The youngest of four children, she was two when her mother died giving birth to a fifth child. Her father had run for the doctor, and when he returned to find the lifeless body of his wife, he keeled over, dead of a heart attack. Angelina and her brothers were split up with neighbors for upbringing. The family who adopted Angelina lived two houses from the DeGregorios, and as teenagers Angelina and Pasquale began keeping company. After Italy entered the war against Germany and Austria-Hungary in 1915, Pasquale joined the army. He ran away once to visit Angelina. "I don't care what they do to me," he told her, "as long as I can see you." Caught, he was ignominiously shorn of his hair and sent back to the field.

After the war, unscathed and discharged with ceremonial medals, Pasquale returned to Cervinara and Angelina. Their son, Giuseppe, who would later call himself Joe, was born in 1922. They were not married. To escape the fury of Angelina's stepfather, Pasquale fled to America. Left behind with her baby, Angelina survived as a washerwoman, taking in the laundry of townspeople to wash in the mountains. But her strength was failing and she begged Pasquale to come home, saying she could no longer provide for their son. Pasquale returned the following year, flush with money earned as a stonemason in Brooklyn. He married Angelina and swept her and little Joe off to Naples and an unacknowledged honeymoon in Venice. Six months later they left Italy for America, this time together.

In New York, Pasquale, Angelina, and Joe gravitated to Bensonhurst, crowded with immigrant Italians, where Pasquale hoped to renew his contacts. They found lodging on the top floor of a three-family house on Thirteenth Avenue. The tenants shared a single hall bathroom, which Angelina cleaned for a little off the rent. Pasquale found work again as a stonemason. Before the year was out, two-year-old Joe had a baby sister. They named her Antoinette. Three years later a restless Pasquale withdrew his nest egg of $2,000 and sailed with his family back to Italy. He was homesick for Cervinara and curious about the powerful new leader they called Il Duce who seemed destined to redeem Rome's lost glory. It was a thrilling time to be home. Joe joined the youth arm of the Black Shirts, learning to march and dreaming a boy's dreams of soldiering. They stayed several years before Pasquale decided that America was where they belonged after all. They sailed back to New York in 1932 aboard the swift new *Conte di Savoia,* pride of the Fascist passenger fleet.

This time conditions were different when they returned to Bensonhurst. The country had plunged into the abyss of the Great Depression. Construction work was scarce. Pasquale couldn't find a job. He was furious with himself. The savings he had squandered on the trip to Italy would have bought them a comfortable house. Instead they were back where they started. Pasquale went on the dole. Eventually he was able to buy an old truck to peddle vegetables. They lived for a while in a two-family house owned by a second cousin of Pasquale's and then a succession of unheated tenements and railroad flats, so cold in the winter that they slept in their coats and socks. And the family kept growing. After Antoinette came Frances, then Dominick, called Mimi. Angelina then suffered two miscarriages before becoming pregnant a seventh time. She dreamed of Gabriel blowing his horn, and when the baby boy was born safely, she took it as a sign of divine favor and called him Gabriel.

Little Joe was transfixed by New York. Bug-eyed, he absorbed the lurid tabloid and radio accounts of the kidnapping and murder of the Lindbergh baby and the frenzied banging of pots and pans by delirious Italian neighbors the summer night in 1933 when their *paesano* Primo Carnera knocked out Joe Sharkey to win the world heavyweight championship.

Pasquale found a construction job in Bay Shore, Long Island, and they moved into a rented house there—next door, as it happened, to another family from Cervinara, Raffaele and Luisa Lengua and their children. He needed a car for work and bought a used 1929 Nash. One Sunday he treated the family to a drive to his construction site, the new Sunrise Highway. In his enthusiasm he drove to the very end and off the macadam into the sand, where the front wheels stuck. Mortified, he had to wait for a tow and vowed revenge. "I'm-a going to kill-a the car," he said. True to his word, Pasquale, a proud man, withheld the car's ration of engine oil from that day on and starved the Nash to death.

When the Long Island job ended, the DeGregorios moved back to Bensonhurst. Now they had a coal stove, but all they could afford to burn was scrap wood, except when Joe and Antoinette could pocket a few nuggets of coal that fell off the Burns Brothers' coal truck chute.

Finally, Pasquale's luck turned. He found a steady job as a mason for Turner Construction. By 1939 he had saved enough to put a few hundred dollars down on a $7,000 house in Bensonhurst. It was a two-story brick building on Fifteenth Avenue near Eighty-second Street, two doors from where Pasquale's brother, Dominick, had opened a fruit and vegetable market. Between them was a butcher shop, and on the other side of Dominick's market was Luke Spano's candy store and soda fountain with its standard Reid's Ice Cream sign. On the ground floor of the house was a small rent-paying dress factory. The house came with a forty-by-seventy-foot lot where Pasquale could plant tomato and grape vines and, perhaps someday, build garages to rent to people in the neighborhood for their automobiles. Best of all, right across Fifteenth Avenue was a large public school, P.S. 204, where the children could get an education.

The house had a basement where Pasquale pressed the grapes from his vines for fermentation into wine, storing it in casks. On holidays he brewed sweet cordials in his bathroom, turning the tub chartreuse, carmine, and cobalt blue with his elixirs, which he bottled and sold or gave to friends as a special favor.

Though well settled now, Pasquale still worked feverishly. After all day on his feet at a construction site, he often straggled home too exhausted to eat the dinner Angelina had waiting for him. He fell into a chair, and she brought a bucket of scalding water for his feet; he would drop into a catatonic sleep, his feet soaking in the bucket. Friday nights the construction crew went out together to drink homemade red wine and lose money at cards to their foreman—they *had* to lose. Many late Friday nights Joe had to hunt down his father, desolate over his losses, and drag him home.

Angelina was forty-two when she went into the hospital in 1940 with yet another pregnancy, her eighth, this one unexpected. Gabriel, her youngest, was already ten, and she and Pasquale had assumed she was beyond bearing another child. The pregnancy had remained a well-kept secret from the children, but Joe, then eighteen, learned about it toward the end. Sixteen-year-old Antoinette knew only that her mother had been taken to the hospital. She was alarmed. What was wrong? she asked Joe. "Take it easy," Joe said. "You're too young to know these things yet. She's having a baby." Antoinette was dumbfounded. She didn't understand any of it. A baby? From where? How did her brother know so much? "I've been around," Joe bragged, dismissing her sputtering questions. "It's not for girls your age to know," he lectured.

As the eldest, Joe was in charge of his brothers and sisters, including the new baby, Louise. Once, when Frances was missing at mealtime, Joe was sent to look for her and found her across the street in the schoolyard riding on the handlebars of a boy's bike. He took the beating for that. "You're the second father, Peppino," Pasquale said. "You got to be responsible. I work to bring food into the house."

Joe, a skinny, bony-faced youth known to his friends as Joe Nose, hung out in Luke Spano's, playing the pinball machine, eating ice cream Mello-rolls, and chattering about girls and baseball. Nights before their own ballgames, someone slept on the schoolyard concrete to reserve the field. Often, too, they hung out in Dominick's grocery listening to Mussolini on the shortwave. They knew Americans called him a clown, him and that beady-eyed German with the square mustache who was storming all of Europe, but the name Il Duce thrilled them. He was Italian, and he was strong and decisive. He was doing something for their people.

Otherwise, Joe and his friends whiled away the hours leaning against the mailbox in front of the school and harmonizing in impromptu barbershop quartets. On hot summer days Angelina gave Joe two nickels for the trolley to Coney Island and back, but often he hitched a ride on the rear, saving the fare for two Nathan's hot dogs. It was about as mischievous as Joe's crowd got.

Joe traveled all the way into Manhattan to Strabenmueller Textile, a vocational high school. He had dreams of becoming a journalist, and the school offered a secretarial course that he thought would teach him note-taking and writing. After graduation he hoped to go on to Columbia University, but Pasquale dismissed it out of hand. College was for rich people. Drake Business School was only $25 a month. He'd learn stenography. Wasn't that what journalists did anyway, write down notes? When Joe finished Drake he rushed over to *The New York Times* on West Forty-third Street to become a reporter. In the newsroom of gray steel desks, clattering typewriters, and tobacco smoke, sportswriter Arthur Daley broke it to him: A reporter's job was hard to come by for an immigrant kid, even one with a steno degree, in prewar 1941. Disillusioned, Joe scaled down his dreams and settled for a clerical job at *Every Woman* magazine.

He was at a friend's house on Coney Island Avenue listening to a record of Charlie Barnett playing "Cherokee" when the boy's father burst in yelling something that Joe couldn't make out. Suddenly the words detonated. "The Japs! . . . The Japs bombed Pearl Harbor!"

Joe's friends were all called up, but he was kept waiting. He visited the draft board and heard for the first time that he was under suspicion as an "enemy alien." He had, after all, been born in Italy. Searching for ways to erase the stigma, he busied himself writing gossipy newsletters from the neighborhood to his friends overseas while keeping his job, somewhat ashamedly, at *Every Woman*.

Then one morning on his way to work he passed a recruiting

table on the sidewalk outside a Broadway auto dealership. The New York Regiment. Impulsively he signed up, and this time to his joy his enlistment was accepted. In September 1942 he was called up, with orders for the West Coast. At Camp Santa Anita in California, where his secretarial skills earned him a corporal's rating, he took the opportunity to officially Americanize his name. If he was going to fight for his country, he wouldn't be Giuseppe anymore. He would be Joe.

But when his unit got orders for Anzio, again he was left behind, suspect as an enemy alien. Instead he was sent to a command head-quarters in the Pacific. Five months after the Japanese surrender he was discharged. His sisters were waiting to greet him at the el station. They scarcely recognized him, now skinny and yellow from the Atabrine tablets. At home Angelina wept. *"Che succèsso? Che ti hanno fatto?"* What had they done to him?

Joe let them know he was no kid anymore. He was twenty-three now and knew a few things. "I may join the Fifty-two—Twenty Club, Pop," he bragged. Pasquale hadn't heard of this. What was this? Ah, Joe told him, home relief, unemployment checks, $20 a week for fifty-two weeks. Pasquale was outraged. "What checks?" he boomed. "You got to go to work!" Through people he knew from construction he found Joe a job as a $75-a-week secretary at the Todd Shipyards.

The neighbors came to see Pasquale's boy back from the war. One of the last to drop in was a pretty, brown-haired girl of nineteen whose family, also from Cervinara, had once lived next door to the DeGregorios in Bay Shore and whose father worked with Pasquale at Turner Construction. Like Joe, Anne Lengua was the oldest of six children, but unlike Joe, she had been born in America, in upstate Troy near Albany. During the Depression her father, Raffaele, had sent the family home to Cervinara while he stayed behind doing construction, venturing for a time as far as Panama where he worked maintaining the canal. Later he'd worked on the roadbed of the Pennsylvania Railroad for a dollar a day. A squat man just inches over five feet tall, he was self-taught, a daily reader of the newspaper. He didn't deal in cash like many of his fellow immigrants but proudly kept a checking account.

Like Joe, Anne had grown up in Cervinara saluting Mussolini and parading in Black Shirt uniform. She was nine when her father brought the family back to New York. She spoke only Italian and had to endure the taunts of "guinea" from classmates. Angelina had long had her eye on Anne as a daughter-in-law. "Now that you're home," she told Joe, "it's time to stop fooling around. I have a hometown girl you should marry."

Joe and Anne began dating and soon were engaged. But if she stayed out too late, her father, Raffaele, still disciplined her with a strap. Joe saw the welts the next day. "Pop," he said, trying to mollify his father-in-law-to-be, "we're going to be engaged. She's going to be my wife. If we wanted to do something wrong, you think I'd take her all the way to New York? We have a hotel right here on Seventy-ninth Street, the Hotel Gregory." He put on a teasing face. "We're going to go there tonight at eight. We'll be home by eight-thirty. It won't take me long."

Pow! Raffaele's strong right hand lashed out and slapped Joe across the face.

Joe got little sympathy at home. "I'm so glad," Pasquale said. "You deserve to get one from me now!"

Three months after their wedding, Joe was hospitalized with a ruptured appendix and a 106-degree fever. Angelina alone radiated a beatific calm. She had struggled too hard to lose any of her children. Brought up a Catholic, she had become born-again, an evangelist. She made the whole family kneel down around Joe's hospital bed and pray. Then she went home and secluded herself in her room. When she emerged days later, she announced, "In six days he will be fine." On the sixth day she entered Joe's hospital room where he lay in a coma. His closed eyes fluttered open. "Can I have a glass of water?" he asked.

The hospital bill came to $2,000. Joe and Anne had no insurance. Although Pasquale always claimed to be broke, they knew he had socked away substantial savings. Joe begged him for a loan, which he made a show of reluctantly granting. When Joe was feeling better, he and Anne went down to Atlantic City for a weekend of recuperation. Pasquale was indignant. *"Che coraggio!"* he thundered. *"You* owe *me* two thousand dollars, and *you* go on vacation!" But Pasquale emptied the commercial space on the first floor of his house and moved his family down, leaving the upstairs to Joe and Anne and, on March 18, 1948, their firstborn, a son they named Patrick, to Pasquale's consternation.

• • •

He was a cherubic, rosy-cheeked baby with bright eyes and pouty, rubbery lips. Patrick, Pasquale and Angelina's first grandchild, was shamelessly adored. Angelina intervened whenever she felt his parents were being unduly strict. Pasquale showed his favor by sending his little grandson to the basement to draw wine from the casks and even letting him taste a little, after which Patrick, rosier-cheeked than usual, would fall asleep in Angelina's sheltering arms. Anne's parents, Raffaele and Luisa, who lived around the corner, were no less doting. It was an idyllic time for the DeGregorios, marred only by the shattering news from the Air Force at Eastertime, 1951, that Anne's brother, Nicholas, a radio operator on a Globemaster flying secret missions out of Roswell, New Mexico, was lost when the plane disappeared with all crew members four hundred miles off Ireland. He was twenty-three.

The house was filling with children. When Patrick was five, Joe and Anne had another son, whom they named Ralph after Anne's father Raffaele. By now, too, Joe's sister Antoinette had married and had a five-year-old son. It was a happy jumble of generations. Pasquale and Angelina's youngest daughter, Louise, was only eight years older than their grandson Patrick. Holidays were particularly tumultuous occasions, with children rampaging through the house while their elders gathered around the table for unending feasts, and blinked in Joe's blinding spotlights as he recorded it all on his eight-millimeter film camera.

Each summer the growing clan drove out to Valley Stream Park for a picnic. The women cooked huge pots of macaroni on charcoal fires, waiting forever for the water to boil, while the men played ball. The meal was served on china and glass; Pasquale wouldn't hear of paper plates. Afterward the women washed the dishes under cold-water faucets while the children ran wild and Pasquale and Joe and the other men played cards in the shade and got tipsy on red wine.

Joe's job at the Todd Shipyards was not enough, especially after Patrick and Ralph were followed by Luisa, named after her grandmother, Anne's mother. Joe took a second job supervising secretaries in an office and then a third job as a bouncer in the Bensonhurst Theater on Saturdays. Finally, when even that proved inadequate, Joe gave them all up for one better job in the printing shop of the Kinney Shoe Corporation. It wasn't journalism, but it was as close as Joe would get since his prewar job at *Every Woman*.

The upstairs of Pasquale's house could no longer hold them. When Patrick was twelve, Joe and Anne moved the family around the corner to the house of Anne's parents, who were retiring to California. But after a fourth child, Joey, was born, with hopes for a fifth before too long, the new house, too, was pinching. They would have to think about moving again. But where? Where could the family find the space they needed at an affordable price? There was an obvious answer, but Joe put it off. He wasn't ready to leave Bensonhurst. The neighborhood exerted an archetypal pull on the family. It was where Pasquale had set their roots. It was home.

Yet many of his friends had already left, Joe realized. The war had changed everything. The boys he had grown up with had met girls and dispersed all over the country. Of his old crowd of over a hundred, he could count no more than fifteen who were still around. Some of them were discussing it over ice cream in Luke Spano's one day in the spring of 1963 when Joe got an idea. Why not a reunion? A dinner! Excited, the group trooped over to Hercules and Carmine Sirico's restaurant on Thirteenth Avenue and arranged it.

Joe tracked down new addresses and mailed out a hundred and fifty invitations to the old crowd; Fat Mike Girgenti, Joseph "Pee Wee" Incivilito, Sal "McGrass" Licata, Angelo "Shoes" Scarpa, Sam "Mouse" Terranova, Noox Indelicato, Luke Spano, Johnny Claps, Victor "Hunch" Virgilio, Jim "Nose" Trombetta, and the rest. To his surprise, ninety-eight of them showed up for the dinner. That night the men sat late around the tables swapping tales of the 1936 subway series, Flying Fortresses, Jack Dempsey, Mayor LaGuardia, and their favorite Miss Rheingold. The wives sat around stiffly, excluded from the action, self-consciously trying to make small talk with other women who were perfect strangers. Sometimes the women looked up, startled, when one of their huddling menfolk, sentimental with whiskey and memories, burst into tears.

The reunion was cathartic, an exorcism for Joe. Attached as he was to Bensonhurst, he could now face leaving. The old neighborhood no longer existed except as an idyll in his mind. Besides, there was no getting around it, the family needed more space. Their fifth child, Louis, was born in 1964 when Patrick was sixteen, a pattern that, consciously or not, echoed Joe's own history in Pasquale's large and widely spaced family. The following year, when Patrick graduated from Bensonhurst's New Utrecht High School, the DeGregorios moved again, this time to Long Island.

It had been happening all over America for a generation—inner-city families, many of them of immigrant stock, pulling up stakes in the postwar suburban land rush. Lured by quarter-acre lots sprouting pastel split-level homes made affordable by the GI Bill, these pioneers, like the homesteaders who had populated the nation's vast interior a century before, reinvented America. They transformed the landscape and, in the process, themselves. Afterward, nothing was the same—not what they had left behind, not what they had come to find. The cities they abandoned were swamped by waves of new immigrants, many of them poor, some of them angry and violent, who speeded the exodus, worsening the cycle. There was no going back. Yet with every new development tract and shopping mall, the beckoning paradise, like the horizon, seemed to recede as they approached.

The house came with a pool, a backyard with lots of grass, and a patch of front lawn big enough for games of touch football. Down the lane was a playground and ball fields with regulation diamonds—a real park, not the standard city patch of rutted concrete with swings, slide, seesaw, and monkey bars. But outside their development, traffic streamed by on Main Street, reminding the DeGregorios that their new freedom was bought at a cost. Everything was a drive away, even the four-block center of Kings Park, which was the only downtown they now knew.

Patrick missed Bensonhurst's familiar chaos, the pull of the streets, stickball games in the schoolyard, open hydrants on hot summer days, his uncle Dom's grocery, and the crowd at Luke Spano's. On moving day, riding in the van, he had cried most of the way to Kings Park. Although he didn't yet have a license, he often borrowed his father's car to drive back to Brooklyn to revisit his old haunts and drop in on Pasquale and Angelina. He felt like a stranger in both worlds.

Joe also sensed a loss. He felt disconnected, cut off from his past.

Here no women leaned out of second-floor windows monitoring life on the street. There were no sidewalk fruit stands where neighbors picked over the produce, exchanging news. People lived invisible lives. Grown-ups no longer held sway over the children—no one knew whose children were whose, where they were, or what they were doing. But this, Joe told himself, was the real America, a place of privacy and property, far from the tenements and push-carts of the immigrants. And it would keep his children away from the malign influence of the hoodlums he called *them*.

Patrick needed a job. He heard about a local trash collection route that was for sale and toyed with the idea of buying it. Joe talked him out of it. It was *their* racket, he told his son. He had never had dealings with *them*, not even when he had to take three jobs to feed his family, and he wasn't going to get involved with *them* now, and neither was Patrick. Why wouldn't Patrick consider college? Joe, remembering his own thwarted ambitions, said he would be glad to pay for it; he'd find a way. Besides, college would keep Patrick out of Vietnam. The war was heating up and kids were being drafted.

But Patrick couldn't face the thought of more school. High school had been hard enough. He wasn't a student, that was all there was to it. Joe didn't force the issue. It was Patrick's life. So he found a job in Farmingdale as a machinist making pendulum parts for tor-pedo heads. It was a defense contract and carried an exemption from the draft. He could make a good career there, which was more important than ever now. Over Joe's vociferous objections, he had gotten married.

The company enrolled him in Farmingdale Agricultural College for a course in reading blueprints, but going back into a classroom was a mistake, Patrick felt immediately. It was like school all over again. Even when he finished the course, he hated being cooped up in the shop. To Joe's dismay he quit to take a job in a gas station. He was pumping gas one day when a passing contractor offered him a job building houses, which was better than what he was doing. He joined a carpentry crew of huge Swedes and came home nights so tired from hauling stacks of lumber that his knees buckled under him. Neighbors gossiped that he was always coming home drunk.

While visiting his grandparents in Bensonhurst one day in 1969, he ran into a former buddy in a police uniform. Patrick was dumbfounded. "I'm in the PD," Al said proudly. They were giving the test again, he said. Patrick should get himself an application.

Mary was worried. She didn't want him to be a cop. But then she thought, if that was what he wanted, she wouldn't stop him. Joe, too, was caught by surprise, but if that interested Patrick, it was fine with Joe. It was an honorable calling.

He took the exam and to his surprise passed. He survived the interviews and screening, and then a budget freeze put everything on hold. No new police hires. If and when city fiscal conditions changed, they told him, they would call. He shrugged and went back to his life on the construction crew.

Four years later, in March 1973, when Mary Anne was nearly a year old, he came home one day to hear from Mary that someone had called and left a number. He called back. "Do you still want the job?" said a voice. He was taken aback. "What job?"

"The Police Department."

He had all but forgotten. "Yeah, sure," he mumbled.

"Next Monday, oh-eight hundred, Police Academy, Two thirty-five East Twentieth Street, Manhattan. Be there." That was it. The voice hung up.

Mary's worries resurfaced. She considered calling the officer back herself to say her husband wasn't interested. But she didn't. He was a grown-up and could handle himself.

Joe accompanied Pat and proudly watched his son being sworn in.

He graduated in October and suddenly was a cop, a freshly minted rookie earning $11,200 a year. A new six-shot police special in a stiff black holster hung off his belt, poking into his right thigh, and a bright silver shield, 31416, gleamed from his jacket, left of his heart. There was a bravado about his wide, relaxed grin and his long brown hair, trailing Elvis-style into fashionable sideburns, but his eyes looked out on the world with a nervous confusion.

3

THE delivery seemed to be taking a long time. Again. De-Gregorio nervously paced the waiting room at Syosset Hospital wondering what the delay was. Wasn't the second one supposed to be easier? Not that anything had been. After Mary Anne was born, they had tried for another child. Mary got pregnant again and was trying one day to coax Mary Anne down from a bureau when the furniture toppled on Mary. She lost the baby. Then in the fall of 1974, she got pregnant again. This time, everything seemed to go fine.

At last there were quick steps in the corridor and a maternity nurse approached. She seemed startled to see him. "Are you . . ." she began, and then stopped in evident confusion. She looked at him closely and began again. "Mr. DeGregorio?"

He nodded.

"Are . . . are either of your parents . . . uh . . . black?"

Black? What kind of question was that? "No," he finally said. "Why?" Was this a joke?

She gave him a compassionate smile. "There seems to be a problem. We don't know why."

He heard the rest in a fog. The baby was dark-skinned, but the mother was white. At first doctors thought perhaps the father was black, or his parents. Now they suspected a circulatory disorder, some lack of oxygen that would account for the baby's livid coloration and the blue circles under his eyes. The doctors didn't like what they saw. He was being tested, but they urged a consultation with specialists.

He, DeGregorio thought. *It was a boy!*

He went in to Mary, who was equally befogged. What happened, they asked each other. What was going on? What could it be? How, *how*, could it have happened? Nothing was wrong with Mary Anne.

He went to see the baby, who was being warmed in an incubator that bathed his small body in violet light. He looked a little dark, DeGregorio thought, but it was hard to tell. Babies sometimes looked dark, didn't they? Maybe it was nothing.

He drove home feeling as if he'd swallowed a rock that left him with a nauseating weight in his gut. There was something wrong with his baby. And as of two weeks before, in this summer of 1975, he was out of a job, laid off.

They started him at the one-oh-nine, a large Queens precinct covering the busy commercial spine of Main Street, Flushing, and the quiet streets of Whitestone. *Usually* quiet. The first call squawking out of his radio was about a possible DOA a few blocks from his footpost. Outside a small row house, a hysterical female was screaming that her old mother was inside dead, with a nurse who had flipped out and refused to open the door. He forced his way in and calmed the berserk nurse. In a corner he saw a figure stretched out and covered in plastic. Gently he peeled away the shroud from an old woman with a rosary clutched in her hands. DeGregorio bent down for a closer look and just about jumped out of his skin when the woman shrieked in his ear. Some DOA! Obviously she had just passed out. But when his heart stopped hammering, he realized that he had begun his police career by raising the dead.

He felt like the dopiest of rookies. He answered a domestic dispute—the scariest of calls because the whole family often ganged up on the cop—but found only an older couple arguing over what the husband kept calling "change of life." He commiserated. Hey, everyone's life changed, didn't it? That's what life did, it changed. That stopped them cold and they calmed down. Case closed. He'd have to ask about that, he reminded himself. What the fuck was change of life?

And then everything seemed to happen at once.

One night when his four-to-midnight tour was over, he and a partner stopped at the Bridge Lanes for a few beers. When the other cop left to get his car, DeGregorio got jumped. They hit from behind, he didn't know how many, knocking him down and working him over, punching and kicking him in the chest, neck, and face, breaking his jaw. They scattered when his partner came back, firing.

Joe, who was getting over a minor knee operation, was at his son's hospital bed when his father, Pasquale, suffered a heart attack at home. Pasquale was rushed to a Brooklyn hospital, but it was too late. He died without recovering consciousness. Joe waked Pasquale in Bensonhurst, then sat with the grieving Angelina in their old apartment on Fifteenth Avenue. It was a hot June day, the fan just shoving around the sodden air. Joe went into a sudden sweat, then started suffering a heart attack himself. Anne called an ambulance to take him to Smithtown Hospital near home; she was adamant about not sending him to the same hospital where his father had just died. Joe missed Pasquale's funeral but he survived, at the cost of his pack-a-day Pall Mall habit. Then Anne fell into a deep menopausal depression. Luisa came home from school one day to find her mother hallucinating and suicidal, holding a razor blade, saying, "Mommy, what should I do now?" The family put her into treatment and she recovered.

Back on the job, DeGregorio was transferred, plunging through the looking glass into the nightmare world of the two-eight, Harlem's toughest precinct, a barren square mile around the decrepit station house at One Hundred and Twenty-third Street and Eighth Avenue. He walked his footpost gamely, noticing crowds of people who melted away as he approached, regrouping across the street, and drifting away again as he crossed back. It puzzled him. What was it, he wondered, a fucking comedy routine? He questioned the patrol sergeant, who gave him a tight smile of exasperated tolerance before explaining that those *crowds* were junkies surrounding heroin dealers. Now, he said, couldn't DeGregorio find someplace better to go? The last thing the two-eight needed was a dead rookie. "This ain't Flushing, kid," he said.

He began to get the hang of the job. Above all, he realized he was a uniform, a symbol. A woman complaining she'd been knifed undressed casually to display the wound. He felt uncomfortable, embarrassed for her. Then it came to him. She wasn't talking to him, she was talking to *the Police*. He wasn't a man, he was a cop.

At the end of June 1975, when the two-eight was about to move into a new fortresslike station house a block away, word came rattling over the teletype from headquarters that 150 of the precinct's 400 cops were being laid off. Rumors had been flying for weeks, but now it was really happening. Nearly 3,000 police layoffs citywide were meant to help cure a critical budget deficit that had sent the city to the brink of bankruptcy. He stared at his name, eyes glazed. So this was how the city treated its Finest! Cursing and joking sardonically with the others, he turned in his gun and shield. The captain himself was teary-eyed. But he made his officers carry their gear over to the new station house anyway. "You guys are going to be back," he promised. "See you in a couple of days."

But the days stretched into weeks.

They named the baby Thomas Patrick—Thomas after Mary's brother, Patrick after him. Mary had little enough family, few enough surviving relatives, and she wanted a way to memorialize them. DeGregorio liked Mary's brother, a charmer despite his alcoholism.

From Syosset Hospital they moved the baby for further tests to the neonatal unit at Long Island Jewish Hospital in New Hyde Park, one of the nation's leading children's hospitals. The campuslike setting, stolid tan buildings set along macadam lanes and strips of grass and trees, was reassuring to DeGregorio, a brave display of normalcy for the abnormalities within.

Tommy was in a large room with other babies in special incubators, one nurse for every four babies. They were allowed to visit him in hospital gowns, but they couldn't pick him up yet. DeGregorio was comforted by the array of medical technology that seemed to bespeak miracles. He felt somehow optimistic that everything would turn out all right. Maybe, he and Mary kept telling each other, it was nothing. Oh please, God, he prayed, let it be nothing.

Cardiologists sent a small camera probe into Tommy's heart and they found the problem, transformation of the main vessels. The arteries taking blood in and out were crossed, doctors explained, sending poorly oxygenated blood through his heart and body. If it weren't for the two compensating but abnormal holes in his heart, they said, he couldn't have survived birth.

Holes in his heart? DeGregorio was reeling. He felt he had taken one through the heart. Through his mind flashed the gruesome image of nature's patchwork that was keeping his son alive, maybe only by a thread.

"He can live for a while the way he is now," a surgeon said, as if reading DeGregorio's mind. "He'll grow. But there'll come a time when we'll have to . . . assist him a little bit."

DeGregorio tuned out. He felt light-headed, dizzy, sick, and short of breath. Poor little Tommy. Had he done anything to deserve this? Had they?

"Assist him," DeGregorio repeated dully. "How?"

"We'll have to take an artery from another part of the body and hook it up," the surgeon said, as if it was obvious. He seemed to be trying, patiently, to say it in a way they might understand.

DeGregorio felt a surge of queasiness. What it meant was they were going to have to operate on Tommy's heart—cut open his baby. The image was unbearable, and he closed his eyes. "But isn't that risky?" he found himself asking. He sensed immediately it was a dumb question and almost thought of apologizing.

The doctor smiled indulgently. "There's no choice," he said.

If she had a new baby brother, Mary Anne kept wanting to know, where was he? They told her he was coming home soon, he was just having some tests. She said that was fine and went on playing.

They brought him home after a few weeks. Mary Anne, intensely curious, stood for long minutes at a time at his crib staring down at this wrinkled invader who was suddenly stealing all the attention. But DeGregorio and Mary took pains to explain that he was her baby, too, and that as a big sister she was going to help take care of him. They didn't say there was anything wrong.

Mary Anne watched breathlessly as they fed bottles to Tommy and changed his diapers and rocked him when he wailed for attention. Soon she was carrying him around, supporting his head the way they had shown her, giving him bottles, and changing him herself. And when he began to sit up and play with toys, Mary Anne played with him like a friend.

DeGregorio still hadn't heard from the job. He found work driving an oil truck, but after a few months he called the builder he knew and rejoined the carpentry crew. The Swedes were delighted to see him, pumping his hand with bone-crushing zeal and welcoming him with beer and sandwiches in the construction trailer.

He moved from site to site all over Long Island. Occasionally Mary brought Mary Anne and Tommy to visit over lunch. DeGregorio was glad to have found steady work and had no quarrel with the pay, the same $1,200 a month he had earned as a cop. But he didn't want to be a carpenter, he wanted to be a cop.

Tommy grew, despite his ailment, just as the doctors said. He was a willful child with an impish grin and mischievous streak, perhaps a rechanneling of the nervous energy he couldn't work off in physical exertion. They had to be careful with him because he ran out of breath easily. He took daily doses of Digitalis for his heart, and every three months DeGregorio brought him back to the hospital for a checkup.

Just walking into the hospital made DeGregorio queasy with anxiety, especially when he saw the children, some hairless from chemotherapy, furiously pedaling their Big Wheel tricycles through the corridors, trailing intravenous bottles. But unlike him, they seemed to accept their condition without question, as if illness, not health, was life's prescribed norm.

DeGregorio, who usually read little besides a lunch-stained tabloid left on the desks in the station house, began leafing through the Bible, looking for answers. They had to be there somewhere, he figured. That was what the Bible was for. Why had this happened to him? Had he done something to offend God? Was this some payback? If so, he couldn't think for what. He thumbed through the book of Job. Maybe there was a message there for him, he thought. Hadn't Job, too, been punished for no reason? Every Sunday he went with Mary and Mary Anne to mass at St. Joseph's, where he always lit a candle for Tommy.

By mid-1977, when Tommy was two and Mary Anne was five, DeGregorio had been off the job for two years. If he couldn't go back, he decided, he could still be some kind of police officer. Roy DeSetto, who had been with him in Flushing and Harlem, heard that the Corrections Department was hiring. Was he interested?

DeGregorio agonized. He had heard that anyone who took a job with Corrections would not be rehired after the layoffs. Did he want to spend his life in jail guarding slimeballs? He wanted to put them in there, not babysit them inside. Still, it was better than hauling lumber. It was a gamble, but he decided to risk it. There was no telling when, if ever, he'd be called back. So when Roy said he was driving over to Rikers Island to sign up, DeGregorio said fine, he'd go too.

On the way Roy stopped for an errand at the one-oh-nine and DeGregorio followed him in. They found the second-ranking uniformed commander, Chief of Patrol Neil Behan, there to turn out the tour. The station house was jittery. Behan was still remembered for his key role in shaking up the department after the payoff and bribery scandals probed by the Knapp Commission.

Someone must have told Behan that two laid-off officers were in the house. He summoned them. DeGregorio shrugged. What did he care? He wasn't even a cop anymore.

"How are you coming?" Behan boomed. He seemed genuinely glad to see them.

DeGregorio was caught off guard. "Not so good, sir," he said uneasily. "I have a family. I can't hold on anymore. I have to join Corrections."

"Corrections?" That seemed to irritate Behan. "I don't want to lose you," he said. He ordered them to stand by while he called Chief Simon Eisdorfen in personnel. "Sy," he bellowed, "tell me when these men are going to be rehired." He read off their names and ID numbers.

Eisdorfen called back minutes later. Behan was beaming. "You'll be back within three weeks," he promised. "And then come see me."

DeGregorio left dazed. Back on the job! He could scarcely believe it. He had waited two years. He had nearly given up. His resentments evaporated. All he could think of now was getting back into uniform, retrieving his shield and gun. It was the best news he had gotten in a long time. Tommy was coming along, and he was going back to work. Maybe his luck had turned.

Two days later a letter arrived from the department calling him back to the academy for a two-week refresher course before a return to duty.

• • •

The turreted Eighty-third Precinct station house on Wilson Avenue was a relic, DeGregorio discovered, so old it had sliding barn doors and a hayloft, from the days of constables on horseback, and a seal, CITY OF BROOKLYN between the green police lanterns. Inside, past the stone columns, up the stoop of slate steps, was a huge front desk with a brass rail and a block-lettered sign commanding ALL PRISONERS STOP HERE. Beyond stretched a corridor lined with dank cells, each with a pallet bed and a seatless toilet. Up a flight of green wooden stairs were squad rooms crammed with gray steel desks and gooseneck lamps, and warrens where murky light seeped through grimy slit windows. The tin-ceilinged basement housed a makeshift kitchen with an old Westinghouse refrigerator, a rusty industrial sink, and a vintage stove where DeGregorio was told he could cook and eat a meal if his stomach could stand it, and where if he had time off he might might flop down on a threadbare sofa to watch TV or catch a snooze.

The CO, Captain George L. Peters, had spent sixteen years in Internal Affairs unmasking crooked cops and was, accordingly, a ballbreaker. He made his men line up for roll call on the street outside the station house despite the risk that some cop-hater with an Uzi might find the target irresistible. DeGregorio came out one day to find the lug nuts on his car wheels loosened. But the men had their ways of getting back at Peters. They stuffed dead rats in his desk, sprayed his toilet seat with chemical Mace, and left their verdict on a men's room wall: "The captain is a scumbag."

Still, for an eager cop itching for calls after two years off the job, the eight-three looked like action. A shadowy Sicilian faction of the Bonanno family held sway out of cafés and brick-front social clubs along the length of bustling Knickerbocker Avenue, and drugs were hawked openly in Bushwick Park by vendors standing on the vandalized benches. In the bodegas, cashiers sat behind thick slabs of bulletproof Plexiglas, and throughout the neighborhood arsonists had burned down some of the old wood-frame houses, giving blocks the look of a rotting mouth with missing teeth.

As one of the rehirees just back from the layoffs, DeGregorio was assigned to radio patrol, rookie stuff. He arrested a motorist who tried to bribe him with $30 to forget about a traffic ticket, drawing the attention of Internal Affairs and a commendation for "furthering the high standards of integrity expected of a professional police officer." And with a partner he charged into a burning apartment building on Bushwick Avenue to evacuate families, a dangerous rescue that won him another commendation.

One August afternoon, when he had just signed back into the house from a run that had delayed his meal, the radio crackled with a call: "Man with a gun . . . One-four Linden Street." He listened with one ear, as he'd learned to do. Linden Street was his sector, Charlie David, but there were fifty gun runs a day like that, usually phoned in by someone with a grudge against someone else. Everyone in New York had to know by now that to get a cop somewhere fast for whatever reason, you called in "man with a gun" or "shots fired" or best of all a 10-13, "officer in trouble." Still, you never knew. There were plenty of guns around, so it was true often enough. But he still had most of an hour coming for a meal. Another sector could take the job.

He heard Central confirm it would be picked up by Adam Boy. That, he knew, was Roy DeSetto, who had been assigned to the Eighty-third with him, and Joseph D. Taylor, Jr., a detective training specialist partnering with Roy.

DeGregorio was taking the last swallow of his Pepsi when the dispatcher's voice rose an octave, turning breathlessly urgent. "Officer down. . . . We have an officer down! One-four Linden. Repeating, officer down . . ."

DeGregorio tore upstairs, three steps at a time, joining the melee of blue pouring out of the station house and into screeching squad cars.

They lurched to a stop in the middle of the street, amid a cacophony of dying sirens from a dozen other cars abandoned at crazy angles, doors ajar and dome lights bouncing eerily off building glass. A ghoulish crowd was pressing in for a sight of whatever mayhem the presence of all these cops signified.

All at once shouting officers were bundling a moaning, blood-soaked figure down the stoop of an old brownstone. DeGregorio shoved his way in. *Taylor!*

DeGregorio could barely recognize him. Taylor was thirty-four, five years older than he was, and had been on the force four years longer. DeGregorio heard just that morning that Taylor had put his wife and three-year-old daughter on a bus for vacation. He planned to join them shortly.

DeGregorio watched Taylor's limp form being lifted into the back of the nearest patrol car and then jumped in alongside Roy. Under his jacket, which had been torn open, Taylor was bleeding through a hole in his chest big enough to hold a football.

"Roy, what happened?"

Forehead striped with streaked blood and dirt, blood-veined eyes popping with fear, Roy panted out the story. They'd taken the call. They didn't have any apartment number, so they went to the top and started down, listening at doors. Nothing. They were ready to call in an unfounded and split. Then Joe listened at a first-floor door, heard something, knocked. The door opened a slit, a twelve-gauge slid through, and *ka-boom, ka-boom!* Caught Joe square in the chest, both fucking barrels. He grabbed Joe's gun, went nuts, and kicked open the door. There were four of them in there, Rastafarians or Jamaicans, they looked like. He emptied both guns into the room, killed one, wounded one. Backups grabbed two trying to jump out the window.

The squad car rocketed and wailed through the city. Roy turned away, crying.

Taylor was dead before they ever reached Wyckoff Heights Hospital. He lay on a hospital gurney littered with the debris of medical failure—stripped-off rubber gloves, torn surgical masks, and squares of gauze sopped with blood. DeGregorio stood with the others around the body, unable to tear themselves away from the vigil.

A cop guarding the door slipped in with whispered news. One of them was there, in the emergency room, right across the hall, *the guy Roy wounded.* Word spread fast. Blood pounding in his ears, DeGregorio joined the others advancing on the prisoner's room, brushing past hospital staff cowering in a corner.

Suddenly the outside door flew open and in strode the super chiefs, the departmental brass, to pay respects to their fallen comrade. DeGregorio saw a flash of pointed stars on collars, gold braid, chests of ribbons, florid Irish faces, grim-set jaws. The commanders quickly sized up the situation. "Get back over there!" one hissed at the fuming officers who, sullen and shamefaced, slunk back to Taylor's room.

The killing, the first in the eight-three since the station house went up in 1895, cast a pall over the precinct. The men draped mourning bunting over the facade and slipped bands of black ribbon over their badges. They crowded into the B & G down the street, the bar now closed to outsiders. It was a cop thing. Civilians weren't wanted.

DeGregorio flayed himself with guilt. It had been his call to take. If he had, would things have been different, would Taylor be alive, would Taylor's little girl still have a father? But would *he* be dead, and Mary Anne and Tommy be fatherless? Who knew?

"Mike Arnold."

The grunted name came from behind. DeGregorio was boiling water for pasta in the grimy basement kitchen. He turned at the voice and looked down to see a meaty hand stretched his way. It was connected to a muscular arm and a stocky shoulder, above which a pair of blue eyes were appraising him critically. DeGregorio had spotted him once or twice around the precinct, a six-footer with closely cropped blond hair who looked, DeGregorio thought, like a model for the master race, an *Aryan.*

He paused a moment before reacting. There was something abrasive about the stranger's approach, yet his gruffness seemed put on for effect. Self-consciously, he shook the extended hand.

Mike said he had been transferred in from Sheepshead Bay, where he'd been assigned before the layoffs. He'd had a hard time finding decent work and had driven a taxi and worked as a bouncer at the disco Régine's. At least he was a bachelor, he said, and didn't have to worry about feeding a family. "I hear you're looking for a partner," he said.

DeGregorio looked at him with surprise. He *had* been looking for a steady partner. How did Mike know? Had he been checking him out? What balls! "Yeah, fine," DeGregorio said noncommittally. Who was this guy? He'd have to check *him* out.

One morning a couple of days later, they were both coming in for roll call when a *chiquita* in a short tight mini sashayed past on the sidewalk. Their heads swiveled as one.

"Nice ass," DeGregorio commented.

Mike shook his head disdainfully. "It's the high heels," he said. "Heels do that."

"Ass," DeGregorio said stubbornly.

"Heels," insisted Mike.

They laughed. He was still looking for a partner, Mike said. He'd heard good things about DeGregorio.

DeGregorio shrugged. Mike sounded all right.

Marty Schwartz was bugging him to be his partner, Mike said, but he didn't pick his partners that way.

DeGregorio was confused. "What way?"

By religion, Mike said. Who cared if Marty was also Jewish?

Also? Mike was a Jew?

Yeah, he said, he was Jewish. What of it?

Nothing, DeGregorio said. He didn't know any Jews. He must have met some in his life, only he couldn't remember any. All he could think of was *a Jew who looked like a Nazi?* He shook his head. "Okay," he said. "Maybe we'll talk to the sergeant."

In the summer of 1978, Tommy was three, old enough for his first operation to have an artery removed from his left arm and implanted in his heart as a shunt. It was a critical procedure, the doctors told DeGregorio and Mary, somewhat risky, as operations always were, but in Tommy's case vital.

The day of the operation DeGregorio was confident it would be a success. He had faith in the doctors; what they had told him had been right so far. He couldn't say exactly why, he just felt optimistic.

They waited outside the operating room until a surgeon emerged in a green scrub suit, his mask hanging around his neck. "I didn't think it was going to work so easily, but it did," he said. "I don't know who you're praying to but keep praying to them. You'll be able to take him home in a few days." He added something about finding some "unexpected complications," but DeGregorio in his jubilation skipped over it. There were always complications. It had gone as well as he had expected. The doctors had been right again.

When Tommy came home, Anne smothered him with kisses. All she could feel when she sat him on her knees were his little bones. She badgered her son with grandmotherly concern. Were they feeding Tommy enough?

Tommy recovered well, but DeGregorio's own wound was deep-seated. Impulsively he made a fateful decision. He didn't know what had caused Tommy's defect. It could have been him, something in his genes, something in the DeGregorios he had never heard about. What if it happened again? What if Mary got pregnant and something went wrong with another baby? He couldn't stand thinking about it. He was haunted by the fragility of life; they were all hanging by a thread. They belonged to a health plan, and he made an appointment at the medical office in Bay Shore. After twenty minutes under a local anesthetic, it was finished; he had a vasectomy. He would never father another child.

After Tommy recuperated, DeGregorio brought him and Mary Anne to the station house to show them around. Tommy, he saw, couldn't keep his eyes off the guns that rode on the officers' hips at his eye level. For a few minutes he put the two of them in an empty holding cell. "This is where they put people who are bad," he said, pretending to close the barred door until their eyes glistened with excitement and fear. When he freed them, they ran eagerly into his outstretched arms.

DeGregorio was well known in the precinct now. Partly to bug the captain, he became an active union member and ran an insurgent campaign against the precinct's PBA delegate. His challenge was easily turned back. But vengeful and unwilling to wait two years for a rematch, he organized a recall vote, attacking the incumbent as a seldom-show and ultimately burying him and another candidate under a DeGregorio landslide. Now anyone with a gripe came to him, and the delegate's job was worth an extra $50 a month.

Mike was shooting for a gold shield. From his first days on the job, he told DeGregorio during their long hours together in the patrol car, all he ever wanted to be was a detective. His cousin, a detective, had gotten shot in the neck and nearly killed by fellow cops who had mistaken him for a perp. Actually, Mike related, he had originally quit the academy to study cooking before deciding he wanted to be a cop after all. He reapplied, this time graduating just in time to be laid off.

DeGregorio nodded sympathetically. It was a familiar story.

Mike confided he had a girlfriend in Canada who worked for an insurance company. He'd known her for a couple of years, he said, and she was on his case, pestering him for a commitment, hassling him, really. He didn't know what to do anymore.

DeGregorio told Mike about Tommy. He should meet Tommy and Mary Anne, DeGregorio said. He should come to dinner.

It was a strained evening. DeGregorio suspected that Mary had had a few before they got there. He figured that Mike would put it down to her preoccupation with Tommy. The next day in the car Mike mentioned that she seemed unhappy, and DeGregorio nodded. "She's cold," he said. "She's a hard woman to get close to." He left it at that. Mike didn't press him.

They were good together, instinctive, working like a team, sharing everything but the driving. Mike seemed to hate driving. Behind the wheel he screwed up his eyes, squinting as if constantly blinded. Maybe, DeGregorio suggested, he needed glasses. Nah, Mike said, squeezing his eyes practically shut. All right, DeGregorio conceded, he'd do the driving. Was it all a ploy, he wondered, to stick him with the driving so Mike could be free? Free to do what? Think like a detective and plan investigations? He never knew. But he was used to driving and didn't mind.

One night, shadowing two figures they had seen leaving an abandoned building on Knickerbocker Avenue, they spotted something being dropped between two parked cars. Mike ran and retrieved it—a loaded pistol. The pair took off, DeGregorio in hot pursuit. He dropped one with a flying tackle, pinning him for Mike. "Click him!" he said as Mike slapped on the cuffs.

Mike always seemed to have some new investigative trick up his sleeve. One night the two responded to a rape complaint at Woodhull Hospital, a young girl with bite marks on her neck. The mother whispered who the culprit was—the father. DeGregorio and Mike went to pick him up.

"I know what happened," Mike told the father sympathetically. "You have a problem. I have a brother like that. It's a sickness. I'm not blaming you. But if you don't look for help, it can get worse. We can get you help."

DeGregorio was aghast. "You have a brother like that?" he asked Mike later.

"Of course," Mike said, laughing. "Sure I do. Every cop does. You have one too." DeGregorio still looked confused. "It's okay to make up a story," Mike said. Detectives did that role-playing all the time.

Another night, answering a call about a push-in robbery on Linden Street, the pair found two old sisters in their seventies in a filthy apartment without heat or hot water. They said two men with knives had pushed their way in and stole $100, food stamps, and the apartment keys.

Canvassing the neighborhood, Mike came up with the name of a teenager who lived in the building and had been locked up before for gun possession. They tracked him down, but he denied knowing the women.

Mike had DeGregorio drive them back to the station house, where he huddled with the detectives. Then, as DeGregorio watched, mystified, Mike covered a police fingerprint form with his own prints, smudging a few and making the rest clearer, and signed out a tape recorder. Then they went back to find the kid.

"I happen to know you're full of shit," Mike told him. "But I tell you what. We don't want you, we want the others that are involved. Here's the deal. When we get the others, we're going to give you two months to get your bags, and I never want to see you around here ever again."

Mike took out the fingerprint card. "See these prints?" he said. "Take a look at this one. Not too good. Here's this one. It's a little bit better, but still not that good. Ah, take a look at this one. This one's going to hang you, this one's going to put you away for twelve years. You want to go away for twelve years?"

It wasn't his idea, the kid said.

"I don't give a shit whose idea it was," Mike snapped.

It was the social worker assigned to the sisters who set it up, the kid said. Mike hit the red RECORD button to get the story on tape.

They went door-to-door tracking down the others, playing the tape. Each in turn implicated somebody else. When Mike was finished, they booked five.

But, DeGregorio wondered, hadn't Mike offered the kid a walk?

"Come on," Mike said, winking. "You know I can't make any promises. Only the DA can do that."

Even Captain Peters paid grudging tribute. "It is requested," he wrote headquarters, "that Departmental Recognition in the grade of Commendation be awarded to officers Michael Arnold and Patrick DeGregorio. While at first blush it may appear that this may be excessive, it must be pointed out that the actions of these officers, having received media attention, resulted in enhancing relations between the department and the community by these arrests. It is also felt that by these arrests there may well have been a reduction of robberies in this area. The awarding of a Commendation in this case can well be countenanced by the provisions of Patrol Guide 120.34."

At the end of 1980, Tommy was five and a half. He was in kindergarten, a blond moppet with large, expressive eyes and a devilish grin. His passion was digging. He loved to dig holes in the yard and haul the dirt into the house in one of his toy dump trucks. That and writing on the walls always got a rise out of his parents. He had a long scar on his chest from his operation, and he showed it off proudly as a badge of honor. Visitors didn't know how to react.

On days when he came home early, DeGregorio often found Tommy sitting impatiently on the curb in front of the house, waiting for him under his sister's watchful eye.

Tommy always had the same demand. He wanted to play ball. "Let's have a catch," he'd beg his father. It took all his energy to chase the ball and throw it back. Tommy ran out of breath quickly and turned blue. He often had to stop to rest. Then he got angry and frustrated. It tore DeGregorio up to watch it, but he pretended not to notice. He tried to distract Tommy. "Ah, let's go get an ice cream."

"No!" Tommy insisted, "I want to play ball."

Maybe because of Tommy, DeGregorio felt close to the kids in Bushwick. He took them for rides in the radio car and let them hit the siren. He felt sorry for them. They didn't have a chance. Drugs were everywhere, and the schools were terrible. "The key to everything in this society is education," he sometimes moralized to his fellow cops, who laughed at him, "the bleeding liberal." He shrugged them off. Did he give a shit what they called him?

One little boy lived with his alcoholic mother near the B & G, down from the station house. She was always in the bar. DeGregorio found her there one night and offered to take the boy home with him for the weekend. She didn't care. DeGregorio went upstairs and helped him pack a small suitcase.

He and Tommy got along fine, DeGregorio was happy to see. Tommy was thrilled to have a playmate for the weekend, someone else to dig holes and play catch with.

It tormented DeGregorio to bring the boy back home Monday. He found the mother where he had left her in the bar. She seemed surprised to see them, as if she'd mislaid something and couldn't remember exactly what until it had unexpectedly turned up. "Where did yez go?" she asked. He realized she had no idea how long her son had been away, with whom and where. It made him sick. He wished he could take care of the boy somehow, but Tommy's deteriorating condition overshadowed everything. He was growing too weak to go to school, and they'd need a tutor at the house. The time was coming to replace the shunts in his heart. The implants didn't grow along with the rest of him, so they had to be replaced. Another operation.

4

THE slate steps were icy, but she took them two at a time, bursting, breathless and frazzled, into the roar of the Eighty-third Precinct station house. It was a cold and dark January morning in 1981, her first day in her first command, and Barbara Adametz was cutting it close. The eight-to-four would be turning out momentarily, and she still had to put on her uniform and get orien*ta*ted, as the cops said. It wasn't her fault, she told herself. How did she know it would be so hard to find? What asshole stole the street signs? They seemed to run out somewhere in Queens. The signs that were still up were all names. Who gave all the streets in Brooklyn names instead of numbers? Wilson Avenue. Stockholm Street. *Stockholm?* What was this, a goof? This looked to be as far from Stockholm as you could get. She had coaxed her beloved blue 1964 Chevy around and around the firebombed blocks and pitted streets, becoming increasingly agitated and depressed. She had never in her twenty-eight years set foot in Brooklyn—not that she could remember, anyway, even though she had grown up not ten miles away in Queens. But Whitestone and Bushwick were worlds apart.

The station house smelled of rusty steam, wet wool, and the BO of men who had spent too many nights and days in their clothes. She unzipped the parka over her sweater and jeans and wished she had pinned up her unruly mass of coppery red hair. The place looked huge to her, as big as an aircraft hangar. Or was it that she felt so small? She wondered if the others had reported in yet. She assumed they had, since she had gotten there late. There were nine rookies assigned to Bushwick in a wave of hiring to bring the department back to strength after the depletions of the layoffs. That was the way the city worked, down the roller coaster, up the roller coaster. Maybe, she reflected, that was why everyone seemed dizzy all the time.

Three of the nine were women—females, as the department called them—the first ever assigned to patrol in the eight-three, although she had heard a woman had been there for some time on desk duty. She guessed they had probably had some "matrons" there, too, over the years, the unflattering term designating the department's women's corps that was used to search and guard female prisoners. It had been ten years since the department had officially broken the sex barrier. There were no longer any "policemen"; now they were all genderless "police officers." But Barbara knew that didn't make them equal.

She presented herself at the desk, gave her name to the lieutenant, and asked where the female locker room was. Past the desk to the left she caught a glimpse of rows of cells, a medieval dungeon.

All conversation stopped, or so she imagined. She thought she could hear the last syllables of her question echoing through the suddenly silent hall. She felt all eyes on her. She could read the amusement on the faces of the cops behind the desk. She knew she attracted attention from men, and she imagined what they were thinking. Would these bimbos get themselves and their partners killed? Was she a good lay? Would there be less overtime to go around? More days off? Roughly in that order.

The lieutenant rolled his eyes in a dumb-question putdown, as if to say how was he supposed to know where the female locker room was. Did he look like a female? Then he pointed upstairs.

As she crossed the cracked green linoleum floor, she felt her body raked by the critical glances of men assessing her walk, her boobs, her ass, her freckles, her hair. Some, she was sure, were checking her left hand, with its bare ring finger. Good, they must be thinking, single, fair game. Let them think, she told herself. She'd been through it before. She knew the drill. She was glad when she reached the stairs.

Generations of heavy cop footfalls had worn depressions in the middle of the steps. She found an old storeroom where the windows were layered with dust and smeared paint, and the ceiling plaster was peeling like fish scales onto barricades of Mission-style furniture. This, she figured, must be it. The two other women were there, but there weren't any lockers. They got a couple of the new men to liberate some empty lockers from the men's locker room, put their stuff away, and changed into their uniforms. She was relieved to find what seemed to be a relatively clean unisex bathroom down the hall—one toilet stall, one shower, and one urinal. It could be locked from the inside, so it would serve the purpose.

When Barbara went back down to the muster room, the other two females and the six male rookies were already there, waiting for the union rep, and she joined them. He walked in a few minutes later, a bulky, long-haired, cocky type who she guessed to be in his early thirties. From his brown eyes, large nose, and olive skin she took him to be Italian, which his name tag confirmed.

"Hi," he greeted them curtly, looking them over with what she sensed was disdain. "I'm Pat DeGregorio, your PBA delegate. Don't ask me what your rights are because you don't fucking have any."

They chuckled appreciatively and a little nervously, knowing that rookies were the butt of endless hazing. Barbara envied his offhand, self-assured style and wondered idly when, if ever, she might be the grizzled veteran cracking jokes to the rookies.

Afterward they were divided up to be shown around the precinct. She saw DeGregorio being called aside, and she heard him grumble, perhaps a little too theatrically loud, "Ah, you got to be kidding, Sarge!"

It was a tall, nice-looking blond cop, Arnold by his name tag, who waved her out into his car for the tour. He said to call him Mike. She slipped into the backseat. Mike took the front passenger seat. Then, to her surprise, DeGregorio squeezed into the driver's seat.

They reintroduced themselves stiffly as DeGregorio threaded the car down double-parked side streets, pointing out precinct landmarks: Bushwick Park with its winos and drug sellers, the Kok Kei on Knickerbocker, a hole-in-the-wall Chinese takeout place that used to be Joe and Mary's Italian-American restaurant where Bonanno boss Carmine Galante bought it, a last supper of lead in the backyard garden eighteen months before. She listened with half an ear, worrying whether she would ever find her way around this maze. She had a lot of questions but was too unsure of herself to ask; she'd better just keep her mouth shut. DeGregorio, too, lapsed into a sullen silence, but a few times she caught him stealing glances at her through the rearview mirror. When he saw she saw, he said, "Just sit there. Don't say anything."

Mike suddenly inclined his head and cocked an ear to the radio, reaching over to turn up the volume. He and DeGregorio exchanged a few words she couldn't catch. Mike turned around to her. "Past burglary," he said, translating the radio code, "Our sector."

When they pulled up outside a building on Knickerbocker, DeGregorio thrust a complaint form into her hands. "This is a sixty-one," he said with exaggerated patience, as if talking to child. "You do know how to write, don't you?"

What was this guy's problem, she wondered? She was tempted to set him straight but decided to shrug it off. She'd be working here a long time, she reminded herself, and shouldn't be too sensitive. "I know how to write," she said quietly.

They went upstairs and spoke to the complain*tant*, as DeGregorio called the victim, and she filled out the report. She could see they were glad to let her wrestle with the paperwork. That, she guessed, was what rookies were for. They drove back to the station house to file it. In the backseat Barbara pulled out her memo book and started making notes on the incident.

"Ah, very good. Put it right in the book," DeGregorio mocked her. "You're going by the numbers. That's good, that's what they teach you in the academy." He turned to Mike and urged him to watch the rookie. She'd show them how to do things right. She reddened and a spark flamed in her green eyes, but she caught herself, set her face in a blank expression, and said nothing.

Another job came over, and with it a rush of adrenaline that washed away her embarrassment. She recognized the code, past assault. Mike and DeGregorio seemed to know the location. They called it Ciccio's Market. DeGregorio floored the car, tickling the siren at the cross streets as Mike squinted out the side window, calling out hazards: "Good on the right . . . okay on the right. . . ."

Barbara wondered if this was for her benefit. Were they putting on a show for her? Past assault, what was the rush? They slid to a stop in front of a fruit and vegetable store on Knickerbocker near the el line and piled out as the inevitable gawkers began to gather. There was a woman out front who looked like the complaintant—

now, Barbara realized, *she* was saying it—and they talked to her. She was the one who had called she said. The man who had assaulted her was inside; he worked there.

Barbara saw DeGregorio march into the store, backed up by Mike, and she followed. In a moment, it seemed, DeGregorio was coming out with a prisoner, a fat white man with his hands twisted behind him. Mike was cuffing him.

Barbara was amazed. They hadn't even taken a proper complaint from the woman. Did she even want him arrested? She questioned DeGregorio.

"If it's going to be cleared up, it's going to be cleared up at the station house," he told her. "You don't wait out here for crowds to gather." He'd had enough bottles dropped down on him. "Here," he said, handing her another form to fill out.

Back at the station house she printed the prisoner, rolling his fat fingers in the ink several times before getting usable prints. Then she led him into a holding cell and slammed the door shut. He glared at her, pulled off his shirt, and began butting his hairy belly into the bars. "You like that, lady?" he shouted. "You like that?"

She didn't like it. She hated disgusting pigs like that. She tried to ignore him, bending her head down and concentrating on the paperwork.

At Flushing High School, Barbara Adametz wore sandals, drank Chianti, smoked pot, and experimented with hallucinogens, not a lot but enough to show her defiance of school, her parents, and society. When she got punished, so, she got punished. Grounded, confined to her room, she read. She loved books, and the house was full of them.

Somehow she managed to graduate. She was hired as a teller by the Whitestone Savings and Loan Association for $65 a week and took an apartment with a girlfriend who was collecting unemployment. When she tired of that, she moved in with an artist and motorcycle mechanic she had dated in high school. John worked for Harley-Davidson and had a 1956 Harley panhead. Barbara found work in a health club. Then in 1972 she announced she was leaving with John. They were off to California.

Grace and Joe Adametz were appalled. Barbara's willful degradation seemed to mock their struggles to escape childhoods of unrelenting poverty. Grace's father, Michael Sheehan, had been an alcoholic, as had been all four of his brothers and their father. When Grace was eight her mother, Anna Carroll, left her drunken husband and prepared to place her three daughters with different relatives, but in the end she couldn't go through with it. Instead she kept the family intact, moving into a relative's attic and eking out a living as a part-time telephone operator. For a while during the Depression, their electric power was shut off, and they had to leave their apartment door open for light. But Anna, whose own father had fled Ireland during the potato famine of the 1880s and ended up on a crew building the New York City subway lines, was a stubborn optimist. "Failure is only when you cease to try," she drummed into her girls.

At nineteen in 1939, with a high-cheekboned loveliness and patrician bearing that belied her wretched circumstances, Grace landed a job as a stock girl in B. Altman's Department Store in Manhattan and began a series of promotions to buyer. At a church novena in Queens one night she caught the eye of a neighborhood boy, a rangy youth with a shy, whimsical manner. Joe Adametz was only an elevator operator, but he hoped to become a policeman or firefighter—whichever service called him first. He had grown up in Long Island City, Queens, where his father, one of eleven children of a Bohemian Czech family that had immigrated to New York in 1888, worked as a storeroom keeper for an oil company.

Joe courted Grace but was soon drafted into the wartime army. The following year he came home on furlough and married her. They had three days together before he shipped out again for the Normandy invasion. He came home unscathed, joined the Fire Department because it had called him first, and their daughter Barbara was born a day after Christmas, 1952.

Joe and Grace scraped together their savings for a small house on the crownlike northern Queens peninsula of Whitestone, a prairie of open land barely discovered yet by the urban homesteaders. By the time Barbara and her younger sister Kathy were teenagers, their refuge had been enveloped by the encroaching metropolis and its ills, but by then the Adametzes had little desire or opportunity to relocate.

Barbara was nineteen when she and John packed the motorcycle, some mattresses, and boxes of books into a van and set off for Sunnyvale in California's Santa Clara Valley where John knew some other bikers from New York. Barbara found work in the kitchen of a hospital, while John repaired bikes. Weeks became months and then years. They felt little compulsion to marry. A piece of paper wouldn't change their lives. They were happy just drifting along. But after six years Barbara was ready for a change. Even she craved some structure to her life, some stability. The life-style had finally gotten to her—the incessant sun, the transiency, apartment leases written for only six months at a time. By the end of 1978 she was ready to go home.

She returned to celebrate Christmas in Whitestone with her family and saw in the newspaper that the city was hiring police officers again after the layoffs. Adventure and discipline together appealed to her. She took the exam the following June, and while she waited for the results found a scullery job in the kitchen of The Honey Tree, a restaurant in Gramercy Park, just down the block from the Police Academy.

Joe and Grace felt blessed. Barbara had found herself. The degradation she had so perversely embraced, piercing Grace with reminders of her painful past, was behind her now. She had grown up.

"Bread cast on the waters always comes back," Grace radiantly assured Joe.

"Oh, sure," agreed Joe with a wry smile. "It comes back as soggy bread."

She had come in for roll call one chilly March morning as the midnight tour was going off, logging in radios, and handing over keys to the radio cars. She was poking stray strands of hair into her hat and making last-minute adjustments in the dopey clip-on tie they had to wear when she overheard someone say something about an apartment. She'd been living at home since she returned from California. It was clearly time to set up house for herself, and she'd been looking for a place.

She traced the remark to a cop doing steady midnights, someone she barely knew, but she asked him anyway if he had mentioned an apartment. He said yes, he was giving up his place in Ridgewood.

He'd been living there while he was separated but now was back
with his wife, and the place was available. Did she want to look at
it? Barbara said she might be interested. It wasn't far and bordered
Bushwick; a corner of the eight-three was actually in Ridgewood.
He offered her the keys so she could take a look. The rent was only
$285 a month.

She was immediately charmed by the building, a chunky, three-
story brick apartment house with a funny green roof and an even
funnier name, Onderdonk Apartments, from its location on Onderdonk Avenue at Himrod Street. Maybe it was the Dutch name,
but it looked almost European to her. She like the gnarled oak that
shaded its facade, and the Italian-German neighborhood, too, the
salumerias, cafés, and delicatessens, the laundromats, row houses,
and low apartment buildings set along sepia toned streets lined with
spindly cypress trees.

When she climbed the two flights of stairs and explored the apartment, she found it spacious, with a big double window in the kitchen
opening onto a fire escape wreathed in branches—the oak she had
admired outside. The bathroom contained another surprise, a real
stained-glass window. She made up her mind quickly to take it.

She bought new furnishings for the first time in her life: a white
Haitian cotton sofa at a Macy's warehouse sale; a small Oriental rug
for the foyer and a larger one for the living room from a remnant
store in Manhattan; a Formica dinette set and chairs, and a brass
bed from a store on Main Street in Flushing; and pillows, plump
squares of peach and orange and lilac and rust and green, a pro-
fusion of color to colorize her life along with the new apartment.
From home she took a padded rocker from her grandmother and
her own books, hundreds of hardcovers and paperbacks—crime
novels, biographies, mysteries, histories, spy thrillers. She never
could bear to part with a book, even after she'd read it. Soon they
were spilling out of the bookshelves, the kitchen cabinets, and even
the bathroom. And for company she had Sam, a fat calico cat she'd
gotten from another policewoman.

Winter had dissolved into spring and bright green shoots were feath-
ering the tree outside her window when Barbara arrived at work
one morning to find the station house bulletin boards plastered with

leaflets about a cop in trouble, a radio alarm that brings fellow officers flocking like no other. She stepped up to read the notice, marred, she noticed, with fewer than the usual number of police misspellings.

FOOD   REFRESHMENTS
"10-13"
IN THE 83RD PCT A SIGNAL "13"
WHOS' GOING?
LOCATION: MOOSE LODGE—ACROSS FROM THE 102 PCT.
87-25 118TH ST.
RICHMOND HILL—QNS.
TIME: 6:30 TILL 2 AM
DATE: MAY 7, 1981—$5.00 DONATION
THE MEN AND WOMEN OF THE 83RD PCT ARE HAVING A
BENEFIT FOR
P.O. PATRICK DEGEORGORIO—83RD PCT.
PATTYS' 5 YR OLD SON IS UNDERGOING HIS
3RD OPEN HEART OPERATION
AND WE ALL KNOW ABOUT MEDICAL EXPENSES.
HELP US ASSIST ONE OF OUR OWN.

5

"Say good-bye to Tommy because he's going to get operated on," DeGregorio called to Mary Anne as she gathered up her books for the school bus that would be honking outside any minute. She came running into the kitchen where Tommy sat in the high chair in his pajamas.

They had told her Tommy needed another operation, but they hadn't said when. She had just turned nine; she didn't need to know all the details.

She seemed suddenly shocked. "Now?" she asked. "Today?" She looked stricken.

DeGregorio nodded. "Tomorrow," he said. "He has to go in to the hospital today to get ready." They'd drive Tommy there and settle him in his room, he explained. Aunt Luisa would be there when Mary Anne came home from school.

"Aunt Luisa?" Mary Anne looked panicked. She'd always liked his sister, DeGregorio knew, but that probably only made it sound scarier.

"Mary Anne, look!" Mary said to distract her. She showed Mary Anne a package of Superman sheets. "We bought these for Tommy as a surprise when he gets home," she said.

It seemed to make her feel better, DeGregorio thought. He watched her playfully rumple Tommy's lanky blond hair and give him a hard squeeze and a tickly kiss that made him giggle and squirm. Then the bus pulled up and she ran off with a shouted "Bye!"

She was so attached to him, DeGregorio reflected. Ever since

Tommy was born Mary Anne had helped take care of him. The two were probably drawn even closer, he admitted, by his fights with Mary. They'd gotten bad, some of them, usually triggered by her drinking. When she had had too much, she took it out on Mary Anne, accusing her of setting him against her. He heard about it later from Mary Anne. She accused him of not caring about her, ignoring her. All right, so he was away a lot, but that was the job. He couldn't control his hours. Besides, they needed the overtime for the bills, didn't they? One night they were screaming at each other and she went into hysterics, yelling that she thought he was going to kill her. She wanted to call the police. He told himself it was ridiculous, he was never in danger of losing control. But once, in his fury, he did something that tortured him mercilessly ever afterward: He swung out blindly with his belt and struck *Tommy!*

Deep down he had always known this day would come, but he had pushed it out of his mind as long as possible. He told himself he was confident. Tommy had always done fine, and the doctors had always been right. Still it nagged him like an open wound, flaring up in unexpected ways. Last Christmas, suddenly overcome with fear and guilt, he had rampaged through a toy store, arriving home with a trunkload of presents as if a lifetime of giving had to be crammed into this holiday. The panic had faded with the new year, but for weeks now in the spring it had been gnawing at him again. The big operation was coming, a large new implant for Tommy's heart. On top of everything else, he worried about the medical bills. The precinct benefit had raised $5,000, more than he had any right to expect, but it still fell short of his needs. He tried to put that out of his mind too.

Tommy looked fine; that was the weirdest part. His sixth birthday was six weeks away. His face glowed like a little crab apple, with strands of blond hair falling across his blue eyes. DeGregorio had to remind himself of what was wrong with him, what had to be done. He had to force himself to bring Tommy to the hospital.

"Anything I can get for you?" he asked Tommy hoarsely after they had registered and had brought him up to his room. Tommy looked pathetically small in the big white bed. An officious nurse was plumping up the pillows and taking his temperature. The surgery was set for the next day.

Tommy asked for some kind of mechanical drawing game that

made lines when you twisted the dials. DeGregorio had no idea what he meant.

"You know," Tommy persisted, "these things you twist."

No, DeGregorio said helplessly, he didn't.

"You turn it, and it goes like this." Tommy fluttered his small hands.

"Let me look," DeGregorio said. He went down to search the gift shop and came back with an Etch-A-Sketch game, the only thing he could find.

Tommy's eyes lit up. "That's it!" he squeaked.

Mike appeared at the hospital shortly afterward. The department had taken him off patrol to stick with DeGregorio through the ordeal. The job was good that way, DeGregorio thought, good in a personal crisis. The rest of the time they could break your balls.

Mike brought a hot chocolate to surprise Tommy. He stuck a straw through the lid and held it for Tommy to sip in bed. Tommy sucked up a mouthful and let out a yelp of pain. He hadn't expected a boiling liquid. He burst out crying, hysterical.

Mike tried to comfort Tommy, apologizing profusely to De-Gregorio. He wasn't thinking, he said; it had been a dumb thing to do. What could he have been thinking of? DeGregorio brushed it off. He had meant well. They hovered around Tommy's bed, distracting him, trying to make him laugh. Soon his tears dried, and he began playing happily with his new game.

It was getting late so they said good night. "See you tomorrow," DeGregorio said, and bent and kissed his son on the forehead.

Tommy barely looked up from the game. "You know, you're great dad," he said. "You're the greatest."

They were back by ten the next morning. Mike had picked up DeGregorio and Mary at home for the trip to the hospital. He'd made himself their driver. DeGregorio wondered, suddenly he could drive? But he was too grateful to question it. Luisa had arranged to stay with Mary Anne a second day, leaving her own two children with her husband, Craig, in nearby Patchogue.

Tommy was excited to see them, but he sounded cranky and tired. DeGregorio was sure he missed his own bed. They said Mary Anne sent him a special kiss, and they talked about baseball until it was time to leave him for the presurgical preparations. Nurses and a doctor were hovering by the door. DeGregorio struggled to sound casual. "We'll see you later," he said.

The operation was set to begin at eleven. The doctors had told them it could take five hours.

They leafed unseeingly through magazines, chain-smoked cigarettes, and paced the corridors. They weren't hungry but took turns going to the cafeteria for coffee, someone always staying behind in case word came. Every time a door opened or footsteps sounded, they automatically tensed and started to their feet. But it was never for them. DeGregorio toted up the reasons to be optimistic. The doctors were the best. Tommy had come through fine before. He told himself he had to be up. Everyone else was down, and he needed to lift their spirits.

At three-thirty they saw a doctor they recognized and rushed up to him. Over his green mask his eyes looked pinched and red-veined.

He didn't stop to talk. "It doesn't look good," he said.

"But . . ." DeGregorio was too stunned to frame a question. The doctor shook his head busily, offered a wave of dismissal or resignation, and was gone.

DeGregorio sleepwalked numbly to a pay phone and called home. Luisa answered. "He's not going to make it," he said flatly.

"What!" Luisa's anguished cry seemed to split the receiver.

"Make some phone calls," DeGregorio said. "Call Mom and Dad."

When he returned to the waiting room, Mike wasn't there. Time passed, and when he looked up again, Mike was back. He said he had gone to the chapel to pray.

More time passed, and then there was a doctor motioning for him and Mary to follow quickly. He waved away their urgent questions and led them down the hall toward a pair of swinging steel doors. *The operating room!* DeGregorio was surprised that they were being let into the operating room. How could they just be let into the operating room? Then it hit him with a terrible force. It didn't matter, that was why. All hope was lost. He entered in a daze.

Tommy looked asleep, centered on the table with a tube between his lips. There seemed to be a lot of people around, but DeGregorio couldn't focus on any of them. He just stared at Tommy. From under gauze wrappings a wire ran to a monitor that bleeped with every heartbeat, sending little peaks of electrical impulse blitzing across a monitor. DeGregorio, mesmerized, stared at the pulsing lines, his baby's lifeblood. And then gradually he watched the lines on the machine flatten out. There was no blood pressure, one doctor said. The operation had failed.

He'd been right, DeGregorio thought desolately. They'd been brought in to say good-bye to Tommy.

As Mary stood across the table, DeGregorio picked up Tommy's limp left hand. It was so small and soft, he thought. As if recognizing his father's touch, Tommy fluttered his eyelids. His eyes opened halfway, then his body went slack.

DeGregorio was prepared to cry but unexpectedly felt convulsed with rage. *O God! Why Tommy, God? Kill me, kill anyone else, kill some motherfucking drug dealer! Oh, no, God, not Tommy! Not Tommy. No, God. God. . . .* His eyes fastened on the surgeon, a little man, he just now noticed, a head shorter than he was. DeGregorio felt a lust to lash out, to hurt someone savagely, the way he hurt inside. The little man in the green scrub suit. He was going to tear him apart.

At that moment an enormous chill shivered through his body. It felt like a bolt of frozen lightning, impaling him to the floor. His boiling fury vanished. When he looked up, the surgeon was crying. "I'm so sorry, I'm so sorry," he blubbered, gripping DeGregorio in an embrace.

DeGregorio was suddenly serene. "It's all right," he heard himself say. "It's not your fault." The grief he felt now was for the surgeon who had tried so hard.

Across the table he saw Mary's face contorted in grief, tears washing her cheeks. DeGregorio looked down. He was still gripping Tommy's lifeless hand.

The ride home was a blur. He wept most of the way, with Mike stony-faced at the wheel. After they pulled into the driveway and stepped into the house, Mike asked him gently where he kept his off-duty gun. He pointed to the top of the refrigerator, and Mike took it. What did Mike think? That he was going to shoot someone? Or himself?

At the wake, Tommy lay in a white suit in an open coffin. His blond bangs fell over his forehead. His cheeks glowed rosily. He looked to DeGregorio as if he was only napping and might leap up at any moment to demand a game of catch. His lips, where the tube had been inserted, were parted in a slight smile. He seemed to be enjoying a small private joke.

DeGregorio was overcome. He threw himself into Joe's arms. How could he have agreed to a wake and an open coffin? He couldn't stand it. His own chest was being torn open, his heart ripped out. He turned furiously on his father. "You should be in there, not him!" he raged.

"You're . . . right," Joe said, bursting into sobs himself. "I . . . wish I could be in there."

Mary Anne arrived with her cousin Joey, the oldest son of DeGregorio's brother Ralph. He was also nine, born seven weeks before her. They had crayoned little cards that said, "You're with God," Silently, they dropped them into the coffin and watched them flutter down on Tommy.

Somehow DeGregorio managed to stay in the room. Mourners seemed reluctant to approach him. A neighbor murmured consolingly, "It's God's will." DeGregorio wanted to scream out, Why, why was it God's will? Who was God that He would kill a child? Why would God let animals live and kill children? But instead he bit his lip and looked away.

Hundreds filled the church for the funeral mass. He had insisted on handling the arrangements himself. Joe and Anne, Mike, Luisa, all offered to help, but DeGregorio had been adamant. It would give him something to do. He went to see their pastor, the Reverend Frank Pizzarelli of the Church of the Infant Jesus in Port Jefferson. The year before, the young long-haired, bearded priest and a dozen volunteers had set up a community service organization called Hope House ministries in a donated hilltop house. It would be a hospice for the dying and a shelter for the homeless, pregnant unmarried girls, and troubled youths. With his biblical beard Pizzarelli had always reminded DeGregorio of Jesus.

He saw cops he barely knew from the One Hundred and Ninth, the Eighty-third, headquarters, and the academy.

"Remember," a sobbing Detective John Medina recalled, "how you used to take Tommy in the radio car and let him hit the siren?" DeGregorio saw Phil Caruso of the PBA weeping along with other mourners.

Father Pizzarelli's eulogy was characteristically simple. "We're here because Tommy's bravery and courage touched us," he said. "He doesn't need your prayers now. He is with God. Pray for yourselves."

Afterward DeGregorio and Mary escorted Tommy on his last drive, to Holy Sepulchre Cemetery in Coram, where they laid him in the spongy ground, green with the shoots of spring. The tombstone they had ordered said, "Let the children come unto me."

Looking for ways to occupy himself, DeGregorio started building a deck for the aboveground pool he'd bought for Tommy and Mary Anne to splash around in. Tommy would have liked that, he thought. And it would keep him busy. He threw himself into the job, planning the design down to the last nail and selecting the lumber and hardware with the utmost care. Evenings he sat at home with the Bible, running his fingers over the lines as he read, as if to feel the words as well. Somewhere in there, he thought, might be some answers. He thought again of the story of Job and wondered if he had been cursed in the same way, but if so, like Job, he couldn't figure out why.

The department, applying standard trauma procedures, secured his weapon and reassigned him to desk duty pending evaluation of his mental state. The department surgeon arranged for him to see a psychiatrist at the academy. He invited DeGregorio to vent his feelings, but there wasn't much he felt like saying.

"What are you doing?" the psychiatrist asked. "Are you drinking?"

"No," said DeGregorio. "I find peace reading the Bible."

"I *do*," DeGregorio insisted, taking the psychiatrist's silence for skepticism. "And it helps. Right now," he confided, "I'm trying to find out where my son is. I feel like Job. That's helped me. Reading Job helped me. What that guy went through! According to the Bible it was a test, a contest between good and evil. Then I got to the part where Jesus says, 'Let the children come to me.' The children were bothering Christ, and the apostles tried to shoo them away. Once I read that, I stopped looking because I realized you have to be like them to see the Father. 'Let the children come to me.' That's what's on Tommy's tombstone."

The psychiatrist offered to prescribe tranquilizers and sleeping pills.

DeGregorio got angry. He didn't want pills.

"You know," the psychiatrist said, "you can't have your whole life revolve around the Bible and church."

"I'm not taking it to extremes," DeGregorio said. "It's just giving me peace."

The psychiatrist suggested a rest, perhaps a change of scene, maybe a trip away with the family.

At Mike's urging he decided to drive with Mary and Mary Anne to Canada. Cops from the precinct had made it easier by arranging for a half-price rental of a large Mercury and discounts at motels along the way. He drove north relentlessly, crossing New England and the border and just going, going, as if to distance himself from his grief. He drove through to Montreal and then on to Quebec. Sometimes they talked in the car, sometimes it almost felt normal, but then they would remember why they were there and one or another would break out weeping. Mary Anne was sullen much of the ride. It was hard to know what she was thinking. It rained almost every day, as if the weather, too, had turned against them.

There were large roadside shrines along the way, to Anne, the mother of Mary, and to many other saints. DeGregorio felt impelled to stop at each one to pray. He took comfort from the peaceful grounds and chapels. He had brought along his Bible and thumbed through it, looking for messages of consolation. Was God testing him, he wondered? Was he cursed? If so, why? He felt ridden by guilt but couldn't think for what. He swung erratically from anger to despair to depression and back to anger, cycles that left him overcome by an exhausted numbness.

After a week of constant driving, they returned home to a pile of medical bills totaling $20,000. The PBA arranged to pick up the hospital bill, and the doctors agreed to settle for whatever the insurance would reimburse. Whatever else they owed they paid with the money they had left. The rest, they figured, just wouldn't get paid.

DeGregorio was called back to see the psychiatrist. Was he angry they took his gun away, the doctor wanted to know.

Of course he was angry, DeGregorio said disgustedly. He was angry they took his gun and left him with his shield. Why didn't they take that too? he demanded, What the fuck good was one without the other? "You know," he said, brandishing his shield, "with this I could go buy a bazooka."

"Do you know why we took your gun away?" the psychiatrist prodded.

"You took it away to protect yourselves, not me," DeGregorio said. The city was worried about a lawsuit.

The psychiatrist smiled and said he was sending DeGregorio back to work. He made perfect sense; he was normal.

Going back was powerful therapy. In the car with Mike, chasing calls, he could forget everything else. Mike even got a chance to talk about some of his own problems. His love life was a mess. He'd broken up with his Canadian girlfriend and had finally found someone else. He'd met Francine, a nurse, in a bar. They'd hit it off, despite some early misunderstandings. Then suddenly it got very serious, and just when Mike thought this could be it, she could be the one, they broke up.

One day Mike told him that the medical examiner had wanted to do an autopsy on Tommy. It was not routine in such cases, Mike knew. If a patient was under regular doctor's care, an autopsy wasn't normally required. Maybe, Mike thought, they just wanted to study Tommy. But knowing how DeGregorio would feel about it, Mike had taken it upon himself to block it. He was going to stop it, Mike said he had threatened, if it meant going to the morgue himself and knocking the fucking scalpel out of the coroner's fucking hand. At that point, he said, the effort was dropped.

DeGregorio couldn't believe it. He hadn't known anything about an autopsy. He felt he'd never be able to repay Mike, never. He wished he knew something that would help Mike straighten out his affairs, but who was he to give advice on romance? Eventually he turned the discussion back to the Bible. Jews, he figured, had to know a lot about the Bible. Wasn't the book of Job in the Old Testament? But Mike somehow seemed bored by his preaching, and DeGregorio finally got the idea he just wasn't very interested.

Instead DeGregorio was persuaded to attend a Long Island meeting of a group of born-again Christians called Cops for Christ. It was something his evangelistic grandmother Angelina might have appreciated, he thought. But Angelina had died in 1976, two years after Pasquale. He listened attentively when a transit cop got up and spoke about saving souls in Times Square. But he realized that he wasn't out to convert others. He needed to find out what was happening to him, so he never went to another meeting.

One night, dozing fitfully in front of a flickering TV, he heard someone talking about death, and he stirred awake. It was some late-night talk show. The screen flashed the name of the speaker, Rabbi Harold S. Kushner, along with a book he'd written, *When Bad Things Happen to Good People*. It was climbing the best-seller lists, DeGregorio gathered. Kushner was asking why, if God was so powerful and good, He let innocent people suffer. Why did He kill children?

DeGregorio shook off his stupor and leaned forward intently to watch.

Kushner, a tall man with a gentle voice, said his own son had been stricken with a rapid-aging disease called progeria that had killed him at fourteen. Like others confronted with such heartbreak, Kushner related, his first reaction was anger at the injustice of it. Why Aaron? Why hadn't God prevented it?

Yeah, DeGregorio echoed silently, why?

Rabbi Kushner continued as if he were talking directly to DeGregorio. He had wondered whether it was punishment, a lesson, or just some unfathomable part of God's plan. He had questioned the goodness of God, even the existence of God. Like others, he said, he believed he had a deal with God; he'd behave himself, and God would treat him well. He had kept his part of the bargain, but God hadn't kept his.

DeGregorio, totally absorbed now, nodded in recognition.

In the end, the rabbi said, he realized it wasn't God's doing, it was fate or nature, whatever you wanted to call it. God was on your side. "He didn't make you have this problem, and He doesn't want you to go on having it. But He can't make it go away. That is something which is too hard even for God."

Kushner went on, looking out at DeGregorio: "God doesn't kill children. People and nature are the killers. God made men free and created nature, which runs by its own blind laws. He chooses not to intervene. If He did, earth wouldn't be earth. It would be Heaven."

Long after the program ended, DeGregorio sat staring at the darkened screen. He didn't know what to think anymore. He still couldn't imagine a God that let the lowliest worm live and let children like Tommy die. Maybe God hadn't singled him out, maybe it was nature, but so what, he thought. Did it matter? Tommy was still dead. He told himself he wanted to be next, that he couldn't wait to die himself. But then he thought of Mary Anne and told himself he had to live for her.

6

THERE is a savagery to mourning, the public display of the mortal remains, the shovelful of earth thrown on the coffin, vigils in the house of the dead. But the harsh rituals serve a purpose. They force the bereaved to confront the finality of death and thereby cleanse themselves for a resumption of living. In mourning there is healing.

Her young years spared Mary Anne the full anguish, and the therapy, of mourning. It was all a blur to her, a terrifying puzzle. Suddenly she was dropped at her uncle Ralph's; she had no idea what was going on. Suddenly Tommy went to Heaven to be with God. She was supposed to be glad, but she felt alone, surrounded by the toys Tommy left behind when he went to be with God. She missed him terribly. Mary Anne was mad at God. God took Tommy away.

She didn't understand what had happened. She didn't know Tommy was that sick or the operation was that dangerous. She was surprised when he went into the hospital so fast. When her mother showed her the Superman sheets they got Tommy, she was happy. She thought how Tommy would look asleep tucked in his Superman sheets. He was so cute and funny!

She was surprised when she came home from school and Aunt Luisa was there. She forgot her parents would be at the hospital. She was drinking a glass of milk with her homework spread out on the floor when the telephone rang. She jumped up to answer it, but Aunt Luisa snatched it up first.

Mary Anne heard her scream, "What!"

She ran over to Aunt Luisa. "What's the matter?" she asked. "Was that Mom?"

Aunt Luisa said, "Don't worry about it."

The house seemed to fill up with people. Her mother's mother and her mother's mother's mother, Grandpa Joe and Grandma Anne, Uncle Ralph and Aunt Kathy, her cousin JoAnne. JoAnne was Aunt Luisa's daughter, named for both grandparents, Joe and Anne. Aunt Luisa was whispering to them all on the side. It was spooky. Mary Anne wondered what was going on.

A while later her mother and father came home. Her mother was bent over, shaking, and at first Mary Anne thought she was laughing. Why was she so happy? Aunt Luisa ran over to hug her father. He seemed to be laughing too. Then she saw he was crying—they both were crying! She heard Aunt Luisa say to her father, "Take Mary Anne in the back."

Her father led her into the bedroom and hoisted her up on the bed. She sat there, calmed by his presence but disturbed by the strange goings-on. He sat down heavily next to her. Aunt Luisa started to walk in, and he jumped up and screamed, "Get the fuck out of here!" He was so angry, it scared her.

Her father looked at her a long time without speaking. Finally he said, "Mary Anne . . ."

"What?" she said, confused. "Tell me."

"Mary Anne . . ."

"What?"

"I have to tell you something."

"What? What?"

"Tommy's in Heaven."

"What?" she said again. She didn't understand. Then suddenly she did. *If you were in Heaven, you were dead. Tommy was dead.*

She sat up straight on the bed, trying to be good, her thin shoulders shaking with dry, hiccupy, girlish sobs. And then her father started crying too.

After it happened she pushed it out of her mind. She didn't want to think of it ever again. But the long car trip her father took them on afterward was so boring. It was like an old people's trip. There was nothing to see but statues. There was nothing to think about but Tommy.

. . .

She couldn't separate her life from Tommy's. She was three when he was born, but she had only the dimmest memories of those years alone. Mary Anne thought she could remember a pond with ducks, the sun shining off the water, her father, big, big, very tall, laughing. She remembered visiting Grandma Anne. She thought she remembered, too, feeding deer at a park for animals and playing at a police picnic in a blue shirt her father put on her. But in her mind the shirt had the numbers eight and three, and Tommy was born by then so that must have been later. And then she thought Tommy could have been there with the ducks too. Anyway, she didn't know whether she really remembered those things or whether she had heard her father talking about them, so she couldn't be sure if she remembered anything from before Tommy.

Her parents didn't tell her right away that there was anything wrong with Tommy, but she sensed something had happened. They would drop her off suddenly at Grandma and Grandpa's or Uncle Ralph's while they took Tommy somewhere. She knew her mother was always worried about Tommy. Watch Tommy, she said. Be careful with Tommy. From things she heard her parents say, she also knew her father stopped going to work as a policeman. He grew his hair long, down to his shoulders, and started driving a truck. At night sometimes her parents' angry voices woke her, and when she called for them to come into her room, their eyes looked red and wet.

She was five when they told her that Tommy was sick. Now they always said, "Watch Tommy. Tommy's sick." He had trouble breathing and turned purple. She carried him around a lot. Tommy didn't understand, he was too little. He was always calm, but she was always scared for him. Once she came home from school to find Tommy stretched out on a lounge on the patio. Her mother said, "I want to show you what happened to Tommy. Don't get upset."

She was immediately terrified. "What happened?"

"Eddie hit him with a bat," her mother said.

Mary Anne started to cry. "Why?"

"They had a fight," her mother said.

Mary Anne went running over to Eddie's house where she sometimes played with Eddie's sisters, Debbie and Ivory. "What did your brother do to my brother?" she screamed. But Tommy just rested awhile, and he was okay.

There were lots of kids to play with in their neighborhood and lots of places to play. Their house was at the end of a street at the top of a little hill, across from woods that looked to her like the biggest forest. A few houses down the hill lived another little girl named Kelly whose father was a fireman. Kelly was three years older and was already going to Catholic school, but she and Mary Anne became best friends. They always played Barbie dolls, dressing them, undressing them, exchanging outfits, and making up stories about their Barbies.

Mary Anne went to preschool at Little Hearts, where she liked building with blocks and chasing around the yard playing ball. She went to church every Sunday. Her mother was very religious, and Mary Anne tried to be religious, too, praying with her eyes closed the way her mother prayed. She liked her mother then. But other times her mother suddenly got angry. One minute she was calm, then suddenly she was angry and slapped Mary Anne. Sometimes her mother mumbled so Mary Anne had trouble hearing her. She yelled about Mary Anne's father, that he was no good. Then Mary Anne felt she had to say something for her father, and her mother yelled, "You're always on your father's side!" Mary Anne felt bad then. Her mother was right, she loved her father more. He was away a lot, Mary Anne thought. Her mother was making him stay away by fighting with him all the time. She was angry at her mother for that, and she was angry at her father for staying away. She missed him more than ever. And when he was home he played more with Tommy.

At night she and Tommy heard them fight. It scared them. Sometimes they went to hide under the crayon table. One time Mary Anne heard her mother scream, "That's right! Kill me! Kill me!" She thought of her father's gun; she knew he kept it on top of the refrigerator. Sometimes he got so angry he hit them with his hands or a belt, even Tommy once. That made her father cry.

There were fights before Grandpa and Grandma came to visit. Her mother didn't want them to come. After Tommy died there was a fight about the little boy her father brought home once to play with Tommy.

One night her parents had to go out. They wanted to get a baby-sitter, but Mary Anne begged to stay alone. She always wanted to stay home alone. It made her feel grown up.

All right, her father said, they weren't going far and would call from time to time.

They called two times, and she said everything was fine. She was sitting in the living room, coloring, when she looked up and, all of a sudden, *there was Tommy!*

It looked just like Tommy. She could see him clearly sitting in one of the red velvet chairs, smiling at her.

Mary Anne was scared. She dropped her crayons and ran into the bedroom to hide. When she came out and looked again, he was still there. She didn't know what to do. She walked slowly toward the chair. When she got there, Tommy disappeared.

As soon as her parents came home she ran to tell them. "I saw Tommy! I saw Tommy!" she cried.

"You did, really?" her father asked. He didn't seem surprised.

She told them the story.

"You mean you left the room and came back, and he was still there?" her father asked. "What was he doing, Mary Anne?"

"He was just smiling at me," she said.

"Were you scared?"

She looked down. "Yes," she admitted.

"Don't be scared," he said. "Be happy. You saw Tommy."

In truth DeGregorio was not all that surprised. It wasn't that he believed in ghosts, although he didn't necessarily not believe in them either. He didn't rule them out or in, one way or the other. But from the job he knew something of the way the mind worked. People see what they want to see. Like all of them, Mary Anne had been haunted by Tommy's death, and like other nine-year-olds she had an active imagination. She wanted to see Tommy, and she saw him. It was as simple as that. Certainly for her he was real.

He carried Tommy with him all the time too. He couldn't pass the curb in front of the house without seeing Tommy sitting there waiting for him. He still saw Tommy everywhere Tommy had been, in every space Tommy had occupied in life—the kitchen, the back-seat of the car, the velvet chair. A day never went by when he didn't talk to Tommy. Tommy, DeGregorio felt, was a constant presence. He could tell Tommy everything now, and Tommy would understand.

It was the same, he suspected, with Mary. However bad it had gotten between them, he never doubted her devotion to Tommy. If anything, she was more obsessive than he was. She had hung on Tommy, he was her lifeline; he gave her her best reason to exist. While he lived and after he died, she had nothing to think of all day but Tommy. At least, DeGregorio realized, he had another life. He had a place to go, the job.

He and Mike had been promoted to anticrime. Now instead of being a slave to emergency calls, flung by a dispatcher from one crisis to another, they began their tour by leafing through the day's unusuals, picking out complaints that pointed to pattern crimes. They brought in robbery witnesses to examine Polaroids of perps and came up with strategies for surveillances and collars. They cruised in plainclothes, in an unmarked car, staking out robbery locations. Mike told him they were on their way to gold shields. They were acting like detectives already.

DeGregorio told himself he wasn't deliberately finding ways to prolong his tours to spend less time at home, it was just that the job required more now. There were lots of collars, and each one tied him up for twelve hours or more at Central Booking and the district attorney's office where the corridors were thick with dozing cops waiting for their paperwork to be called. He told himself the overtime was good, they could use it. Then there was always PBA business, disciplinary cases to be grieved, picnics and parties and fundraisers to organize.

He often wondered what had really happened with Mary. Where did it start? Tommy, that was the obvious answer. But it had started before Tommy. He only made it worse. It had started before Mary Anne too. She hadn't brought them closer. How could he have thought she would? He had known about Mary's troubled family ever since they met, but he had foolishly thought her ordeal had made her stronger. Actually, it must have undermined her. If it was truly genetic, as he'd read, then she didn't have a chance from the beginning. He thought he had never really noticed her drinking in the early years. He couldn't remember seeing her take more than an occasional drink. Now he admitted to himself that he had realized even one drink seemed to send her off, but he had pushed it out of his mind. The clues were there, but since he hadn't wanted it to be true, he closed his eyes to it. It didn't just start suddenly, he thought; she had been drinking all along. He was the blind one.

Either way, the thread connecting them had snapped. The marriage now existed in little more than name only. They had turned off to each other. They shared the same bed but there was no longer anything between them. Should he blame himself for not being more understanding, not catching on sooner? Would it have made any difference? Maybe it was no one's fault, an error of judgment. People make mistakes. But they had made a vow for life. Their union had been blessed by the church; it was sacred and couldn't be tossed aside when it proved inconvenient. He believed that. Anne, he knew, often boasted, "In my family there is no divorce." If nothing else, how could he hurt his mother? Dutifully, he knew, she continued to intervene, trying in her way to rescue his marriage, pleading with Mary to get help, talking to the neighbors, even Mary's mother. But that only seemed to alienate Mary further.

And what about Mary Anne? She needed him more than ever now. After Tommy, was he going to walk out, leave his little girl? She was beginning to look more like him, with the same wide forehead, full lips, and heart-shaped face, tapering to a delicate chin. All his love was funneled to her now. How could he ever imagine abandoning her? He was trapped between misery and guilt.

He was hardly unique, DeGregorio realized. Millions of his fellow Americans were stuck in unhappy marriages. Millions more had split from their spouses and were living as singles again or had remarried, once, twice, three times. Rare, it seemed these days, was the *un*broken home, the once-conventional family—first husband, first wife, their own children, *none from a previous marriage.* Life the way he remembered it from Bensonhurst and "Father Knows Best" now seemed the aberration. DeGregorio was the norm. What had gone wrong with the times, with themselves?

But what made him special or at least *seem* special, he realized, was his uniform. Every week on the job he handled family *dis*putes, the way cops said it, but here his own life was a mess. Other people could call the cops. Who could he call? He couldn't call the cops, although Mary had threatened once, picking up the phone and starting to dial. He had torn the phone from her hand.

Others could plead ignorance, but as a cop, wasn't he supposed to be a mind reader, a psychiatrist with a gun? He knew, or was supposed to know, when to shoot and when to talk or walk his way out of a jam. If that wasn't intuitive in cops, didn't they at least learn it on the street? More than anything else, cops were supposed to know things civilians didn't and see things civilians missed.

He liked to think that the department had taught him how to see. On one of his first days in the one-oh-nine, he remembered, they had put him into the car of an old plainclothesman named Doyle who seemed to see everything. Cruising Northern Boulevard one day, Doyle suddenly said, "Whoop boop," and spun the car into a screeching turn. "Mutt there," he said, pointing to a hooded figure on the corner. "He's got drugs."

"Come on," said DeGregorio skeptically. They had just flashed by. How could anyone tell anything about the guy?

Doyle stopped the car and shooed DeGregorio out. "Grab him!" he shouted.

DeGregorio, still confused, piled out and threw the guy up against the wall for a frisk, turning up a single pill. "This?" he showed Doyle in disbelief.

"Behind the tire," Doyle said patiently.

DeGregorio searched and found a vial of pills just where the keen-eyed Doyle had said.

But just because cops were screened for criminal pasts and psychopathic tendencies, tested for intelligence, drilled in ethics, trained to spot what civilians overlook, and sworn to keep the peace didn't mean they were any better at life than other people.

Professional skills were not transferable to private life, he realized now. Doctors had a higher rate of drug addiction than the general population. Lawyers stole. Priests screwed. Cops were like everyone else, more so if their high divorce and suicide rates meant anything. Maybe the job was a marriage killer, maybe it took such a toll that there was nothing left to give at home. Maybe it attracted certain types who liked to tell other people what to do. The badge didn't confer immunity from the human race. DeGregorio never thought that it did. He just hadn't thought much about it before now. He was a good cop, and he'd always assumed that meant he'd be a good husband and father. But now that Tommy was gone and his marriage was crumbling, he was beginning to wonder.

7

BARBARA had missed the precinct's benefit for DeGregorio's son's operation, although she'd kicked in the $5 donation anyway. She didn't socialize much around the precinct. She wasn't the type to stop in regularly at the B & G for a few beers before heading home, although she did occasionally, and she hadn't seen much of DeGregorio since he'd showed her around the precinct her first day. She had long since brushed off his rude comments. The eight-three was an off-the-wall place, she'd found. Everyone there was a little crazy, so this was his craziness; she didn't hold it against him. Maybe, she figured, his attitude had something to do with his son, although she wondered why he had taken it out on her. Yet it was strange. Underneath he seemed nice enough. He was certainly an attractive guy. There was something vulnerable about him, something warm, something forceful too. She hadn't felt any personal animosity on his part; it was more like some kind of role he was playing, the usual macho bullshit she saw regularly in the department. Guys, they never grew up.

Barbara was at the soda machine in the basement when she saw a cluster of cops whispering and shaking their heads. Joan was there, one of the two other women sent to Bushwick with her. She walked over and asked what was going on. "Didn't you hear?" Joan said. "Patty's son died in the operation."

Barbara was dumbstruck. She knew from the benefit and word around the precinct that the boy was sick, but she had no idea it was that serious. She tried to remember whether DeGregorio had ever brought his son in, whether she'd ever met him. Could she picture him? She didn't think so, although she had a dim recollection of once seeing DeGregorio with his wife and daughter in the station house. They had been at the zoo or something, and he came in to pick up his paycheck. He'd asked her to show his little girl where the bathroom was. Barbara couldn't recall whether she ever heard the girl's name. The wife looked haggard, Barbara remembered.

She could follow the news ricocheting around the station house like a stray bullet, striking incredulous cops numb. It was horrible, she thought. How must DeGregorio feel? She couldn't imagine what it was like to lose a child. Maternity was not one of her drives, and she'd never thought much about having children. But you didn't have to be a mother to know it had to be the worst horror. She wondered what she could say if she saw DeGregorio. For all her reading, she was often unsure of herself when it came to expressing nuances of feeling. But when she didn't know what to say, at least she knew enough not to say anything. That, she figured, immediately distinguished her from people who didn't know when to keep quiet. Sometimes there just wasn't anything right to say. Anyway, she wouldn't be bumping into him for a while. From what she had heard, he was taking some time off.

She was working her way into the job and felt good about it. Her social life was coming along too. John was back from California and she still saw him occasionally, but as a friend. Their long romance had mellowed into the platonic fellowship of onetime lovers who hadn't quarreled but had just grown apart. She also went out with a few guys from the precinct. A lot of them were divorced—she was surprised how many—and there was no shortage of offers from them. Some had wasted no time trying to put moves on her, even married ones. What did they take her for, a dummy? She had made up her mind long ago never to hook up with anybody sneaky enough to cheat on his wife. Going out with anyone from the precinct was bad enough; word got around fast. And if something blossomed but died after a while, then what? They'd have to stare at each other every day. But she wasn't a hermit, she liked going out. What was she supposed to do?

As it was she spent a lot of time alone or with her family. Often after work or on days off she went to visit Grace and Joe in Whitestone, or had dinner with Kathy. Mostly, though, she retreated to her homey little refuge in Ridgewood. She loved to kick off her shoes and sit out on the fire escape with a book and a glass of wine. She adored her old-fashioned, big, boxy apartment with its high ceilings and large kitchen, although she almost never cooked. But best of all was the iron perch in the boughs where, through the summer and fall, she often took her supper, nibbling on a salad or takeout chicken as regally as a Park Avenue socialite dining on her penthouse patio. She didn't need anyone else to be happy. She treasured her independence.

And then one day, coming in for roll call, she ran into DeGregorio, almost literally smashing into him outside the muster room. She had forgotten all about him. Seeing him suddenly reminded her of his terrible story. She was flustered and didn't know what to say. "Hi," she said weakly. "How are you doing?"

He looked at her so blankly, she wondered for a moment if he remembered her. Then he smiled a little stiffly and said he was okay, that it was good to be back on the job. It gave him other things to think about.

"Yeah," she said, and then didn't know how to continue. She looked away, embarrassed.

He broke the silence, saying he'd been out a month, a long time. He'd had a lot of time to . . . think.

She waited for him to go on, but he seemed to find it difficult to say more. He shrugged. "It's hard," he finally said.

"Yeah," she said again, immediately angry with herself for sounding so moronic.

Well, they were waiting for him upstairs, he said. He didn't know if she'd heard, but he was in anticrime now.

Suddenly more at ease, she offered congratulations. She had heard something about it, she said. Was Arnold with him?

"Wouldn't go anywhere without Mike," DeGregorio said.

"Like American Express?" she said.

It took him a moment to get it, and then he smiled. He had a wonderful smile, Barbara thought, noticing for the first time how his lips curved sinuously into laugh lines both earnest and a little wicked.

Whoa, she thought, catching herself quickly. *After what he's just gone through, you can't think of him like that.*

• • •

She was easy to talk to, DeGregorio thought. She didn't seem to know or care that he was cursed. She treated him like a normal person. There was something gentle and relaxed about her—her throaty way of talking, her billowy red hair, and the way her eyes kind of brushed over him when she looked at him. He couldn't help noticing that she was slender, with a tautness to her body, and sharp, pretty features. Built nicely enough, too, her snug turtleneck certainly didn't hide that.

He remembered the day she had first come in. She looked blitzed and he'd shaken his head. *Oh, Christ, what they're turning out of the academy these days.* But if nobody looked good in uniform, as the cops liked to say, well then, she didn't look bad. When they had to pick a rookie to show around the precinct, Mike asked him who he wanted. He said, "I could give a shit. Pick the best-looking one." And Mike did.

The anticrime office on the second floor was the size of a closet, barely big enough for the two steel desks and chairs wedged into it. Ten members of the unit turned out of the tight quarters, but since they worked different tours, they were rarely there together. But in January 1982, Sergeant Jerry Longarzo called DeGregorio and Mike and the others together for an important meeting on "assimilating females." The department had decided to end the male monopoly in many of its elite units. The Eighty-third had been selected as a pilot precinct for the introduction of women to anticrime. One would come in to start, and others could follow. Now, Longarzo wanted to know, who did they want? "Remember," he warned, "you guys are going to have to work with this broad."

There weren't a lot of possibilities—three to be exact. The men ruled one out immediately, which made it between Barbara and Joan. DeGregorio tried to remember when the females had come into the precinct. About a year ago, he figured. Wow, he thought, anticrime in a year. Nice for them. It had taken him eight years. They went over the women's qualifications. Joan wasn't bad looking. Barbara wasn't bad looking either. They kind of looked the same. Maybe Barbara was a little better looking; it was hard to decide. "If anybody," said DeGregorio, "I vote Barbara." He added, lest he be seen as too compliant, a ritual putdown, "Least of three evils." The tally was two for Joan and eight for Barbara. DeGregorio was designated to give Barbara the good news.

She was stunned. *Anticrime!* She wasn't ready; she felt panicked. It was too soon. She wasn't experienced enough. And then she had a worse thought. Oh man, everyone's going to talk. Everyone's going to say that I screwed somebody to get this. I'm going to hear all kinds of shit from everybody.

"Great!" she told DeGregorio, keeping her thoughts to herself. "Thanks."

It was a different world upstairs. Instead of the tumultuous main floor, busy with blue-uniformed patrol cops, it was something out of Mickey Spillane, with clusters of steel desks divided by wooden barriers, glass-windowed offices, and airless cubbyholes, and thickset men with cigars and shoulder holsters grunting into black telephones.

Barbara felt a little awkward in the resolutely male enclave. And some of them, by the looks they shot her, seemed to think she should. Well, tough shit, she thought. This was her home, too, now. She could take care of herself and didn't have to take anyone's crap.

Her first partner in anticrime was Frankie Cammarata, a kibbitzer and practical joker. Then Frankie's old partner Buzzy came into the unit, and Frankie and Buzzy went back together. She got Carmine Napolitano, an experienced, shrewd cop, and a nice guy, she thought. Everything was fine with her. She got along with everyone, although all the men seemed to know one another from way back. The unit was tight.

DeGregorio and Mike hung out mainly together, but she saw them a couple of times a week in the office. DeGregorio sometimes asked her how she was getting along. If she had a question about who to call in narcotics or anything else, she saved it to ask him. He seemed to like talking to her, too, she thought, and she looked forward to their encounters. She wondered how things were coming along at home for him but wouldn't dream of asking. Mostly she let him steer the conversation, encouraging him with nods and smiles and simple questions to keep him talking, keep him from leaving.

Sometimes the unit went out together for breakfast, and she found herself jammed into a booth with DeGregorio. She noticed again how his smile lit up his usually grave expression. She watched his expansive gestures and thought how thick and brown his forearms were, how surprisingly hairless and soft they looked. He was like a grown-up boy, she thought, no longer bothering to deny how strongly he attracted her.

"Barbara!"

He caught up with her at the coffee maker. It was early, and no one else had turned out yet. He always enjoyed seeing her; his spirit did a little quickstep. He didn't know exactly what it was about her, but her presence always gave him a boost. Even though they'd had only a few conversations, he felt he could tell her anything and she would understand. He'd felt like a worthless wretch for so long that he wondered why anyone would even want to talk to him. But she was so receptive, so warm and *knowing*, such a wonderful person.

"Barbara," he said, "I've been thinking." He saw her eyes widen with what might have been surprise. Amber, he thought. Wasn't that what they called that color? Or were they green? Sometimes they looked more green.

"You know," he said, "about the precinct dinner dance?"

"Yes," she said, smiling.

"You're such a nice person, and smart. There's a guy I think you should go with, Kevin. You should meet him. He's single, too, and—"

He stopped when he saw her expression. The smile had frozen lopsidedly on her face, and her eyes now suddenly shot sparks.

"Do you think," she said slowly, "I need you to get me dates? Do I look that desperate?"

"He's a college graduate!" DeGregorio said, still thinking he was doing her a favor. Then he flushed with embarrassment. Desperate? That wasn't what he meant at all. Why was she so pissed? He liked her, he protested stumblingly. He wanted to do something nice for her. This guy was a nice guy. He'd just thought . . .

"Well," she said firmly, cutting him off, "you thought wrong. What am I, a charity case?" She walked off in a huff.

He stood there feeling like a complete turd. Now what was that about? he wondered.

When he ran into her over the next few days, she seemed deliberately cool to him, so when the transvestite dropped in at the station house, as he did periodically to parade his voluptuous siliconed breasts to the ogling cops, and Frankie got an idea like a light bulb going off above his head, DeGregorio willingly went along. Barbara definitely needed to loosen up, he thought.

Frankie called over the transvestite, a neighborhood character who had become a kind of mascot to the precinct. "So," Frankie asked, "when are you going to go all the way? You know, cut off the penis?"

He treated it as a serious question. "I know, I know," he said. "I just have to do it."

Now, said Frankie, making a show of theatrically whispering into his ear, here's what they wanted him to do.

He protested, giggling, "No, no, no," but Frankie persisted. "Well . . ." he said, batting his eyelashes. The men cheered.

DeGregorio put a call over the air.

Barbara and Carmine, out in the car, heard the 10-2 come over the radio and looked at each other. Report to your command. What was that all about? She called in. DeGregorio had asked for her, the desk said. They had a woman prisoner who needed to be searched.

Barbara offered a muttered curse. Always when she was at the fucking other end of the precinct, they called her in to search women prisoners. Where were the other females?

She was still annoyed with DeGregorio. Getting her a date—he must be from Mars. She could get all the dates she wanted. He was the one she was interested in. But as much as he seemed to like talking to her, he wouldn't, or couldn't, take the next step. He seemed locked in his own miserable world.

Outside the anticrime office back in the station house, Barbara looked at the hooker—or Las Vegas showgirl or whatever the hell she was—they had brought in, and shook her head. Tacky! This one was an Amazon, six feet at least. Barbara instinctively compared her own body to this overstuffed sausage. Then she motioned her to the bathroom where she could lock the door and give her a good frisk.

Barbara pushed her against the stall. "Take everything off and hand it to me," she said.

The Amazon didn't move. Was she deaf? Barbara repeated the

command louder. She still didn't move and looked as if she was going to laugh. Very weird. Barbara got nervous. This one could pull something, she thought. This one could definitely pull something.

Then she heard a muffled noise, some commotion outside, a knocking. With one eye on her prisoner she inched backward and unlatched the door.

They were all crouching there: Frankie, Buzzy, Mike, Ralph Autino, Mike Geddes, and, yes, DeGregorio, giggling like schoolboys.

"Did you find it yet?" Frankie cackled.

Only Carmine stood apart, scowling. "I had no part in this," he said.

Then it dawned on her. It was a setup. This was a *guy* she was supposed to be searching. "Very funny," she said. "Very, very funny."

On a warm May evening in 1982, the unit declared a moratorium on crimefighting and gathered at Shea Stadium to watch the Mets play the Montreal Expos. They bought cheap seats in the right-field mezzanine, settling not far from another contingent of cops who had had the same idea. Under the strong lights the field was shamrock green, and the perfume of cut grass mingled with the familiar ballpark theme of da-da-da-DA-da-DA and the answering coda of roars from the fans.

Barbara had taken the seat next to him. DeGregorio saw she was wearing jeans and a short-sleeved blue-and-white-checked cotton shirt that showed her bare arms with their sprinkling of freckles. Her fleece of red hair, unpinned and hanging loose, cascaded to her shoulders.

She had come with a goatskin filled with red wine. He couldn't believe it. He'd never seen one before, except maybe in commercials about skiing in Switzerland. What was she, a hippie? Who brought a goatskin to the ballpark? She saw him eyeing it and, perhaps misunderstanding the look, eagerly passed it to him for a drink. He was holding a quart cup of ballpark beer but put it down on the concrete and accepted the bladder. Trying to imitate her, he squirted it toward his mouth from an arm's length away. He missed, spraying a stream of Gallo, or whatever the hell she'd filled it with, into his face.

She was laughing so hard, she practically fell over the seat. The others whooped that if he wanted to kill himself, he'd have to use a better weapon. Jesus, he was fucking dangerous with that thing. He should take it to the range and qualify with it before he killed someone. They'd put DeGregorio with a loaded wineskin against some hump with an Uzi any day.

He tried to keep his composure. "I wanted to do that," he said, wiping his face with his sleeve. Then he looked at Barbara, who was holding her sides and weeping with hysterics. "Hey, Barbara, don't wet your pants," he called out. Then he, too, cracked up. He realized suddenly he was laughing, he was *laughing*. He couldn't remember the last time he had really laughed.

When the game was over and they filed out, hoarse and red-eyed from cheering and laughing and drinking and smoking, DeGregorio felt a letdown, a dull ache of loss, of dissatisfaction. He reached into his mind, struggling to track the feeling to its source, and discovered to his surprise, a regret that he had arranged his ride to the ballpark with Ralph Autino. He had left his car out on the island and had come in with Ralph who would drive him back. Otherwise, DeGregorio wondered, could he have gotten a lift with Barbara? She had come alone.

The realization that the thought had not only crossed his mind but had also found some deeper resonance disturbed him somehow, to the point where he began prodding his psyche like a still-tender wound to test the limits of his pain and confusion. He discovered a feeling he hadn't been aware of before: It was a long time since he'd taken pleasure in a woman's company or even longed for her presence.

He and Mary still lived under the same roof, but that was about it. They were no longer living as husband and wife, as DeGregorio had confided to his sister Luisa. Tommy's death had been the final blow to them. The loss of a child does that to parents, DeGregorio had heard. You'd think it would be the opposite, that grief would unite couples. It often didn't work that way, certainly not in their case. As it was, their relationship was stretched thin; there was no slack, no reserve of love and affection to draw on. One crisis and it all snapped.

She was starting the cocktail hour earlier and earlier, he figured from the circumstantial evidence. She wasn't that obvious. She didn't stand around with a bottle of Seagram's; she didn't have to for him to notice. He could see it in her mood swings. She'd be suspiciously talky, and then something would make her fly into a rage and curse him. He had abandoned them, she screamed. She had to do everything. He was a fool and was turning Mary Anne against her. Somehow, maybe from the time he had brought home the little boy to play with Tommy, she'd fixated on the idea that he wanted to adopt a child. "You'll not replace my son!" she railed.

He dreaded coming home. He insisted to himself that it was the job that kept him away, but he was thankful when a collar kept him at the DA's office overnight. If the unit went out after work for beers, he told himself he had to be there. Sometimes he even went out alone for a few. But it didn't affect him like it affected her; he could hold it.

Thinking about Mary Anne was the hardest thing. He knew she was caught in the middle, that Mary was trying to drive a wedge between them. He was convinced that Mary took the bond between father and daughter as a reproach, and resolved to break it, tormenting Mary Anne in the process. He could survive, but what about Mary Anne? It had to be destroying her.

Weekends when he wasn't working, he took Mary Anne out of the house, to Sunken Meadow Park or the beach or for drives, just the two of them. DeGregorio could see that she clung to him more and more. She sometimes threw herself at him when he came home. Out of exhaustion and guilt, one night he shoved her off.

"Get away from me!" he shouted, sending her running off, shocked and wailing.

"You hit Tommy!" she screamed, as if she knew there was no crueler taunt she could throw in his face.

He was checking the bulletin board outside the muster room—who was retiring, what cars were for sale, what genius new directives were there from the puzzle palace at One Police Plaza—when he saw the notice about the precinct party on Queens Boulevard. He was wondering, should he go?

"You going to the racket, Patty?"

He hadn't seen Barbara step up behind him. He whirled around. "I don't know," he said. "You?"

"I guess," she said.

"Maybe I'll go."

"We can go in my car," Barbara said, "go together."

He felt a rush of joy. He hadn't looked for this, he told himself. He had, in fact, ruled it out. He'd convinced himself that Barbara was a friend, that he just liked talking to her. He didn't want to feel deeply about anyone. Feelings equaled agony. Everything ended with pain, so he had ruled out feelings. Tommy's life had been snatched away, and his joy with it. God had punished him. Why, he still couldn't understand. So it was better not to care. But now unexpectedly, with or without his permission, the ashes of his feelings were being disruptively stirred into life again.

He was scarcely aware of what it was or when it started. It was subtle, an imperceptible shift of the wind, a rearrangement of molecules. It was soothing to be around Barbara. Something dormant stirred within him, an excitement he'd begun to associate subliminally with her perfume, a citrusy fragrance that struck him somehow as deep and passionate. He didn't stop now to question the feeling. Maybe he was afraid it would go away if he confronted it, and he didn't want it to go away.

She'd been drawn to him from the beginning, Barbara admitted now, although it broke all her rules. She knew that he was married, although it seemed hardly a marriage by his account. He had confided as much to her. She had made up her mind never to take up with someone else's husband. If he was so great, the wife would never let him go. If he was a loser, she'd still never let him go, and who wanted him? Marital infidelities had never titillated her. They were nice for the cheater, who had it both ways. But why should she share a lover with anyone? She was selfish; she wanted someone all to herself. She was straightforward and expected to be treated the same. No bullshit, no lies, no sneaking around. She had been spoiled. She and John had had a long and loving romance and had been honest with each other. Anyone else had a lot to live up to.

She had also resolved not to hook up with someone from her precinct. There were no secrets in the station house, and hurt feelings lingered long after a romance died. She had heard too many stories about partner romances—nice and cozy while they lasted, just the two of you in the car all day or night, but afterward, then what? Ask the sergeant for a new partner because the two of you stopped sleeping together, or keep sharing a car with an ex-lover, someone you now hate or who hates you?

For all these reasons, Barbara was determined not to be attracted to DeGregorio. So naturally she was.

His aloofness had intrigued her, challenged her, from the first. Had he been another of the drooling, hungry-eyed clods who mentally stripped and fondled her as she passed, she would have blown him off in a second. But she was intrigued by his deep reserve, his aura of suffering, his vulnerability, and his shield of privacy, which she respected and did not attempt to transgress. She wouldn't have dreamed of asking about Tommy, and he didn't volunteer much. It was his tragedy, and she sensed enough not to invade it. That alone, she realized, seemed to impress him, and so she was pleased to provide a friendly ear when he needed to unburden himself. But who was she kidding? She didn't want to be just a buddy. He moved her too much for just that.

So she made the first move, offering to drive him to the racket. Now she needed an excuse, some way to get him up to her apartment. She had nothing dramatic in mind, although she had sprinkled a few drops of Shalimar on her pillow just in case. She just wanted him to see her place, to have this intimacy between them. She was driving her car home from the precinct, and DeGregorio was following in his car. They would drive to the party in her car.

"Oh, wait," Barbara said after he parked. "I just want to change into sandals." She was wearing her usual summer uniform, jeans and a billowy white T-shirt.

"You want me to wait here?" he asked.

"Oh, come up," she said, "I may be a minute."

And then she thought, Oh shit! The place is a mess! She'd left in a hurry in the morning. Had she made the bed, put away the dirty laundry? But it was too late, they were on their way upstairs.

He had often tried to picture where she lived but couldn't quite conjure the right image. He had not been in a single woman's apartment for many years, not since he and Mary started going out seriously—fifteen, sixteen years ago? He had no idea how they lived today. Did they live like guys, like slobs? Barbara probably didn't, he figured. She was smart, and he imagined her to have good taste.

He looked around, marveling: the polished oak floor, the white cotton sofa, the multi-colored pillows, the books piled everywhere. He had never seen so many books outside a library. It beckoned with a warmth beyond his imaginings.

"What a pretty apartment!" he said.

She seemed pleased and asked if he really liked it.

He nodded. "It's . . . so . . . pretty," he said again, guiltily contrasting the serenity of it to his own turbulent household and feeling suddenly a little awkward. To cover it up he walked around and discovered the cat.

He peered into the kitchen and said, "Wow!"

"What?" she said. "Did you meet Sam?"

"The window, the tree."

"Oh," she said, "you like my penthouse?"

"Um," he said absentmindedly.

"I'll be a minute," she said, retreating into the bedroom. "Help yourself to a drink."

He opened the cabinets and looked for scotch or vodka but found nothing. Finally, under the sink behind the Tide and the Windex, he spotted two bottles and maneuvered them out—a dusty, half-empty crème de menthe and an even cruddier-looking old Galliano. Shaking his head, he put them back and opened the refrigerator, looking for a can of beer or a bottle of wine. He stared for a minute, unbelieving. Bare. The entire refrigerator was empty. He had never seen an empty refrigerator, except maybe at Sears. Where did she keep food, on the windowsill? He'd settle for a glass of ice water. He struggled to open the freezer compartment. Had it ever been defrosted?

"What are you growing in here?" he shouted to her. "Ice?"

"What?" she shouted back through a closed bedroom door. "You helping yourself?"

"What do you have," he shouted in again, "besides cream de mint and Galliano?"

"Can you make something with that?" she shouted back.

He shook his head in amazement. He walked back to the living room and then, on a whim, took out his keys and dropped them on an end table.

• • •

DeGregorio knew the bartender. "Will you sell me a bottle of wine?" he asked him as the party was winding down. The bartender stuck a bottle in a plastic bag and slipped it to him. DeGregorio tucked it under his windbreaker. She could invite him up for a nightcap, he thought. Then what? They could die of thirst.

He had it planned now. On the drive back he patted his pockets, then clapped a hand to his forehead. "Uh-oh," he said earnestly. "I must've left my keys in your apartment."

"I was going to invite you up anyway," she said.

The cat greeted them at the door and then ignored them. DeGregorio took out the wine. "You do have a corkscrew?" he asked.

"I do have a corkscrew," she said.

He joined her on the sofa, knees brushing casually. She had kicked off her high-heeled sandals and tucked her long legs gently under her bottom. They clinked glasses and sipped. He felt jittery, a little unsure of what he was doing there and disconcerted by her closeness and what it was doing to him. He became intensely aware of the baby powder freshness of her skin, the fleeting trail of her deeply stirring perfume—Shalimar, she'd told him when he'd asked—the jingling of her earrings tangled in strands of her hair, the scratching of the denim as she moved her legs, the soft plunge of her neck into her shirt, and the firm breasts outlined underneath when she moved.

"So," he said, looking around desperately, "you did all the decorating yourself."

"Um-hmmm," she said.

And suddenly their lips were brushing and their bodies fused in a long, caressing embrace. He felt the yielding softness of her body against his chest, the tickle of her eyelashes on his cheek. He wanted to hold her like this forever, inhaling her delicious warmth.

"Patty," he heard her say, "why don't you stay over?"

8

DEGREGORIO was in love. There was no mistaking the rapture he felt from that night, and he told Barbara so. "You're in lust," she kidded him. No, he insisted, he was serious. He had never felt this for anyone, ever. In fact, he thought, their ecstatic lovemaking had been secondary. What had moved him beyond words was their harmony. They seemed always to have been together, psychic partners, two halves of a whole so serenely and blissfully in tune that they seemed hardly to touch but danced off each other's body. It was—how could he explain it, even to himself? It was *effortless!* Never had he felt so self-assured, so gloriously powerful, so giving of love and so loved in return. She had given him back his manliness and his sense of worth. If she could love him, then he was worth loving, he was not an outcast.

He was not troubled by any need to explain his absence at home. Mary was used to his unpredictable schedule, he reasoned. She'd just assume he was out on a collar or doing a turnaround and found it easier to sleep in the station house rather than drive home late and go back in again early. He could always say he had stayed at Mike's. The way things had been going, he told himself, he had not really been married for years.

He felt guiltier over Mary Anne. She wouldn't understand. How could she, at ten? With Tommy gone and Mary battling her demons, he was about all she had left; he was her mother and father. He could see the consequences in her already. She'd always been such a breezy, self-confident kid, but now she seemed moody and clingy, maybe because he wasn't around much. Often when he came home late she was asleep. Then she'd leave for school before he got up. He didn't know the answer. To be around meant getting into fights with Mary. To be away meant missing Mary Anne. And now he wanted to spend more time away, to be with Barbara. All he could tell himself was that he wasn't seeing much of Mary Anne anyway because of his hours, and besides, his happiness helped Mary Anne. If he was happy, he'd be a better father, and it would be better for Mary Anne. Being miserable at home served no one. They'd manage without him. He'd find a way to make it up to Mary Anne down the line.

He stayed over at Barbara's apartment every few nights. She made him a set of keys, joking, "Just be sure to call before you come," as if he might surprise her with a rival. He chuckled. He wasn't worried. He trusted her.

And then he was reassigned, out of the Eighty-third. In the summer of 1982 drug crime was raging out of control all over the city. New antidrug teams were spearheading vast roundups. In Brooklyn alone teams were racking up more than a thousand arrests a month. The overwhelmed Narcotics Division was being beefed up with anticrime officers. DeGregorio, Mike, and some of the others were moved to Brooklyn North Narcotics, operating out of the Seventy-ninth in Bedford-Stuyvesant.

His first panicked thought was of Barbara. They'd be separated. But she told him it was actually a blessing. There were no secrets in the station house. She'd always been afraid theirs would leak out even though they made an elaborate show of barely nodding hello in the station house and picking places outside Bushwick to meet. This, she told him, would ease her mind. They'd still keep seeing each other, only they wouldn't have to be so worried about covering their tracks. And since Brooklyn North covered the eight-three as well, there would still be many chances for them to meet.

She was right. They often ran into each other at the old station house when processing arrests, and at Central Booking with their prisoners. Sometimes, while they waited to be seen by a prosecutor, they drove across the Brooklyn Bridge to Chinatown for dinner. They had to keep an eye on the clock, but they were happy with every stolen moment together. Often they spent their free time together in Barbara's apartment, watching television or just cuddled up in bed. Often he came over with a bouquet of flowers and a bottle of wine. They had no need for constant diversion. They were each other's diversion.

Other nights he would cook. He already knew that if he waited for her to feed them, they'd starve. He brought over a chicken from the supermarket and broiled it expertly in her oven, once he got the oven to work. He doubted she had ever opened it until he arrived on the scene. Sometimes he brought over a box of linguine and a jar of his mother's clam sauce, or just improvised a sauce with canned tomatoes and mushrooms.

But he liked to take her out. The drug beat was a great provider. He was racking up eighty to a hundred hours of overtime a month, and even after he paid all the bills at home, there was a lot left over for dining out and Broadway shows. One night, on their way to the theater, he remembered the famous picture of a sailor kissing a girl in Times Square. "I'll bet," he said, "you wouldn't kiss me right here on Broadway."

"Oh yeah?" Barbara said. She spun his shoulder around, dipped him down, and pressed on his lips a smotheringly juicy, dramatic, passionate kiss.

He asked her often about the old unit, and Barbara kept him posted. Her partner, Carmine, she reported, continued to take a brotherly interest in her. Carmine couldn't understand how she stayed single. He kept asking her if she was dating anyone. Oh, yes, Barbara assured him—someone who took her to Broadway shows and good restaurants. Carmine seemed impressed, she said.

DeGregorio was at the eight-three not long afterward and ran into Carmine. "You hear what happened to Barbara?" he asked DeGregorio.

He was suddenly alarmed. What had happened to Barbara?

Carmine grinned. "She must be going out with *some* guy," he said. "She's going to plays and all."

DeGregorio tried not to laugh. "Really?" he said. "I'm happy for Barbara. She's a nice person."

"Patty, sit down," he heard her say with unaccustomed abruptness as he walked in her door one night. "There is something we have to talk about."

He was puzzled by her tone; it didn't sound like her. They were going to spend the evening together, maybe call for takeout or go to a local place in Ridgewood for dinner. He lowered himself onto the sofa, not taking his quizzical eyes off her.

"Patty . . . I . . ." she began and then trailed off. Whatever it was she was trying to say was difficult for her, DeGregorio could see. He began to get a sick feeling in his gut.

"I don't want to do this anymore."

He recoiled and then for a moment almost felt like laughing. This was so ridiculous, it made no sense. What was she talking about? *I don't want to do this anymore.* Do what anymore? He was having trouble focusing his thoughts.

"This!" she said impatiently, circling an arm to include them both. "This, all of this, you, me, us."

Us? But what was wrong with them? He struggled to get it. Everything was wonderful. He'd never been happier, *she'd* never been happier. How many times had she told him so herself, breathing those words against his neck as he held her close?

"Patty . . ." Her voice caught raggedly as if on a nail, and she began crying. "It . . . hurts too much. I'm caring for you too much, Patty."

He slumped, wrenched by her anguish yet too numb and desolate to take the few steps toward her to comfort her. He was still in a fog. *Too much for what?*

She wiped her eyes with a tissue. "You know me, Patty," she went on, quaveringly. "I'm not a nut about planning ahead." She sniffled and managed a slight smile, drawing an answering smile of recognition from him. He often kidded her about her impulsiveness, her forgetfulness of life's little details, like buying groceries. She seemed to live for the moment, like the hippie she used to be. It was one of the things that always charmed him. This was just like her, he thought, to blurt out something without warning, not to give him a clue beforehand. Many times, he realized, he didn't know what she was thinking, so maybe he didn't know her that well.

"Barbara," he finally said, "what are you saying?"

"I'm getting too attached to somebody who's married to somebody else," she said. "It's going to hurt too much. I don't want to get this attached to someone who's married. I just can't do it anymore."

So, DeGregorio thought, that was it. How could he argue? That was the way she felt. Over, just like that. Two months of happiness down the sewer. Of course, he thought bitterly, what did he expect? He was always getting fucked. He *was* cursed. There was no point in prolonging the torture. He told Barbara he'd see her around and walked out, closing the door behind him.

The next day brought a busy afternoon of collars throughout Brooklyn North, so hectic that he had little time to brood about the breakup with Barbara. Late in the day he was back in the eight-three processing a batch of prisoners when he felt a light hand on his arm. "Hello, Patty."

"Barbara!" He was so disoriented that he didn't know immediately how to react. He felt awkward, yet thrilled to see her so unexpectedly. He couldn't help it, he felt happy. He hadn't expected to see her so soon again. In her jeans and T-shirt, with her red hair piled under a police baseball cap, she looked terrific, he thought.

"Shhh!" she cautioned him, looking around. But he noticed, thrilled, that she was smiling. "How are you?" he asked.

"You mean since I last saw you?" she said, still smiling.

"Yeah," he said. It seemed like ages ago.

"I'm okay," she said. "You?"

"Oh, wonderful," he said, "magnificent, never better."

She looked away, guiltily, he thought. "What are you doing here?" she asked.

"Shitload of collars," he said, motioning toward the back where the prisoners were being printed and handcuffed to chairs. "You?" he asked.

"I got a collar, too," she said. "You going to Central Booking?"

Yeah, he said, they were leaving shortly for the eight-four.

"Me, too," she said.

They arrived at the precinct a few minutes apart, lodged their prisoners, and handed in their paperwork, waiting to be called by an assistant DA. The room and corridors were jammed with cops asleep in plastic chairs.

"You want to wait in the car?" he asked.

Outside, he sat behind the wheel, lit up two cigarettes, and took one out of his mouth and handed it to her. "So?" he said self-consciously. It was awkward, he felt; they seemed a little like strangers now.

"So," she repeated.

"Fate," he said. "You see, we can't get away from each other."

She laughed.

"You know what I think we should do?" he said.

"What?" she asked tremulously.

"Go for coffee," he said. "They're so fucking backed up in there, we'll be here for days."

"Barbara," he said when they had their coffee and the waitress had left, "what do you feel about me?" He was studying her carefully, staring into her eyes, trying to read her thoughts.

"I . . . I love you, Patty."

"Well, I love you. I haven't felt this good in a long, long time."

"Me, too," she said.

"Barbara," he continued, "you know my marriage has been over for a long time. The only thing in your mind is a piece of paper, and you know you don't care about that."

"I'm not anxious to get married," Barbara admitted. "But there are . . . other people involved."

"You mean Mary Anne," he said. "I told you about Mary Anne."

"Not much," she said. "You haven't told me a lot about her."

This was too much to deal with now, he thought. "We don't have to decide that now," he said. "Let's just turn back the clock, go back the way we were."

She seemed unconvinced. "This is too haphazard. I can't live like this. I can't see anything but heartbreak ahead. I don't want to be hurt, Patty—attached to somebody who's married to somebody else."

"But," he argued in desperation, "you're hurt now. Aren't you hurt now?"

"Yes," she admitted.

"So," he said, pressing on recklessly, "you're hurt either way. Why don't we keep seeing each other because it hurts too much not to?"

She seemed to ponder that for a moment. "You mean," she said, "postpone the hurt for a little while?"

"Right," he said eagerly. "you don't have to deal with the hurt right away." He saw her smile and knew he had won her back.

She started in on him as soon as he opened the door. Where had he been? He'd abandoned her, left everything for her to do. She was stuck there. He was useless, worse than useless, he was a stupid fool.

DeGregorio saw the shape she was in. He could smell her breath and hear her slurred speech. He tried to calm her, explaining that he'd been out on collars and slept at the station house. But she was unrelenting, building up to a rage. She chased him through the house hurling accusations. He listened to her rant. Everything, he noticed, was *I, my, me, mine*. Where, he wondered, was the *us*? There was no *us*. She saw everything as directed against her; even Mary Anne wasn't mentioned. She couldn't stand it, she'd had it. He was doing nothing for her, he was never there, he didn't live there anymore. He might as well get the hell out now. What the hell good was he anyway?

He was prepared to be a little contrite. He did feel some pangs of guilt about Mary Anne if not Mary. He tried to hold out for Mary Anne's sake, but this was too much to take. He tried to control his temper, but it escaped. He took a breath, puffed up like a bullfrog, and then felt himself explode with fury.

"All right! All right!" he shouted. "You got your fucking wish. I'm out of here!" He wrenched a suitcase out of the closet and dumped his bureau drawers and toiletries helter-skelter into it.

He found Mary Anne cowering in her room. He was sure she'd heard everything. "I'm leaving for a little while," he said, trying to modulate his voice but succumbing to a telltale tremor. "Mommy and I are having problems. I'm going to live with Mike in the city. You'll stay with Mommy. I'll come on weekends."

She started crying. "Aunt Kathy and Uncle Ralph aren't getting divorced," she wailed. "Why are you getting divorced?"

"We're not getting divorced," he said, trying to soothe her. "We just need some time apart. I'll see you soon, honey." He kissed her and left.

He spent the night at Mike's and the next night at Barbara's. He spent a few more days at Mike's, two nights at Barbara's, then back to Mike's. Then he was spending three nights a week at Barbara's, then a week, and then he hardly went back to Mike's at all. Finally, without much discussion he just moved all his things in one day.

Barbara sat on the bed watching him unpack. "Yuk," she said, wrinkling her nose in mock dismay. "Don't you have anything that's not Banlon?"

PART
Two

·

9

LONG before he became a cop DeGregorio knew who they were, the ones his father called *them*. He had a friend who worked for them, running football bets back and forth on the subway. "I got to move some slips," he told Pat one day. "You interested?" Fourteen-year-old Patrick automatically shook his head. He didn't have a clear idea of what exactly his friend did or who was paying him, other than somebody working for Joe Colombo, whose paternalistic presence seemed to overhang everything illicit in their part of Bensonhurst. But it didn't sound like anything Patrick should be doing.

He had heard about drugs too. One day he was walking to the park with his friend Dennis. Patrick wanted to play ball, but Dennis wasn't interested. "Nah," he said. "Want some of these?" He flashed Patrick a palmful of little colored beans. "What are they?" Patrick asked, intrigued. "Tuinols," said Dennis. Patrick was dumbfounded. Two-in-alls? *Pills!* Where did Dennis get pills? Patrick thought of what his father would say. His father had smacked him for sneaking a cigarette. What would he do if he caught him with pills?

Joe knew *them*, the ones from Bath Avenue whose names were mentioned only in whispers. Growing up in Bensonhurst in the thirties and forties, he had seen a lot of them. Joe Colombo, who was Joe's age, played on the Bath Avenue baseball team against Joe and his friends. The round-faced Colombo, with slicked-back black hair, ran a social club called the Sons of Italy on Thirteenth Avenue. He and his cohorts played cards there and hatched the schemes that in coming years would propel him to the top of his own Mafia

family, and, ultimately, to death from a hitman's bullet in Columbus
Circle.

But Joe wasn't interested in Colombo's club. "What the hell am
I going to join for?" he questioned. "I'm an American." He cele-
brated his Italian heritage when the DeGregorio clan filled their
house on Fifteenth Avenue. But he didn't need to join a club for
that, not one of *their* clubs. He hated the way they were all equated
with *them* just for the similarity of vowels in their names, and for
that he blamed *them* more than the ignorant people who made the
bigoted judgment.

But they were hardly a myth the way some of his countrymen
tried to insist. They clearly existed, any fool knew that, although
they were not the way you saw them on television or in the movies—
suave, well spoken, and devilishly handsome. They were piggish,
crude, and violent, and once they got their hooks into you, you were
finished, you were part of them forever. He despised their arro-
gance, their lordly airs, their criminality. The next generation was
already being corrupted. He knew that some neighborhood young-
sters were runners for their gambling rackets and that others found
work as enforcers. He knew that storekeepers opening up in the
morning found little cards from a "protective agency" wedged in
the doorjamb, and that once a month collectors came by to pick up
the $50 or $100 extortionate tariff of the racket, depending on the
size of the business. Those who refused to pay risked a broken
window, a fire, or worse.

Dominick's market down the block, owned by Joe's uncle, Pasquale's brother, had to pay like the rest. But one day Dominick's
wife, Maria, saw an ashman's horse and wagon bearing down on an
old woman crossing the street and pulled her to safety. She was the
mother of Frank Uale, better known as Frankie Yale, one of the
Bath Avenue boys. From then on Dominick no longer found protection cards in his doorjamb. But he still had to buy the Mama
Mia–brand olive oil, which was another of their rackets.

Joe's brother-in-law, Al Venditti, who had married his sister, Antoinette, knew Colombo too. Al, nicknamed Monk for his simian
swarthiness and vigilant dark eyes, had joined Colombo's Italian-
American Civil Rights League, the ostensible antidefamation group
that Colombo ran out of a chapter on Bay Fiftieth Street. Protesting
what they called the government's anti-Italian Mafia slurs, Al and

other followers often picketed noisily outside the Manhattan offices of the FBI at Third Avenue and East Sixty-ninth Street.

Al had mixed memories of Colombo, with whom he, too, had grown up. He liked to note that "I went this way, he went that way." Al remembered that in the days when needy Italians didn't have many places to turn for help, Colombo gave them introductions on a calling card that magically produced jobs. Colombo sent families away on free trips to his well-equipped vacation camp in upstate New York. He gave out free turkeys on Thanksgiving—Al helped distribute them. And Colombo didn't demand favors in return, not immediately anyway. Sure, he knew that Colombo was deep into the rackets, gambling, loan-sharking, hijacking, shakedowns—but no drugs, Al thought, not then. Anyway, he thought the Sons of Italy and the Italian-American Civil Rights League were clean. Even the boss of bosses, Carlo Gambino, dropped in on Colombo in his chapter. Al saw him there. And Al was in Columbus Circle, ten feet from Colombo, the day in 1971 when he was fatally shot by a gunman who was then himself quickly and mysteriously murdered. Al never forgot the scene. "There were more FBI there than people. Suddenly, PAW! PAW!"

In later years, Joe's family heard, Al had cause to draw on some of his connections when a business opened by one of his sons was the target of a shakedown. Al appealed to a certain man of respect who arranged a sitdown that was resolved with an order to leave the son alone. Later, while Al was working as a commercial building super in lower Manhattan, he got into a dispute with a city street-repair crew and was roughed up by some of the Italian workers whom he dismissed derogatively as "Zips," Sicilian immigrants. He made a phone call, and the next morning two enforcers wiped up the street with Al's tormentors. He relished the story. "Monk," he said he was told, "you get a chair and sit in front of the building. If they look at you, call me right back." Al wasn't sure he understood. "Did you really mean if they look at me, because they're passing here seven hours?" "If they even look at you" came the response. Al sat out there every day until the street-repair job was finished, he later recalled triumphantly, and the crew never looked at him.

Joe, who didn't get along with Al, was not amused. He had no patience for *them,* any more than Pasquale did. Pasquale had had a falling out with Al going back to the time Al had helped him build his rental garages between the house and the vegetable garden. Al complained that he had never been properly paid. Then once when Al and Antoinette were house guests, Pasquale asked them to move out to make room for Antoinette's brother, Gabe, who was coming in for a visit from Mississippi. Al was so angry that he threw a spaghetti bowl across the room and stormed out of Sunday dinner. He and Antoinette, he vowed, would sleep outside in the car.

Sundays, Joe dressed little Patrick up in a suit and took him to the sprawling Shrine Church of St. Bernadette on Thirteenth Avenue in Dyker Heights. The pews bore little brass plaques of benefactors, including some, Joe had reason to suspect, who sought to take the curse off their criminal fortunes by donations to the church. Joe always marveled at the acres of gleaming marble, the grotto built of massive slabs of rock that overhung the altar, and, outside, the maze of thick hedges that encircled the grounds like an enchanted forest. There was plenty of money, too, for a Pee Wee Baseball League and football teams, all fully uniformed and accompanied by the church's fifty-piece drum and bugle corps. What would Jesus think of this spectacle? Joe wondered. Even young Patrick seemed cynical. Placing a coin in the collection basket, he piped up one Sunday: "He took the money, Papa. Let's go home."

The success of St. Bernadette's seemed little short of miraculous. The church had been founded as a storefront mission a mere twenty years before by a young priest, himself an immigrant whose father, a baker, had brought the family from Italy to Brooklyn when the boy was a year old. Now the cleric, Monsignor Francis P. Barilla, a large man who liked to plant himself outside the church, sitting backwards in a chair and glaring at the impious, was feted by Mayor Vincent Impellitteri, and other notables at hotel banquets, and led parishioners on pilgrimages to Rome, where they were received by the Pope. But Joe suspected there was more to Barilla's success than miracles. What was a priest doing smoking long Havana cigars and driving a Cadillac?

Joe thought he knew where some of the money was coming from. One Christmas, Barilla drafted him to pick up a benefactor's contribution for the church's building campaign. "And don't accept nothing less than ten thousand," he commanded. Joe, with ten-year-old Patrick in tow, wound up at the ordinary-looking house of Tony Anastasia, the waterfront boss and brother of Murder Incorporated's Albert Anastasia, slain in a barber's chair the previous year.

The door of the plain house on Eleventh Avenue was opened by a slit-eyed bodyguard. "Who is it?" demanded a gruff voice from the back. Anastasia came out. He was smaller than Joe expected, with brush-cut hair and penetrating eyes. Joe nervously explained his mission, and Anastasia said, "Tell the good monsignor I'll take care of it," airily dismissing him.

Joe reported back to Barilla, who was incensed. He ordered Joe and Patrick into his tail-finned Cadillac, and together they rode back to Anastasia's. This time the bodyguard was friendlier. "Oh, come in, Fadda," he said, ushering Barilla, Joe, and Patrick into the house. Now Joe could see that the outside was misleading. The interior was crammed with lavish antiques, Oriental rugs, and oil paintings.

Barilla got right to the point. "Tony, I want ten grand." Anastasia seemed chastened. "No problem," he murmured, counting out a pile of hundreds and handing them to Barilla. Then Anastasia's glance fell on Patrick. "You Joe's kid?" he asked. Patrick nodded. "I need a kid to shovel snow," Anastasia said. "Ten bucks every time it snows, no matter how deep. Okay?" Patrick looked up questioningly at his father. Joe had no real objection. What harm could there be in it? But it hardly snowed at all that winter.

Patrick never doubted where his father stood. At twelve he was in the candy store on Seventy-ninth Street one day when his father came in for cigarettes. Joe seemed surprised to see his son there— and more than surprised, suspicious, to also see Bunny, the neighborhood bookie, modish in a pressed brown suit and his sandy hair topped rakishly with a snap-brim fedora. It had been an innocent encounter, but Joe immediately assumed the worst. As Patrick looked on amazed, his father turned on Bunny. "You better not be taking action from my son!" he warned. Patrick was in shock. Bunny operated under important protection. Here was his father telling Bunny off. Patrick was afraid and embarrassed, but to his astonishment, Bunny backed away, murmuring, "No, Joe. I wouldn't do that." Patrick looked at his father with a new worship. Maybe, Patrick thought later, Bunny realized he had no power over Joe because Joe had no respect for him and didn't fear him. Maybe that was the way to handle *them*.

• • •

DeGregorio, new in Brooklyn North Narcotics, was trained in buy-bust by a smooth Spanish undercover pro named Joe. He showed DeGregorio's team how to approach a cluster of dope dealers on a corner and buy something from each of them, then wander off and radio descriptions of the sellers to the backups who would sweep down for the busts. They all took turns playing the buyer. The rest of the time they did the busts. DeGregorio found it exciting. Mike was less enthusiastic. He didn't care much for narcotics; he wanted to be a detective solving crimes.

Some of the team's better marijuana buys were out of a trio of smoke shops in Brooklyn's desolate Bedford-Stuyvesant section. The faded boxes of rice, canned soup, and evaporated milk wouldn't fool a moron, DeGregorio thought, not with the store windows displaying glass pipes and rolling papers.

For the busts, DeGregorio learned, the teams liked to come on terrifyingly as the Dirty Dozen. Intimidation worked. It reduced the danger of resistance. DeGregorio's partners wielded crowbars and sledgehammers. One swung an axe handle, another wore a hat with a pig face, snout, and ears. DeGregorio greased his hair to spike it up crazily and went unshaven, his jowels dark and as scraggly as barbed wire.

Staking out one smoke shop on Franklin Avenue, they busted the storekeeper, a small, wiry black man wearing a multicolored African shirt and a flat floppy hat that sat on top of his head like a giant icebag. Jamaican, DeGregorio guessed. He called DeGregorio "Constable" in a reggae lilt and smiled, showing a mouthful of gold teeth. He gave his name as Frankie.

With a practiced air, Frankie swept prepackaged bags of mari-juana and a pile of money into a shopping bag. Evidence. It occurred to DeGregorio that Frankie probably had been doing this a lot longer than he had. Probably he didn't want angry cops to trash his place and beat the crap out of him. A wise man.

Frankie motioned him aside, away from the others. Perhaps, he suggested, they could come to some *arrangement?*

DeGregorio played dumb and Frankie spelled it out. He could take care of DeGregorio and the cops could kind of forget about him. You mean, DeGregorio asked, like money? The constable had it just right, Frankie said.

DeGregorio said he'd see what he could do and carried the offer back to his command. Internal Affairs liked the idea. Frankie might only be a mutt but he had to have contacts. DeGregorio was put on a controlled pad. He would only pretend to be on the take. He was wired and sent back to the smoke shop, alone.

Frankie had $250 for him.

The next time he met Frankie at his other shop on DeKalb and again pocketed $250. But the following week he handed the envelope back. It was getting too hot, DeGregorio insisted. He needed more.

This time Frankie paid him $500.

He went back each week to one shop or another, gradually raising the ante to $1,000. He had to take care of other people, DeGregorio said. He was surprised how easy it was. There seemed to be no limit to what Frankie was willing to pay.

The next time he went back to the shop on Franklin, Frankie had a gun tucked into his pants. DeGregorio called him closer to admire it. It was a new nine-millimeter automatic. Frankie said he could get lots of them.

DeGregorio asked how many.

Well, Frankie countered, how many did he want? They were $60 each.

DeGregorio calculated. He ordered twenty instead of the payoff that week.

He went back a few days later to pick up the guns. The next week he went back to buy two hundred more, a few of them nine millimeters, the rest Colt thirty-eights, this time for cash. But he wanted to know where they came from.

Frankie shrugged, clearly reluctant to say.

Where? DeGregorio pressed him.

He had someone in the Colt factory, Frankie said.

DeGregorio was ready with a proposition. He could work directly with the guy in Colt. It was perfect, he insisted. Frankie would still get his cut and if anything went down, Frankie was out of it. Besides, DeGregorio threatened, hadn't he already taken enough risks for Frankie? Did this scumbag have any idea?

Okay, Frankie agreed, okay, he'd make the introduction.

It was a big breakthrough and DeGregorio discussed it excitedly with Federal agents from Alcohol, Tobacco and Firearms. The captain in Brooklyn North Narcotics was dubious, reminding DeGregorio what he was there for. "If you want to play silly fucking games with guns and bribery, okay," he said. "But you got to keep your numbers up." So what if DeGregorio was building a big Federal gun case? He still had to make his share of street busts, that's why he was there.

But then the case stalled. DeGregorio waited impatiently for word that the agents had made a contact inside Colt's Connecticut factory but it never came. DeGregorio never understood why.

Frankie and a partner were rounded up on bribery and marijuana charges. Three smoke shops were shut down and ten thousand dollars in bribe money and three hundred guns confiscated. But the source of the guns remained a mystery. How many other guns had gotten onto the streets that way? DeGregorio wondered. It left him with a sour aftertaste. He'd been onto something, he was convinced. The case was bigger than Frankie, but when he tried to take it further, the plug had been pulled. For that he'd risked his life? Disgustedly, he went back full time to buy-bust.

Still, from what Barbara was telling him about his old anticrime unit in the eight-three, what he was doing was more exciting than her cases. He wished he could get her into narcotics too. When the lieutenant in Brooklyn North said they were looking for people to fill in temporarily, DeGregorio asked the guys on the squad about Barbara from the eight-three. Mike certainly was for her, although he was on his way out of the unit. The precinct detective squads were being beefed up and needed volunteers. Mike had signed up immediately and was being posted to the eight-three detective unit, with the gold shield he had coveted for so long. The others also remembered Barbara from anticrime and said she'd be good. "She's great, Lieu!" DeGregorio raved, pointedly omitting the fact that he was living with her. The lieutenant put in her name.

Sergeant Jim Mullally, a genial, outgoing former pharmacist, shared DeGregorio's frustration over the gun case. They had traded conspiracy theories many a night. In the late summer of 1983 he and

DeGregorio brainstormed over where they could go from there.

DeGregorio knew Mullally as a crusader, a zealot, maybe a little wild but irrepressible and honest, a supervisor who was always trying to cook up new investigative strategies. The war against drugs hadn't failed, Mullally always said; it had never been tried. Now some so-called experts were saying that traditional organized crime was out of the narcotics business, Mullally told DeGregorio. That was crap, he said. "I want to get into the Italians," he said. All he needed, he said, was a good undercover.

DeGregorio immediately thought of Joey. He had been a great trainer in buy-bust.

Mullally waved away the suggestion. "Been tried," he said. Joey had gotten as far as a Sicilian named Dino, an intimidating associate of the Guidices, a tough family of drug dealers. Joey was his best on the street, Mullally said; he didn't mingle with the *goombahs*. "We need an undercover who fits into that world," Mullally said. "Like you."

DeGregorio was flattered but was put off at the same time. What did he know? He'd barely done one case. "I'm not an undercover," he said.

"Bullshit you're not. Bullshit!" Mullally protested. What about the gun case? he reminded DeGregorio. "You're a natural," he said. "Now who do we know who could give us a CI?"

DeGregorio played along. There was Detective John Medina of the eight-three who had come to Tommy's funeral. He'd been there twenty years. If anyone had a confidential informant, Medina did.

10

BARBARA liked the way Patty watched over her career. He'd been at it a lot longer than she and knew the strange ways of the department, although he'd given up his union delegate's job when he left Bushwick. She was grateful when he appointed himself her mentor. He had told her about all the buy-bust action around the city, how anticrime was being raided for bodies for thirty-day undercover stints, how it would be a good career move. She put in for it through channels and waited to hear.

She was happy to see that he was delighted. She was pleased he was pleased. They'd been living at her place for a good part of a year, getting along beautifully once she had persuaded him to lose the worst of his polyester wardrobe. In turn, she was a little embarrassed to admit, he had introduced her to the concept of cooking. His first household purchase was a blender. He was an intuitive chef, she noticed enviably. Without reading recipes he seemed to know just how long to leave things on the stove and how much to add of this and that. It always came out tasting delicious. Of course he never ventured too far afield from pasta and sauces and soup, things he could make in a blender, and sometimes poultry, but that was already a lot more than she knew how to make. He was romantically attentive, too, never seeming to take her for granted and often arriving with a bouquet. Or he'd tell her to change quickly, he had tickets for a show. Weekends he went to visit Mary Anne, and that was good, too, Barbara thought. It gave her some time to herself—time to read and shop, get a manicure, and have her hair done. But he often returned a wreck, worn out from Mary's harangues.

She wasn't as worried about people talking as before. Her partner, Carmine, had once spotted DeGregorio's car parked by her building. He'd called DeGregorio excitedly afterward, complaining, "You bastard, why didn't you tell me?" Still, she thought, it was good that Patty had been moved out to narcotics. Serving together with him in anticrime at the eight-three had been a strain. She had to keep reminding herself that in the precinct he was just another cop. Now, separated during the day, they found it more special when they reunited. But then she heard from the captain that her month in narcotics had been okayed, and she was happy about that too. They'd be together again.

They assumed she knew nothing, which was close enough to the truth. In fact, she had a certain familiarity with the subject from her high school days but had long since put that behind her; she figured that products and packaging and jargon had changed in fifteen years. She needed a refresher. She was turned over to Joey, the hip Hispanic detective and legendary street-buy whiz she remembered hearing about from Patty.

He told her about needles he called "works" and the different powders and weeds and pills and capsules. There were infinite varieties in color, purity, and countries of origin, he lectured. Junkies knew what they were after. There was no shrewder consumer than a dopehead desperate for a hit. To ask for the wrong stuff or to be gotten over by a seller dangerously marked a buyer as a cop. To make it more complicated, he said, different neighborhoods sold different brand names. To ask for the wrong product in the wrong neighborhood could be a fatal mistake.

Barbara found it hard to keep up. There was so much to remember, and the stakes were so high. She must have looked dazed because Joey told her not to worry, she'd catch on. All she had to do was watch. In the beginning she wouldn't have to buy anything; she'd just stand there looking like his girlfriend.

She had to leave her gun behind, which made her nervous. She couldn't hide it on her body, not in the summer. She was told that the first thing the men did was look a woman up and down, any woman. She could be ninety years old, they looked at her body. "And," Joey said, eyeing her lithe, trim form, "you're skinny. You have no place to hide it." Barbara guessed that was a compliment. She asked about keeping it in her purse. Joey told her to forget it. "Women in the ghetto don't carry pocketbooks because they'd just get snatched," he said. "The worst thing you can do is carry a pocketbook. You might as well carry a sign: HEY, I'M A COP."

When they went out together, he showed Barbara how to spread her purchases among a number of sellers for maximum impact. "You buy coke from one guy and heroin from another, to make a speedball," he explained. "Then you buy your works from a third guy. That way you hook up three people." Joey also showed Barbara and some of the other newcomers a few of his favorite tricks. They watched as he went out in a bloodstained apron, pretending to be a butcher on a break who had to score quickly and get back to the store. Sometimes he was a teacher with a briefcase who needed to cop before the school bell rang. The sellers were unfazed, Barbara noticed. Clearly, their clients came from all walks of life.

When it came time for Barbara to work alone, Joey showed her how to apply dark makeup under her eyes to look sickly. Her red hair would attract attention, so he showed her how to hide it under a ratty kerchief that went with the tattered clothes of a white-trash junkie. She was nervous, but that was nothing to hide, he said to encourage her. It came off as authentic. Junkies were often jumpy and hyper.

Her knees shook the first few times, but the buys went off smoothly. It was easier than she'd expected. Patty was in the team doing backup duty, and after she made her buys and radioed in the description of the sellers, he and his partners rushed in for the roundups. She stayed out of sight so the sellers couldn't put her together with the arresting cops. But then Patty got involved in an undercover bribery sting at some smoke shops in Bedford-Stuyvesant and did fewer busts. Before she knew it her month was over, and she was recycled back to the Eighty-third.

Medina's informant was close to the Guidices, a family of heroin suppliers in Queens. Supposedly he was an ex-addict who had a personal grudge against them for addicting his brother. But he'd have to be carefully checked out. Informants were notorious slime-balls. DeGregorio heard of one who had offered to turn in his mother for $100. This one could turn around and sell them out to their targets. DeGregorio and Mullally arranged to meet him and check him out.

He was a strange duck, DeGregorio thought, effeminate and whiny. DeGregorio and Mullally exchanged uneasy glances. This guy wasn't wrapped too tight, but at least he didn't seem to be in it for the money.

"All we want, basically," Mullally said eagerly, "is an introduction to the . . . the . . ." He fished for the name.

"The Guidices," their guest said, pronouncing the name *joo-DEEsees.*

"Guidices," Mullally picked up. "We'll take it from there."

How high-level were they? DeGregorio wanted to know. Were they big-time?

"They're mid-level," came the answer. "They're from Ridge-wood."

Ridgewood! Shit! Of all the luck, DeGregorio thought. He and Barbara lived in Ridgewood.

"They run a lot of holes in Bushwick," the informant went on. "They get their shit off somebody else. I don't know who."

That would be his job, DeGregorio figured. Run it up as high as it went, to the importers if he was lucky. This hump would just get them in the door. "Let's get this clear," he warned their informant. "Once you get me an introduction, you're out of the picture, *capisce?"*

He nodded. "I got another guy too. Nicky. He's also got holes in Bushwick and Williamsburg."

When they talked about it later, Mullally was all excited. "Patty," he said, "you're going from zero to sixty right off the bat."

DeGregorio would be a big heroin buyer from the island with a lot of customers of his own. For his undercover name he liked the sound of Pasquale Greco. He was supposed to have been named Pasquale anyway. It was close enough to his real name so that if somebody called him, he wouldn't forget to turn around, an im-portant consideration. His uncle, Joe's brother Mimi, was a singer who had gone by the stage name of Johnny Greco. DeGregorio had always liked the sound of that. Then, too, he knew, Greco was a big name in Sicily, especially among the Corleonesi. One of their bosses was Michele Grego, known as "the Pope." It wouldn't hurt for people to think they were related. Yeah, he decided, it was definitely a good name. He went into headquarters to pick up a driver's license and credit cards made out to Pasquale Greco, a telephone beeper, and a car, a beige Chevy whose license tag, in case anyone traced it, would come back to Pasquale Greco.

A few days later, his sport shirt open to expose a jangle of flashy gold chains, he went to meet Nick. Distrustful, Nick said they'd meet first on the street; he named a corner. DeGregorio knew the location well. It was in front of the ivy-covered Episcopal church, only two blocks from where he was living with Barbara. Nick, he knew already, lived just down the block in a yellow-brick row house.

He was repulsive, DeGregorio decided instantly. Long limp hair, a wispy mustache under a long bony nose, half-closed eyes, and a sickly pallor that gave him the look of an excavated corpse. With obvious caution Nick walked him around the block, questioning him about his background and associates, details that DeGregorio and Mullally had made up beforehand and that DeGregorio was now prepared to dribble out with convincing reluctance. They exchanged beeper numbers.

DeGregorio, jubilant, felt he had passed his first test. He was getting over on *them*, slime bastards. They had always disgraced his people, branding them all criminals. Well, it was payback time. It was surprisingly easy. He *felt* like Pasquale Greco. He suddenly knew everything about him, what he wore and drank and ate, how he leered at passing babes and threw around money from his thick wad of cash. He didn't have to grope for the right emotions; they seemed to flow out of him naturally. Maybe Mullally had it right. He was a natural.

Next he arranged to meet the head of the Guidice clan who lived in the same neighborhood, just a block from Barbara. Catherine Guidice's face could stop a clock, DeGregorio thought. It was long and sad and topped by a bleached blond bouffant. And she had a voice that sounded like tires on a gravel driveway. He'd heard she was separated from her husband, Frank, who police intelligence files said ran gambling operations for an ambitious young captain in the Gambino family, John Gotti. She supposedly had two sons and a daughter working with her.

He began by asking for a "taste," a $50 sample that "his people" could test. Catherine readily obliged, providing a pinch of heroin that came in fairly pure. But his first two small buys were diluted, heavily cut. DeGregorio feigned indignation. They'd been badly stepped on, and it had hurt him with his customers. "That makes me look stupid," he complained to Catherine. She was apologetic, offered to make amends, and invited him up to her apartment for another buy.

It was a simple second-floor walkup, he saw, but on the dining-room table, unlike most families, they kept a scale. He watched Catherine weigh the heroin as her daughter Donna's eight-year-old son took it all in wide-eyed. "Does the kid need to be here?" DeGregorio objected, as if he might be a witness someday. Actually, it gave him the creeps. Why wasn't the kid in school? What were they, animals?

He started buying small amounts from both Catherine and Nick. They knew each other, he figured, and he made no secret that he was buying from both of them. If anything, he thought, it would enhance his credibility and bargaining power. Each would think he had to be okay since he was buying from the other as well. But when Nick made a few remarks, DeGregorio could see it was bothering him. DeGregorio asked him what was wrong, and Nick invited him up to his apartment to talk things over.

They sat in the kitchen. From what DeGregorio could see past a wall divider, the living room was a mess, kind of what he had expected from Nick. In a chair in the corner he spotted a young blond woman with a blotchy face. She was moaning with pain and looked terrible. Nick said not to bother about his wife; she had cancer. She whimpered and begged Nick for some coke. Nick taunted her: The shit was for sale, not to be wasted. He grudgingly shook out some grains for her to snort. "Now shaddup, bitch," he said, turning back to DeGregorio.

They talked awhile, until Nick said something about making a call and stepped around the half wall to the other side, out of DeGregorio's sight. DeGregorio heard him dialing, and then his side of the conversation. "Yeah, Chickie, yeah," Nick said. He paused. "Oh yeah?" He sounded surprised. "Oh yeah?" DeGregorio heard the phone drop, and when Nick came back, he was holding the scariest gun DeGregorio had ever seen, a forty-five-caliber Thompson machine gun, all black, with a round magazine. It looked like something last used by Al Capone. Nick was pointing it at his head.

His stomach reacted first, twisting instinctively into an excruciating knot. Pain was tearing his bowels. The muzzle of the gun looked as big as a howitzer.

"You know," he dimly heard Nick say, "I was talking to my friend . . ."

"Yeah?" DeGregorio struggled to keep his voice under control while his racing heart threatened to pound though his chest. His eyes flicked back and forth compulsively from Nick's ghoulish face to the muzzle of the gun.

"He says you're a fucking cop."

DeGregorio's stomach churned with a sickening heave, and he nearly threw up. "Really?" he managed to say. He was unarmed. No wire. The backups who had followed him there were useless. "Is that right?"

"That's right," Nick goaded him. "Where the fuck do you come from?"

"I told you, I come from the island. What do you want me to tell you? Listen, Nick, if you don't want to do business, that's fine with me. I'll just go somewhere else. No problem." He tried to get up slowly, as if he were untroubled and could just wander out of there.

Nick stared and lowered the gun. "Ah," he said, "I was only fucking kidding. There was no one on the phone."

DeGregorio's flood of fear and relief funneled into fury. "You know," he said, "I think you are fucking crazy!"

"Calm down," Nick urged, laughing.

"Fuck you, calm down!" DeGregorio was enraged. "Forget it! Forget everything!" he said and stormed out of the apartment. He'd had it with this psycho. He'd gladly deal with the Guidices instead.

The next time he met Catherine he said, "Know what, Catherine? I even like you. You're a nice person, I'm a single guy, so let's you and me go into business. I'm doing my business out on the island. It's growing. Take me to your guy." When she seemed to hesitate, he pressed, "Let me deal with him. I'll get a better price, better merchandise." He lowered his voice for the clincher. "We'll make more money." She said she'd think about it. Meanwhile, they could do some more business.

He was on his way to see her a few days later when he ran into Nick. Instantly his stomach constricted. He was back in Nick's kitchen with the machine gun. "Where are you going, Pasquale?" Nick taunted him, singsong. "To the fucking Guidices?"

"Yeah, that's right," DeGregorio mumbled, hurrying off.

Now that DeGregorio was making regular buys from Catherine, the bosses at Brooklyn North Narcotics decided it was time to bring in the feds. The DeGregorio-Mullally operation, they agreed, would henceforth be run by a joint FBI and police task force under the code name Ridgenarc, for Ridgewood Narcotics, out of the bureau's Brooklyn-Queens offices in a bronze-glassed commercial building on Queens Boulevard.

DeGregorio shared the general police paranoia about the FBI, which was notorious for big-footing its way into high-profile cases, edging the local authorities aside, and stealing the credit. But working the gun case had broken down some of his reservations. He was impressed with the professionalism and resources of federal agents. If they could help him make this case, he had no objection. They sure had the money. They showed it by presenting him with a white Thunderbird, courtesy of a hapless trafficker who had lost it by forfeiture to the government. He was moving up in the drug business, wasn't he? Well, here was proof.

He made more buys from the Guidices and sensed that Catherine liked him but that her daughter, Donna, a moon-faced, sad-looking girl, was distrustful. Warily, she let him tag along one day when she resupplied her holes in Bushwick, where junkies working for her passed dime bags through crevices in slum walls. Because the sellers couldn't be trusted with more than minimal quantities of drugs at a time, she had to keep resupplying them. But Donna wasn't comfortable around DeGregorio. He was in the Thunderbird with her and her mother one day when Donna abruptly said, "How do I know you ain't a cop?"

It took him by surprise and he almost lost control of the wheel, but he caught himself quickly and said leeringly, "Tell you what, Donna. We're going to drop off your mother now and get a bottle of wine and a motel room in Ridgewood. We'll take all our clothes off, and after you find out I ain't got a wire on, we're going to do the right thing."

Catherine thought that was funny, cackling, "Heh, heh, heh," in her sandpapery voice. Donna just gave him a dirty look.

It was a dangerous bluff. He *was* wearing a wire, a Nagra recorder taped to his crotch, where he figured Catherine would be least likely to touch him. But that was the end of that, DeGregorio vowed. This would definitely be the last time. They'd have to come up with a safer way to bug his meetings.

The bureau had the answer. Swiftly, technicians from special operations bugged the Thunderbird with a tape recorder in the dashboard and a wireless transmitter in the sun visor.

Catherine finally agreed to take him to her supplier. Slumped down behind the wheel outside her building that day waiting for her, he saw her approach with a stranger, a tall, glowering, sleek-combed Italian-looking guy. When Catherine got into the car, he climbed in, too, uninvited.

Was this a setup? He'd better come on strong, DeGregorio figured. He turned to Catherine. "Who the fuck's this guy?"

Dino, said Catherine. DeGregorio made the connection. This had to be Dino, the Sicilian who had intimidated Joey the undercover. DeGregorio hated him already. "I'm a friend of hers," Dino grunted.

"Well, you ain't a friend of mine," DeGregorio said. "Get the fuck out of here."

Dino pierced him with a fierce stare, and DeGregorio tensed for a fight. "I don't know who you are," he repeated. "Get out of the fucking car." When he still didn't move, DeGregorio said to Catherine, "If you want to do business with me, get him out of the car."

Triumphantly, he saw Catherine shrug and tell Dino he'd better leave.

They drove awhile, Catherine guiding him through the blue-and-white-bannered streets of Greek Astoria to where she said her supplier was waiting. "Don't worry," she assured him. "He's a big guy, he's dealing with kilos." She told him to stop down the block from a tavern called My Place while she went inside.

He leaned back against the seat to wait. Down the street, a dark figure exited the tavern. DeGregorio eyed him through the sideview mirror as he melted away out of sight. He smoked a cigarette, then another. Waiting, that was always the worst part. Suddenly the car door was yanked open, and he jumped with surprise.

"You see how people lie! What a liar he is!" Catherine was back, empty-handed, raging.

"What? Did he stiff us?"

"He didn't have it. He went to get it."

"That was him?" DeGregorio wished he'd seen his face.

"Yeah, the guy all dressed in black." She snorted in disgust. "I should bring it in myself, then I wouldn't need assholes like that."

"So then why don't you?" he prodded.

"My son chickened out."

DeGregorio stayed silent, letting her talk into the dashboard mike. She was bemoaning her fucked-up kids.

"My son, Joseph, was going to shoot up. I detox him three times myself. He hocked his sneakers, his stereo system, everything. He went and sold everything, he sold his jewelry, too, for being a nose junkie." She looked around nervously. "Where's this guy? Hurry up, pain in the ass."

DeGregorio rushed to agree. "I hate hanging around like this, you know. I'm getting nervous now."

She was muttering, "This bullshit . . . get the hell out of here. . . ."

"This is bullshit, you're right." He worked to keep her talking. "I remember when it was seventy-five hundred an ounce," he said. "That wasn't long ago, right?"

"Yeah, but right now there's all shit. . . ." Her voice trailed off.

He looked up to see what had distracted her.

There was a dark figure at his side window, a man all in black—black jacket, black shirt, black pants.

DeGregorio felt he had been dropped into a foreign movie. Thrown off balance, he tried to sound casual. "Hi, how you doing?"

"Did you get it?" Catherine asked.

"Yeah," the man grunted, climbing into the backseat.

"What's your name?" DeGregorio asked.

"Franco." The accent was Italian.

DeGregorio stuck out his hand. "Pasqual'." He watched as Franco gave Catherine a package, which she eagerly tore open. She sprinkled out a few white grains and peered at the color.

Franco looked insulted. "What are you, stupid? I'm telling you it's good, it's good." At $200,000 a kilo, he said, she was lucky to be getting anything at all. Supplies had dried up. The people bringing it over used to charge $35,000 a kilo for transport but now they wanted $55,000, he complained. He had a kilo waiting that he couldn't get over here.

DeGregorio saw an opening. "How much you give me to bring it over?"

"Fifty thousand," said Franco.

"I got my own plan," DeGregorio said. "I'm not stupid. I know how I could do it. I got a way I could bring it over here, in my own mind, if I had with me a guy about eighty-five, ninety years old. What do you think of that?"

"No," said Franco contemptuously. His ideal mule was a woman traveling with five kids.

They dropped Franco off to see Catherine's daughter, Donna. He and Catherine were alone again in the car, and DeGregorio said it would be good dealing with Franco. "He knows me now, so that's good, you know," he said. "He knows me now."

It was after 1:00 A.M. and Catherine said she wanted some coffee at a diner. She complained about Donna. She was selling speed now, and using too. "O, dear God, this girl. What is she? What is it, they got to put speed in the coke? You don't know these kids. They'll do anything."

"I know," DeGregorio commiserated.

11

MARY Anne, eleven, told herself it didn't matter. It didn't matter that her father didn't live at home with them anymore, that her mother had savage tantrums, that Tommy had died. Nothing mattered. She was okay. Everything was all right. She could handle it. Pretending made her feel better. It covered up the hurt and loss and confusion. But really she didn't understand why her father had left and what was going on with her mother.

Her father's absence filled her with shame and guilt, as if she were somehow responsible for his departure. In a way she couldn't explain, she thought it had to do with her deep feelings for him. She loved him so much, maybe too much. Maybe the way she felt about him was wrong, and that was why he left. Maybe this was his way of punishing her for her feelings. It would explain why her mother seemed so angry with her. Maybe it was all her fault; her feelings had caused everything. But then she reminded herself that she didn't care, it didn't change anything, it didn't matter.

She was having trouble in school, struggling through the sixth grade in Coram Elementary. Sometimes she wished the bus would forget to pick her up in the morning. She had trouble concentrating and preferred looking out the window, daydreaming, or playing with her friends in the schoolyard. She liked her teacher, though. He was nice and seemed to know about her trouble at home. He took extra time to explain the homework to her, and if she got something wrong, he didn't yell at her. He said she had to make more of an effort if she wanted to graduate. But she didn't feel like making an effort. School wasn't that important. She felt all used up from making an effort at home.

It wasn't always that awful with her mother, Mary Anne thought. There were times after her father left when her mother seemed to try. She took her shopping and explained things to her—about becoming a woman, about the changes she would be feeling and seeing in her body, about her first period. At times like that she seemed like a real mother, a mother like her friends had.

There were times, too, when her mother parted the curtain that hid her past and gave Mary Anne a glimpse of her own childhood— just her, her mother, and her two brothers, and how hard it had been for her watching over her brothers all the time. Mary Anne was hungry for more. She was curious about her mother's family, but her mother wouldn't say more. Mary Anne knew her mother's mother, who lived in Kings Park. Mary Anne thought she blamed her for making her mother crazy. Mary Anne wondered about her mother's father and why she never mentioned him. She sensed a deep sadness in her mother, but she couldn't break through it. It made her feel sorry for her. It surprised her, but then Mary Anne realized she was supposed to love her mother.

Mary Anne knew her mother had some problem with her drinking. She had heard them arguing about it before her father had left. She had dim recollections of terrifying fights even when Tommy was still alive. She remembered hiding with him under the crayon table. For a long time her father's yelling about drinking made no sense. Everybody drank, she thought then. What was bad about drinking? She saw her mother and father pouring drinks from a bottle. She saw her mother's mother drinking beer; there was nothing wrong with that.

She now knew when her mother had been drinking, because she could smell it on her breath. It had a special smell, sour, a hard smell that made her head shake. She made a connection between that smell and her mother's bad moods. When she could smell the drinking smell on her mother's breath, Mary Anne knew her mother would blow up over anything—if she couldn't find the keys or if her little kitten Pepsi peed on the floor. Sometimes she insisted it was late and Mary Anne had to go to bed right away, even though it was only seven-thirty or eight o'clock. Mary Anne refused. Her mother was crazy. Who went to bed at seven-thirty? Other times her mother shook Mary Anne awake in the middle of the night to complain that the truck hadn't picked up the garbage or the phone bill was too high. Did Mary Anne make all those calls?

She was forced to listen as her mother cursed her father as useless, a fool who didn't care about her, didn't care about Mary Anne, ran out on them, and didn't leave them enough money. His family was the problem, her mother yelled. There was heart trouble in his family. Maybe Tommy's problem came from his side of the family. It could be their fault he died. Yeah, her mother said, Mary Anne's father couldn't deal with that so he ran out on them. He couldn't bear to live there anymore because it reminded him of Tommy. He wasn't man enough to stay there and deal with it.

She blamed Mary Anne for always defending him. She told Mary Anne he had to be sneaking around with some other woman. He wasn't living with Mike but was probably off with somebody else, the liar. Of all the things her mother said, Mary Anne thought that was the most ridiculous. Her father wasn't like that; he wouldn't do that. Her mother was wrong about everything else, so why should she be right about that?

She wanted to defend her father, but her mother would say that was what she always did, that Mary Anne always loved him more. It was useless, Mary Anne thought, but she couldn't stop herself from twirling her hair, twisting it around a finger above her ears, and twirling, twirling, twirling. Often she didn't even realize she was doing it. Sometimes, too, she blinked her eyes uncontrollably.

They had fights, but her mother wasn't strong enough to hit hard. It was pathetic, Mary Anne thought. She almost wanted to laugh— her mother, barely able to stand up, trying to hit her. But then Mary Anne would run to the phone and frantically call her father. She usually got his answering machine and left a message. He would call back later, telling them to calm down, but sometimes he came in person.

From things her father said, Mary Anne had a feeling her mother had a bottle hidden somewhere. Her father would often question her: Did she see her mother drinking? Was she still drinking Seagram's? From the Spanish chest? She didn't see any bottles in the Spanish chest now, but Mary Anne gathered from the questions, the way her mother's breath smelled, and the way she was mumbling and angry that she had to be drinking secretly because Mary Anne didn't see her drink. She was curious about where her mother got the drinks.

Once while her mother was busy in the kitchen, Mary Anne went through her bedroom. She dug through the closet and through the drawers, looked under the bed and behind the curtains, and then pulled aside a pillow, a yellow cushion with armrests sitting on the floor. There it was, a long-necked brown Seagram's bottle.

She stared at it, amazed, and terrified to see her suspicion suddenly take form. She didn't know what to do—steal it or tell her mother she found it. If her father were around, she thought, she would tell him. He probably would get mad, and there would be a fight. She thought she heard her mother coming and panicked. She quickly replaced the pillow on the floor and tiptoed out. Her mother was still in the kitchen. She reached into her mother's purse, sneaked a cigarette out of her pack of Marlboro's, and carried it outside to the garage.

She had started smoking a few months before. Her friend Kelly sometimes bought cigarettes and gave her some. Or she just took some from her mother. Her mother couldn't care much. She once told Mary Anne, "I know you're smoking because I saw them." When Mary Anne denied it, her mother didn't seem too upset. "I'll let you smoke, but you're too young yet," she said. Mary Anne ignored her. Who cared what she said?

She liked to smoke in the garage. Along one wall ran a long wooden ledge covering a narrow slit down to the floor. She could stub out her butts on the sill and drop them through the slit where they disappeared. She could be alone there in the musty dampness with the cobwebby cartons and rusty tools. She could hide in there and smoke, and no one would bother her. She felt her father's presence too. *His car used to be right here.* She fantasized that he would drive up one day, feel bad he had left her there, and move back in with them again.

One day her mother was working herself into a rage, banging pots and pans in the kitchen, howling that Mary Anne was driving her crazy. Mary Anne tensed, dreading what was coming. She started to twirl her hair and then blurted, cruelly triumphant, "I found it! Under the pillow on the floor."

Her mother stopped in mid-cry. She looked stunned, staring open-mouthed at Mary Anne. Then she seemed to catch herself and tried to brush it off as nothing, just an old bottle she'd forgotten about. What was the big deal? After that the bottle was gone from behind the pillow. Usually now it was right there in the Spanish chest.

Kelly saw many of the fights. Often she was playing when Mary Anne's mother went into a fit and chased Mary Anne around the house. Loyally, she took Mary Anne's side, pleading, "Leave her alone!" Kelly was still Mary Anne's best friend, although she was already in the ninth grade.

They usually played together after school. Mary Anne's mother had taken a job driving a taxi and sometimes didn't get home until eight o'clock. Kelly's mother also worked and didn't get home until after six. Her father was a fireman and was away a lot too. After the school bus dropped her off, Mary Anne walked down the hill to Kelly's house or called Kelly to come over. Mary Anne often made her own supper, heating up leftovers or just nibbling on things she found in the refrigerator.

One afternoon in Mary Anne's house Kelly was talking about some dances she'd gone to. There were drinks there, whiskey, and she'd had some. She'd tried beer too. "Well," Mary Anne said, "my mother has whiskey. Want to drink some?"

Kelly didn't care, she said. It might be fun; it was up to Mary Anne. Sure, Mary Anne said, she knew where it was; they could try some. She got two glasses from the kitchen, opened the Spanish chest, and found a bottle of Seagram's. She poured them each a little. It was funny, she thought, going to her mother's chest and pouring out some of her whiskey. She waved the bottle like a drunk and burped. Kelly did her own imitation. They horsed around, laughing, then Mary Anne lifted the glass dramatically and took a sip. It tasted like paint and she choked and coughed. She felt like vomiting. "Nas-*ty*!" she said, gagging.

Kelly took a swallow and also made a face. "Not so good," she wheezed. "Awful," agreed Mary Anne. With Kelly she didn't have to pretend.

It was clear they had to move. DeGregorio worried all the time about running into Catherine or her kids or, worse, Nick. What if his drug suppliers saw him with Barbara? He was supposed to be living out on the island. What would he be doing walking around Ridgewood with some redhead? Barbara would attract their curiosity for sure. She didn't exactly melt into the scenery, DeGregorio realized. If they ran her plate, then what? To make matters worse, the informant had seen DeGregorio enter her building one night and so had discovered where they lived. He was fooling around with drugs again, and when he needed money he sometimes planted himself under their window and howled up at them. It couldn't go on like that.

He knew how reluctant Barbara was to give up the apartment. She was sick over it. They had both been happy there. It was where their life together began after he had schemed—the way he remembered it, anyway—to forget his keys there. No, she always insisted, she had already decided to invite him up. What about the ruse of changing shoes? But the choice was inescapable. She could only stay if he left. It was either that or leave together. She agreed with him that it was no choice at all. After more than a year together they were closer than ever. They couldn't imagine separating.

A policewoman he knew from Bushwick told him about a Queens apartment complex where she was living. She liked it, she said, and there were vacancies. Spurred by the urgency, he drove there impulsively for a look. It was an unadorned redbrick blockish garden apartment cluster near Main Street in south Flushing, not far from a cemetery and the borough's spaghetti tangle of parkways, expressways, turnpikes, and boulevards. He was shown a one-bedroom apartment on the top floor of a three-story building. It looked okay. He called Barbara.

She seemed surprised he had moved that fast on his own but had no objection. If he liked it, she told him, he could sign.

Her first look at the place was the day they moved in. That may have been a mistake, he realized quickly. Her eyebrows went up in dismay. She berated him. Wasn't it a *project?* Stubby low-rise bunkers, scraggly hedges, balding, brown-patched strips of grass—didn't he see that? Across the street was the same, she said—cheap wood-frame cookie-cutter multifamilies. Didn't he see kids who ought to be in school sitting on the backrests of benches, clowning over the blaring of a suitcase-size noise machine? For this she had given up her charming apartment in Ridgewood, the place *he* loved so much?

He watched her shake her head in disappointment and disbelief, as if surprised that a smart cop could be so blind.

He shrugged, crestfallen. It didn't seem so bad to him. It was basically a Jewish area, the managing agent had told him, with a few low-income families. "It's near Queens College," he said hopefully, as if that would make it better for her. Besides, he insisted, stung, it wasn't really a project.

"It's not?" she said. "Oh, what is it?"

"It's private," he said. It was definitely not a city project for the poor.

She seemed unconvinced, and when she let Sam out of his cat carrier, he didn't seem to like the place much either. DeGregorio tried to mollify her: It was only temporary, until they could find something better. At any rate, it was too late; he had already signed the lease starting May 1984, and even then movers were carting their furniture in. He had also ordered phones, two lines under separate listings, each hooked up to its own answering machine. That way he could still maintain the fiction that he was living with Mike Miller. It was a harmless fib for Mary Anne's sake, DeGregorio told himself.

Her mother told her to go to bed, which was ridiculous. It wasn't even eight o'clock. Her mother was in her nightgown. She'd been drinking again; Mary Anne could smell it. Maybe she thought it was later than it was. But it was before eight. She refused. It was her house too. She could do what she wanted, she said. Was her mother stupid that she couldn't see the clock? Her mother should just get off her back and leave her alone.

She saw her mother's pale, red-rimmed eyes widen in fury. Leave her alone, her mother repeated with mounting hysteria, slurring the words. Leave her alone? That was the trouble; she had left Mary Anne alone, and now she was turning into a . . . a . . . She was working herself into a frenzy, Mary Anne could see. Her mother cursed her. She was just like that lying father of hers who ran out on them, leaving them with nothing. Maybe she should leave Mary Anne alone, alone for good, instead of working her fingers to the damn bone driving a cab, and for what, for a pig of a daughter who left the house a mess?

Mary Anne couldn't stand it. *She* left the house a mess, she retorted. Half the time her mother didn't know what she was doing; she must be drinking again. Maybe, Mary Anne thought instantly, she shouldn't have mentioned the drinking. Maybe that was too much. But her mother had pushed her too far this time. She was sick and tired of being yelled at; she was beyond control now.

Her mother knocked over a chair and came at her. Mary Anne put up her hands defensively to block the blow, then suddenly flailed out, connecting with her mother's cheek. Mary seemed stunned and put her hand to her face, dabbing distractedly at the reddening bruise. Mary Anne, also shocked and a little frightened, started to run. Her mother lurched after her. Mary Anne ran through the kitchen, followed by her mother. When Mary Anne turned, she saw her mother had picked up a steak knife!

In her next circuit through the kitchen, Mary Anne instinctively snatched up a knife too, a carving knife with a foot-long blade. Immediately she was terrified about what she might do. She dropped the carving knife and on another dash through the kitchen picked up a fork. Her mother kept coming, weaving unsteadily with the knife outstretched. Mary Anne ducked, and her mother stumbled off balance. Mary Anne stooped and stabbed the fork deep into her mother's right calf.

She crumpled with a shriek of pain and dropped the knife. Mary Anne, blind with hate, fear, and rage, kicked her. She kicked her own mother.

While her mother sat up groggily and yanked the fork out of her flesh, moaning and gripping her calf to stop the blood that was bubbling out of the four little puncture wounds, Mary Anne ran to the phone and with shaking hands dialed her father's number. It rang and rang until the answering machine cut in with her father's recorded message. "Thank you for calling," it said, "I'm not in right now, but if you'll leave your name and number at the sound . . ."

At the beep Mary Anne shouted, "I hate Mommy! I don't want to live here no more!"

Her mother glared at her, muttering threats. "Yeah, call him. Call your stupid father," she ranted. "Get out of here and take all your shit."

Mary Anne tried her father again every few minutes, each time leaving a frantic message. Finally on the fourth try she reached him. He must have just walked in. At the sound of his voice, his real voice, she dissolved into hysteria, overcome with relief. "Help me! she screamed into the phone. *"Come and get me out of here!"*

She must have scared him to death, because he shouted, "What happened? What happened?" When she started sobbing and telling him about the fight with the knife, he said in a hard voice that he was coming. She should wait there. He was leaving right away, this minute.

"He's coming," she taunted her mother. "He's coming here!"

"Get out," her mother said. "Wait for him outside."

Mary Anne scooped up Pepsi and ran out the door. The June night had turned chilly. Shivering in her T-shirt, she sat down on the steps. A salt breeze off Long Island Sound clacked mysteriously through the tall weeds in the woods across the street. Down the hill she could see the lights of Kelly's house. She felt like walking down there—she was dying to have someone to talk to—but she was afraid she'd miss her father.

She felt completely mixed up. Did she really want to leave? She wanted her father home, but she didn't know if she wanted to leave. Where would she go? Where would he take her? What about all her things?

She waited and waited. A few times she saw the lights of approaching cars and jumped up nervously, but all the cars turned off into driveways. Finally she saw lights that kept coming. It had to be him! But she didn't recognize the car. It was a white car, a Thunderbird. What was he doing with a Thunderbird?

He skidded to a stop and jumped out, almost before the motor stopped running. "Da—" she started to say, but he was already bounding into the house. She heard angry shouts—his voice, then her mother's, then both screaming at once.

She waited in the shadows, not knowing whether to show herself. When she saw him approach, his face was set in a furious scowl. "Get your stuff," he commanded. Get her stuff? What stuff? She had so much. How could she get all her stuff? It would take a moving truck. "But I . . ." she began.

He ignored her. "Get your stuff now," he demanded. "Pack your stuff. You're leaving. And you shut up," he said to her mother.

Suddenly she was afraid to go. "I don't want to leave!" she cried. "I want you to stay!" She tried to throw her arms around him, to hold him there. She loved him so much. Why had he ever left?

He stroked her hair and pried loose her arms. She smelled his aftershave, Canoe, and tobacco and the manly smell of his body. Then he broke away, and she saw him haul a suitcase out of the closet and tramp into her room. In a few minutes he reappeared with the suitcase. He grabbed her by the hand and pulled her out to the car. He opened the door for her to get in, then heaved the suitcase into the backseat, climbed in behind the wheel, spun the car around the circle that dead-ended the street just past the house, and shot down the hill past Kelly's house.

They drove awhile in silence. When they passed a 7-Eleven, he turned to her. "You want something?"

She nodded, afraid to trust her voice.

He pulled into the parking lot and started to get out. Then he sat back down heavily. "I'm not living with Mike," he said. "I'm living with some lady."

Mary Anne recoiled as if he had slapped her. Her body snapped back involuntarily against the seat. All she could think of was throwing herself out of the car. She grabbed the door handle and tried to leap out.

"What are you doing?" He reached across the seat and grabbed her arm.

"I don't want to meet her!" she screamed. "I'm not going!"

He grabbed her arm and pulled her back inside.

"Let me out of the car! I'm not going to see this lady!"

"Calm down!" He was squeezing her arm.

"I hate you!" she yelled. "I don't want to live with the lady!" Her mother was right. How did her mother know? She thought her mother was wrong about everything, but if her mother was right about this, maybe she was right about other things. Maybe he was the wrong one.

"Stop it!" he ordered. "Calm down."

"You lied to me!"

"I didn't lie to you," he said, unconvincingly, she thought.

"You said you were living with Mike."

"I was," he said. "For a while, in the beginning."

She couldn't believe it, he was such a liar. "See," she said, "you're still lying. Why didn't you tell me?" She looked at him angrily, staring him down. He couldn't even look at her straight, she thought.

"Because . . ."—he groped for words—"I . . . Why should I get into my personal life with you?"

"Your personal life?" she screeched. *"Your personal life!"* She couldn't believe him. "What about *my* personal life? I'm the one who's been living there with Mommy. I'm the one she's driving nuts. What about me?"

"That's why I'm taking you out of there," he said, trying to sound reasonable, she thought.

Wasn't that what she wanted—to get out of there? she wondered. She didn't know anymore.

"Where am I going to stay?"

"You'll . . . you'll stay with us."

Her head was spinning. How could she stay with him now? Who was *us?*

She wasn't sure how long they drove, but suddenly, it seemed they were out of the car and he was walking with her suitcase down a pathway between a bunch of apartment buildings. There were lights in some of the windows. It looked like the city—a lot of people living all together on top of each other. Inside the building she noticed that people had painted their names in big balloon letters on some of the walls. It looked scary, out of control. They walked up a lot of stairs and down a dim hallway to an apartment door. She expected him to open it with a key, but she was surprised to see him ring the bell. It buzzed like a dentist's drill. She jumped at the sound.

In bed in her *project* apartment, Barbara stirred and groaned. There was a bee buzzing around her ear, and through the gauze of sleep she tried to brush it away.

It kept coming back. It wasn't a bee, Barbara decided. It was a something else. What was that horrible sound? She ducked under the covers and pulled the pillow over her ears to shut out the racket. Someone was breaking in somewhere. Probably a car alarm. She suddenly realized it was a buzzer. *The door!*

She got out of bed and groped for her watch on the bureau, trying to read its face in the dark. It looked like midnight. Where was Patty? Then she remembered that Mary Anne had called, frantic. He had rushed out there. Who the hell was ringing their bell at midnight? She snatched a robe from the armchair, wrapped it around her, and ran for the door.

She peered through the peephole, automatically ran a hand through her sleep-tangled red hair, unbolted the door, and swung it open.

"Why didn't you use your key?" she asked, befuddled.

He didn't answer. Finally he said, "Mary Anne, this is Barbara."

Blinking in the harsh light, Barbara struggled to make sense of the scene, gazing from him with the suitcase to Mary Anne and back to him again. Stupidly, she couldn't keep her eyes off the black kitten that Mary Anne was carrying. What about Sam, she kept thinking. Would two cats get along? Her mind wasn't functioning. She was about to ask about the key again when she realized that it didn't matter. He'd already rung the bell, and she was up.

Now what? For the first time she looked closely at Mary Anne. She seemed crazed, her eyes blinking fast and darting wildly around the room. She thought she should say something gracious, but her mind was stuck. Finally what came out was "Are . . . are you going to live with us now?"

Mary Anne shrugged, as if to say, How should I know. It's out of my hands. Immediately Barbara felt a spasm of guilt. She was thinking of herself. How did the poor girl feel? Barbara thought Mary Anne might have remembered her from the station house. She thought she detected a spark of recognition in the girl's eyes, as if she suddenly knew who Barbara was and understood that their casual encounter—was it two years ago?—was a glimpse into the secret life her father had been living.

"Well," said Barbara with forced cheerfulness, "let's make up a bed." She got some sheets, a pillow, and a blanket from the closet and spread them over the couch in the living room. They should all try to get some sleep, Barbara said. They could talk in the morning.

Mary Anne watched them go into the bedroom and, overcome with misery, threw herself down on the makeshift bed and wept into the pillow. It smelled from *her* perfume, she thought, a heavy scent she disliked immediately. She ached for her own house, her room, her things. She thought about Tommy. She always thought about Tommy more around May. May was when he died. One minute she was at home, the next minute she was in a strange apartment with a strange lady her father was living with. Married to? She didn't know. She didn't know anything about her. Had she bewitched him with her striking looks, her red hair? His *lady,* he called her. What did that mean? How could he have lied to her like that? And she was a liar, too, if she was with him. How could he be in there with *her,* Mary Anne wondered furiously, when his own daughter was out here crying?

She didn't remember sleeping. She thought she had cried all night, but she must have slept because suddenly it was morning and her father and Barbara were walking around dressed, getting ready to leave. At the realization, she gave a little frightened whimper. Leave? Leave her alone? He said he was late, and Barbara, too. They had to go to work. "Stay here," he said. "Don't go anywhere." *Go anywhere?* Where would she go? She didn't know where she was, and she didn't know anybody. She was scared to death to go out.

Over a bowl of cereal that she scarcely touched, Mary Anne eyed Barbara straightening up and trying to make small talk. How did Mary Anne sleep? Was the sofa comfortable? She was sorry it had to be the sofa, but as Mary Anne could see, they were a little cramped. It was only temporary because they didn't like the neighborhood, and now maybe they would need more room.

At the suggestion that her arrival had set off big changes, Barbara seemed to catch herself in embarrassment, Mary Anne thought. She changed the subject. When she had off, she'd take Mary Anne shopping. Would she like that? They could go to her hairdresser too. And before Mary Anne could say anything, while her mouth was a big open O, they were out the door.

Mary Anne told herself that she could see through the friendly talk and false smiles, the little normal acts to win her over. Did they think she was a dummy? She could see through their lies. She'd play along, but she wouldn't be happy. Maybe Barbara thought that Mary Anne would accept her if she got to know her. Well, that was not going to happen. She'd humor them, but she wouldn't be won over.

She spent the day watching television. When she got hungry, she went to the refrigerator. There didn't seem to be a lot to eat—some lettuce, a box of crullers, a jar of mayonnaise, bacon bits, steak sauce, Aunt Jemima pancake mix, a Kentucky Fried Chicken bucket with a half-eaten drumstick. She nibbled a few of the things and sort of filled up. When her father came home that night after eight, he brought Chinese takeout food.

The next morning the ringing phone blasted her out of a fitful sleep. Where was she? She was completely disoriented. She groped around in the unfamiliar setting, falling over an end table before she grabbed the receiver. There was no sign of her father or Barbara. They must have left for work. "Hello," she answered groggily.

"Hello?" said a woman's voice. "Barbara?"

Uh—no."

The voice paused. "Who's this?"

"This is . . . Mary Anne."

"Mary Anne?" There was another puzzled pause.

"Yeah."

"Well, okay." The caller sounded thoroughly confused. "Mary Anne, could you tell Barbara her mother called? Thank you, Mary Anne."

She wondered if she should explain what she was doing there, but before she could decide, the caller hung up. She spent the rest of the day as she had spent the first, watching television, waiting for her father and Barbara to come home.

The next day Barbara said she was off and could take her shopping. And they could get to know each other. They went to a mall and to Barbara's hairdresser, where Mary Anne got a perm. Barbara said it looked great. Mary Anne didn't say anything.

The next day she was alone again. They had left her a key and a note about where the laundromat was if she wanted to do the laundry.

"C'mon, Pepsi," she said. "Let's go do the wash."

She pulled on a sweatshirt and jeans and jammed her feet into laced-up sneakers. She coaxed the little black Persian into a carrying cage and snapped it shut, then grabbed the laundry bag, a box of detergent, and a stack of quarters.

Outside it all looked unfamiliar. She was in something called the Kew Gardens Hills Apartments, a cluster of low, reddish buildings dropped like Lego blocks on little patches of greenery criss-crossed with walkways and benches. She saw some kids breakdancing in front of one building.

"What do you think, Pepsi? Which way?" Mary Anne peered up and down the street, shrugged, and headed down Seventy-third Avenue alongside the flow of traffic.

She reached Main Street two blocks later. Here at least there were some signs of life and stores wherever she looked. "Know what, Pepsi? I'm glad you're here," Mary Anne said. She turned left at the Kosher Corner and looked for the laundromat, which had to be close by. Across the street was a Baskin-Robbins that looked good, she thought. There was Benjy's Pizza, a movie house, a bedding store, a cleaners—and the laundromat.

She put in the wash and settled herself on a bench in front of the machine. It felt good just to sit. She watched the laundry slosh around in the froth of soap, and when it was finished, she put it in the dryer and watched it spin. It was soothing and hypnotic. She tried to see how far the clothes would go up the side and onto the top of the drum before they collapsed to the bottom. They were like bodies falling, except for some reason they didn't drop right away. She thought of Tommy.

When the dryer stopped spinning, Mary Anne unloaded the machine, picked up Pepsi, and walked out.

She forgot which direction she had come from. All ways looked equally strange. She thought it might have been by the savings bank, which had a tower that looked like a church steeple. "You remember this, Pepsi?" she said. "Me too." After the bank she crossed right, expecting to see the low red buildings. But they weren't there. "Let's walk another block," she told Pepsi. "Know what I wish? I wish Kelly was here."

Some of the houses here were bigger, like mansions, she thought. Down side streets were lines of row houses, all the same, with two downstairs windows and two upstairs windows. It was spooky. She wondered how the people who lived there ever found their way home. She walked to the corner to look up at the sign. She could barely read it, never mind pronounce it: V-L-E-I-G-H PLACE. She tried to say the name and couldn't. "We're lost, Pepsi," she said.

When she finally found her way back, she felt lonelier than ever. Were they worried about her, she wondered. They weren't even goddam home.

12

"THE next block, make a left," Catherine growled.

"Why, where are we going?"

"I got to pick up my nephew," Catherine said. "We're taking him with me."

Nephew? DeGregorio had never heard her mention a nephew before. What was she pulling? Was she setting him up? Keep calm, he told himself. They weren't onto him. He was getting paranoid. He had to keep his mind clear. He was Pasquale Greco.

All that stuff with Mary Anne was making him crazy. She was moping around, sullen, not talking. He tried to draw her out. At night sometimes when his beeper went off, he'd ask her to get his tape recorder so that when he called Catherine or Franco back, he'd have a record for evidence. She showed a spark of interest then, but clearly she was torn between pleasing him and punishing him for what she thought he had done to her. He had a guilty conscience. He knew he hadn't told her the truth, but what choice did he have? It was for her own good that he took her out of there.

His judgment was confirmed on the few occasions he had taken Mary Anne back to visit her mother. They were tense encounters. He couldn't even leave her alone with her mother but felt he had to stay there just to make sure it didn't explode into violence again. And he could see that Barbara was suffering, although aside from a few remarks she seemed to be keeping it to herself. Once she asked him if Mary Anne was going to stay with them from then on. He blew up at her. How did he know? He didn't plan this. For Chrissake, what did she want him to do, leave the kid there? They were about to kill each other, her and her mother. He reminded Barbara that they had talked about custody. What were they, he thought, two kindergarteners? They'd been together for three weeks already. Couldn't they learn to get along? *Women. Always bickering.*

He caught himself again. If he couldn't keep his mind on what he was doing, he warned himself, he was going to fuck up. It was bound to happen. He had to stay cool, just play the role. Everything would work out if he just didn't lose it.

On this June afternoon in 1984 he was carrying a big wad, $7,500 in marked bills, for another ounce from Franco, the man in black. Catherine set it up after he had bitched about the first buy. Dilute shit. It had been stepped on so many times, it was like fucking Sweet'n Low. She said they would have to complain to "Freddy." It sounded like another supplier, maybe above Franco. Now he had someone else to shoot for.

Driving around with Catherine, DeGregorio was still wondering if she was playing games with the nephew when she suddenly yelled in his ear, "*Cops!*"

DeGregorio swerved. "What?" His nerves were shot. He was shaking.

"Cops! Make a right!"

She had spotted a patrol car. With panic that was only half-feigned, DeGregorio screeched around the corner.

A few blocks down, she said, was Michael, her nephew.

DeGregorio pulled up to a kid waiting on the corner. He looked young and alone. It looked legit. The kid just stood there, ignoring them.

"What are you looking at?" DeGregorio demanded. "Get in the car."

"He can't see, you know," Catherine said. "He was mugged, and with a gun."

DeGregorio saw the kid feel his way to the car, open the door, and slide in the back. He was uneasy. A stranger who was supposed to be blind was sitting right behind him in the backseat. He couldn't see the guy's hands.

They pulled away from the curb, with Catherine giving directions. They were meeting Franco, and DeGregorio pretended he was still pissed off over the last batch.

Catherine nodded. That was why Michael came along, as the tester, she said. "Michael, you snort a little bit. Would you be able to check it?"

"Yeah," said Michael.

So that was it! The guy was a fucking junkie guinea pig. These people were such animals, DeGregorio could puke.

"I want to ask you something, Patty," Catherine said. "What kind of cut do you use?"

DeGregorio hesitated. Was she testing him? He ought to sound knowledgeable. "What do you use?" he asked, stalling.

Catherine asked Michael the name of the powder he used to dilute the heroin.

"Lactose," he prompted.

DeGregorio mumbled that he used the same thing.

But Michael was a connoisseur. "There's two kinds," he said.

DeGregorio was vague. Someone else did the cutting for him. "I don't bother with that. It's not my problem."

DeGregorio was still acting grouchy, saying Franco had better be there this time and the stuff had better be good, when Catherine suddenly said, "I don't know why, Patty, that everybody that sees you thinks that you're a cop."

He summoned up an angry indignation. "Who thinks that I'm a cop now?"

"Everybody."

He worked up some outrage. "Who's everybody? Who else?"

Catherine turned to Michael. "Don't you think . . ."

To his relief, Michael said, "No, this ain't the one I was thinking about."

"Oh, thanks," said DeGregorio with what he hoped was the right tone of sarcasm and hurt.

Now he was curious as well as alarmed. "Who else?" he asked. "I want to know who else thinks that."

"My boy did," Catherine said. DeGregorio figured she was referring to her strung-out son, Joseph, who was at the apartment one day when DeGregorio was there.

"Well, he's just dizzy and you're dizzy," DeGregorio said, calculatingly going on the attack. "Maybe you're a cop," he said. "How do I know? Maybe *he's* a cop? I never met Michael before."

Catherine wanted to drop it. "Get the hell out of—"

"Oh, get the hell, but you can say that and that's okay," De-Gregorio insisted. "I'm not supposed to be mad about that."

"Yeah," said Catherine disgustedly. "I'm a cop."

"What do I know?" said DeGregorio.

They picked up Franco on the street and drove to a diner. When Franco, who was again all in black, got out of the car, he told them to get a cup of coffee and wait for him. Catherine grumbled about something. She argued with him in Italian. DeGregorio couldn't catch much of it. Franco seemed to get angrier and angrier until he shouted, *"Ba fa goola!"* and stalked off.

DeGregorio was stunned. Had she blown the deal? Franco was a step up; he couldn't lose Franco. Making a rash decision, he sprang from the car and caught up with him.

"Hey, listen, *paesan'*," he said soothingly, walking Franco out of Catherine's earshot. "I came here to meet you. You're arguing with her. I got nothing to do with her. She's crazy."

"Yeah," Franco agreed, looking him over appraisingly. "You want to do business?"

"Yeah," said DeGregorio. "I just got to get away from this crazy bitch."

"Okay," Franco said, scribbling on a piece of paper. "Here's my beeper number."

Down the street in a backup car, monitoring transmissions from the Thunderbird's hidden mike, Jim Kearney of the FBI and Police Sergeant Charlie Dean saw DeGregorio bolt from the car and chase after someone. Then, alarmingly, they heard Catherine and her nephew searching DeGregorio's car.

"What do you think?" they heard Catherine say. "Who is this guy?"

"You sure he ain't a cop?" Michael asked.

Dean started to jump out. What if they found the transmitter?

"Where are you going?" Kearney demanded.

Where was he going? The undercover was in grave danger. If they found the wires, DeGregorio was exposed. He had to be warned. Dean had misgivings about the case from the beginning, and this could be a disaster. They could collar the two and shut the case down.

Kearney was appalled. Shut it down? Was Dean bonkers? He pulled the sergeant back into the car. "Wait!" he commanded. "We don't know he's in danger. Wait it out."

They waited, and Kearney blew a sigh of relief when he saw DeGregorio return to the car before Catherine and Michael turned up anything in their rummaging. DeGregorio's secret was safe, which was the good news. The bad news was that they suspected him.

DeGregorio arranged to meet Franco on his own the next day. "No more Catherine," he said when Franco climbed into the Thunderbird.

"No more!" Franco agreed. She was greedy. Who needed a middleman taking cuts from both of them? "This motherfucker wants three hundred from you. Three hundred! And six hundred from me."

"Nine hundred dollars!" DeGregorio said.

"Nine hundred," Franco repeated. "I can't believe it!"

"I believe it," DeGregorio said.

From now on, he and Franco agreed, they would deal directly. But, DeGregorio warned, the stuff had better be good. Franco told him not to worry. If it wasn't good, he'd take it back. Franco had DeGregorio drop him off under the Triborough Bridge in Astoria, and when he came back, he had an ounce that he promised was pure enough to cut five ways.

Kearney later told him it tested at ninety-two percent pure heroin. "Wherever he's getting it," Kearney said, "he's a main guy."

DeGregorio was impressed. They had to be getting close to the source.

But Franco told him he couldn't get more. DeGregorio figured he was either holding out on him or he wasn't high enough up to assure a steady supply.

"Nobody have the wine," Franco insisted. All the yelling and screaming in the world wouldn't help. The supply had dried up. He was down to two ounces, which he couldn't sell without approval. "Because me no fucking cocksucker, no!"

"Am I a cocksucker?" DeGregorio demanded.

"No, no, me no cocksucker. I want that you believe me."

"Two months ago everybody got it," DeGregorio pressed.

"Yeah, two months ago, no now."

"When your wine coming again?"

"I don't know, Pasqual'. Maybe next week." He was going to be away in Texas, he said, arranging a new smuggling route into the country, but he might be able to turn it over to the boss.

The boss! DeGregorio liked the sound of that. It could be the break he was waiting for. When they talked on the phone later, Franco asked, "You want to come tonight, talk to my friend?"

DeGregorio was so excited he almost dropped the phone. "Who is this? What's his name?"

"Federico."

Then there was a strange voice on the phone. "Hello, Pasquale?"

"Yeah. How you doing?" DeGregorio replied cautiously.

"What's going on?" said someone named Federico. "I don't know. I don't want to send nothing anymore." He sounded fed up with all the complaints.

DeGregorio instinctively went on the offensive. "Okay, first of all, the last time we did business, remember, the wine was shit."

"I know," Federico said. "I was telling—"

"It was shit, shit, shit, shit, shit." His customers were yelling, DeGregorio said, but he wanted to be reasonable. "If you want to talk, I'll come and talk."

"Ah, you want to come to my restaurant?"

It was the invitation he'd been hoping for.

It was the Figaro, Federico said, One Hundred Fifty-three West Forty-fourth Street. "What time you come?"

DeGregorio tried to mask his excitement. "All right. What time is it now? I need a little time to get ready."

"There is no rush," said Federico calmly. "I want to talk to you. Is all right if you be around eight to nine."

"Yeah, all right. Listen, where can I call you? I want to call you back in about ten minutes."

Federico dictated his home number and the number of the restaurant.

DeGregorio felt a surge of triumph but forced himself to sound cynical. "But there can't be no problems no more. Business is getting good. I need a lot more wine for the restaurant, understand?"

Federico started to say something, and DeGregorio cleverly cut him short. "No, I don't want to talk over the phone."

DeGregorio had the home number checked out. It belonged to a Federico Spatola on Twenty-fourth Avenue in Astoria, where FBI surveillance teams had often tailed Franco. But who was Federico?

That night, backed up by Kearney and other FBI agents staked out in casually parked cars, DeGregorio visited the Figaro Restaurant off Times Square. It was a typical Italian joint, he thought: dim, red, the usual celebrity photos on the walls, a nice-looking bar. He asked for Federico and was directed to a squat, disheveled man in his forties with an ample belly, bushy hair, and a mustache. They took a table in the back. In his nervousness DeGregorio came on strong, complaining about the quality of earlier buys.

Federico, thrown on the defensive, protested he had told Franco not to sell the bad stuff and promised to make it up the next time around. DeGregorio grunted grudging approval, and they spent some time drinking espressos and Sambucas before DeGregorio begged off. He had a chick waiting, he said, pumping his fist back and forth. Hot to trot. Federico laughed understandingly.

The next day Franco led DeGregorio into a back room of the Café Commercio on Steinway Street in Astoria and handed him a package with two ounces at the bargain price Federico promised, $16,000. DeGregorio handed him $9,000 and said he'd owe the rest.

When the three of them met again a few days later, in the red-roofed Neptune Diner under the elevated N train line at the Queens end of the Triborough Bridge, Franco said he was leaving for Texas to put together his big shipment. In the meantime, he said, DeGregorio should deal with Federico.

"You think there'll be any problem getting the wine?" DeGregorio asked.

"No," said Federico. "I buy direct."

Federico was definitely the bigger guy, DeGregorio thought, coming up with a quick gambit. Seizing his chance when Franco left the table to go to the toilet, DeGregorio leaned over the Formica and said conspiratorially to Federico, "You know, this guy is charging me too much money. I can't make money like this."

"How much he charging you?" Federico asked, suspicious.

"Nine thousand, eighty-five hundred. Every time it changes," DeGregorio said, exaggerating. "Sometimes ten thousand."

"That's what he's charging you?" Federico asked, taking the bait. Franco had to be profiteering, pocketing the difference.

When Franco came back from the bathroom, Federico barked, "What the fuck you charging him?"

Franco innocently turned to DeGregorio. "Tell him what I'm charging you."

DeGregorio held his ground. "It's always different," he said. "And every time it's different quality."

Franco cursed savagely. With Federico and Franco now heatedly arguing, DeGregorio excused himself to go to the toilet. Let them fight it out. When he came back, Franco was gone.

"I'll deal with you now," Federico said. "Cheech have to go away anyway. I take care of you now."

It was what he wanted. Finally, thought DeGregorio, he was moving up.

"You're supposed to be doing well in the drug business," FBI supervisor Lew Schiliro said. "You have to move up a little bit with your car." They were in the bureau's garage under Manhattan headquarters on Foley Square, and Schiliro, slight, with closely cropped hair and a sinister droopy mustache, was leading him past gleaming ranks of fancy confiscated cars. "Whatever you want," he said, waving expansively.

"Yeah," DeGregorio said casually. "I'll take a Cadillac."

"We don't have those," Schiliro said with disdain. "How about this?" He stopped at a midnight blue Mercedes 300 SL with tan leather upholstery.

DeGregorio was impressed. This was a $30,000 foreign car. "Sure," he said quickly.

The first weekend he drove it home to his parents, Joe's eyes widened in disbelief. DeGregorio could see his evident suspicions. What the hell was Patty up to? How could a cop afford a Mercedes? DeGregorio hadn't told his father what he was doing, and Joe, he was sure, wouldn't ask. "Don't worry about it, Pop" was all DeGregorio said. His father would have to trust him.

• • •

Near the end of June, DeGregorio went back to the Figaro to pay Federico $8,500 he still owed. "Pasqual', listen," Federico said. "I got to go to the other side for some business. Don't you worry. While I'm gone, my brother will take care of you."

His brother! DeGregorio knew Federico had a well-connected brother, and he had been hoping to meet him as well. "Can your brother handle more weight?" he asked.

"Anything you need. Even kilos."

Federico said warmly that when he got back from Palermo, they should go into partnership. DeGregorio promised to consider it. "C'mere," he said. "I want to show you something." He pointed down at his Mercedes on the street.

"Aah, that's-a nice, Pasquale," Federico said.

"That ain't mine," DeGregorio said. "A guy owed me money. Now it's mine."

"Really?" Federico sounded impressed.

"Yeah," DeGregorio said. "Fuck him. He owed me twenty-five thousand, didn't pay, and now I have his fucking car."

"Aah," Federico sighed appreciatively. "When I come back, Pasquale, we got to talk."

In the meantime, he said, DeGregorio could deal with his brother, Joseph. He would set it up.

Fidgeting at the Figaro bar, DeGregorio resisted the urge to check his watch again. He didn't want to look troubled or overeager. Joseph was three hours late. Had something gone wrong? Were they onto him? Were they waiting for the last customers to leave so they could whack him? Which direction would they come from? From behind? They usually came from behind.

Joseph finally strolled up, grinning. "I'm fashionably late," he said. The family resemblance was impossible to miss, DeGregorio thought. Joseph had the same stocky build as Federico, but he was clean-shaven and better looking. There was something boyishly *simpatico* about his flashing dark eyes and quick smile.

He led DeGregorio upstairs to an apartment over the restaurant, a cramped second-floor studio with a sleeping alcove. They had some unfinished business to complete. DeGregorio handed over $8,000 he still owed for a previous sale, carping over the lousy quality—the stuff had tested at a mere thirty-one percent purity. Joseph apologized and offered to shave a thousand off an ounce next time. DeGregorio shrugged agreement.

"That's great!" Joseph said, beaming. He popped the cork on a bottle of champagne to toast their first deal.

Joseph suggested that they meet next time at a Korean restaurant near the Figaro, the Woo Lae Oak on West Forty-sixth Street. DeGregorio got there early to check it out. He had never seen a restaurant like it before. It was as big as a ballroom, and in the center of each large wooden table were gas grills where customers sat barbecuing their own food, served by diminutive Korean waitresses in maroon-and-white dresses and schoolgirlish white anklets.

DeGregorio took a stool at the long bar. "Waiter!" he bellowed. "Chivas!" He sat and waited and waited. Joseph showed up two hours late.

"How come you're never fucking on time?" DeGregorio grumbled.

"I'm fashionably late," Joseph said with a cherubic grin.

"What the fuck do you know about fashion?" said DeGregorio, charmed despite himself. They both laughed.

DeGregorio ordered the maitre d' to show them to a good table. When they were seated, he demanded the wine list and scanned it with disdain. "Don't you have anything better?" he complained.

"Yes, sir, but it's like a hundred doll—"

DeGregorio jerked his head up, glaring. "Did I ask you how much the fuck it is?"

Joseph got the message. "Oh, you're doing good," he said.

"Don't worry about it," DeGregorio said cavalierly.

They ate and drank like old buddies. Joseph said he had three kids, including a little girl, and that his wife, Sara, was several months pregnant. He said he liked to cook and was a seventh-degree karate black belt. More to the point, he confided he was dealing with a big heroin distributor in New Jersey and Connecticut.

"You know," he said to DeGregorio, "Greco is a big name over there."

Over there, DeGregorio knew, meant Italy. "Yeah, I know," he answered casually. "I think it's my uncle."

A few nights later they arranged to meet at Figaro's for another dinner. As usual, Joseph was late. DeGregorio didn't even bother checking his watch. He'd be there when he got there. Joseph finally arrived and they went through their "fashionably late" routine, which had become a joke between them. When Joseph opened his jacket, DeGregorio noticed the butt of a pistol tucked into his pants.

Then Joseph said offhandedly, "You're a cop, right?"

DeGregorio was so stunned that he didn't react immediately. Setting down his scotch so his hand wouldn't shake, he managed to look back levelly. "Yeah, that's right," he said, deadpan. "And you know what, Joe? I'm going to fucking lock you up."

Joseph laughed.

DeGregorio joined in, tentatively at first, then uproariously.

13

"IT's just for now, just until we find a place out on the island." Barbara listened as DeGregorio explained it once again to a sullen Mary Anne, who slumped glumly in the backseat with Pepsi on her lap, staring out the window. He steered the big blue Mercedes through the expressway traffic, past cars of tanned beach-bound teens with iridescent sailfish and surfboards poking out of open hatchbacks. Barbara sat next to him, depressed enough herself. Seeing Pepsi reminded her that she had had to give Sam away. The two cats didn't get along. Pepsi got to stay and Sam went to the FBI's Queens garage. Once again now, Barbara thought, Mary Anne was punishing them with her silence, and she was getting fed up with it. For two months, crammed into their little project apartment, she had endured Mary Anne's tyrannical moodiness. They had tried to do everything they could for her. They had recently taken her to Macy's for new fall clothes and school supplies, but they couldn't give up their jobs and babysit her all day long. They couldn't give up their lives.

DeGregorio was often out late on his undercover case. His beeper sometimes went off in the middle of the night, and he ran out to meet someone. He was under a lot of pressure, she could see that, but she worried about him more than he seemed to worry about himself, although, she thought, he could be laughing off her concerns just to keep her from worrying.

Both of them had enough on their mind, without worrying about Mary Anne too. Now they had come up with a stopgap decision. Clearly they needed more space. Also, the 1984–85 school year was starting soon. Unless they were willing to send Mary Anne to the local Queens public school, they'd have to move. Mary Anne was adamant about not starting junior high there, and her father was sympathetic. He knew and Barbara knew, too, what went on in city schools, especially junior highs. How could they think of sending her there after Coram?

But Mary Anne's plea to go back to Coram, where all her friends were, wouldn't fly either. Mary had agreed to a divorce and the surrender of Mary Anne's custody to her father in exchange for keeping the house and, Barbara suspected, the relief of being rid of her daughter. Mary had insisted on keeping the house where Tommy grew up, DeGregorio told Barbara. He cherished Tommy's memory, too, she knew, but in a choice between a monument and his flesh-and-blood daughter, there was no question what he'd choose. He had jumped at the deal—a house for a divorce and his daughter. "Absolutely!" he told Barbara he'd said to Mary. "Done deal!"

The solution they had hit on now was to take Mary Anne to her uncle Ralph and aunt Kathy in Kings Park while they looked for their own place there. Mary Anne could start junior high in September and come back to live with them when they were resettled. She wouldn't have to change schools again. It was a good compromise. Ralph, an electrician, and Kathy, a nurse, lived right next door to Joe and Anne. So Mary Anne wouldn't have only her father's brother and wife and their three boys to keep an eye on her, she'd also have her grandparents.

And not a moment too soon, Barbara felt. They needed a breather. At least she did, and she suspected he did, too, although he kept telling her how glad he was to have Mary Anne with them now. Barbara knew how attached he was to Mary Anne and how guilt-ridden he was over having abandoned her. But Barbara felt that Mary Anne's arrival had happened all too suddenly for her. She hadn't wanted to make a big issue of it because he had enough on his mind right now, but she was angrier than she let on. Nobody had asked if this new arrangement was okay with her. She didn't know whether Mary Anne was a permanent part of their household. They couldn't even use the living room anymore. Barbara felt like a prisoner in her own house.

Contrary to his recollection, she didn't remember discussing the custody of Mary Anne. If they had, it was only fleetingly and then for *someday* in the future. In her mind it was something hypothetical, a distant goal *if* their future went that far. She was still perfectly happy to take things one day at a time. They weren't even a couple in any legal sense, not that she was eager for marriage. She had never cared much for society's formalities. What was important to her was how much they loved each other, how well they got along as friends as well as lovers, how clearly devoted he was to her, and how she responded to him as to no other man.

But apart from the shock of Mary Anne's arrival in the middle of the night and the crude way he had buzzed her to the door, Mary Anne's addition to the household had complicated their lives immeasurably, Barbara felt. Overnight, literally overnight, they lost their privacy. With Mary Anne camped in the living room, they could barely exchange a few personal words, let alone feel comfortable in their intimacies. One or the other of them had tried to be home for Mary Anne as much as possible, but their work schedules were hard to mesh. On the rare occasions when they were both off together, they couldn't leave Mary Anne alone and go to a Broadway show or even out for dinner. Mary Anne showed little interest in being included, so they generally just hung around the apartment, awkwardly aware of one another's presence.

It was no secret that Mary Anne resented her. It wasn't surprising either. Barbara had read enough about the stepmother syndrome to have an idea of what to expect, but she thought she could win Mary Anne over. She realized who was at the crux of this competition, but she had thought, perhaps naively, that Mary Anne would understand they were not rivals for her father's affections. They were, in a way, partners in each other's happiness. If he was happy with Barbara, then he would be a better father to Mary Anne. And the same went for each of them in this awkward triangle. Barbara, for one, was glad that he could reestablish his relationship with Mary Anne. It would make him happier all around. She was willing to do her part, she told herself, and from the time of Mary Anne's arrival, she had tried, really tried, to establish a rapport. But Mary Anne's long silences and monosyllabic replies left little doubt that she was miserable. Barbara had expected that at the start, but it hadn't gotten any better. It had surprised her. She thought for sure that Mary Anne would have warmed to her by now, but it seemed she was determined to be unhappy.

She didn't know whether Patty saw it the same way. Mary Anne was different with him, more forthcoming certainly, even possessive and coquettish, and sultry, if a twelve-year-old could be sultry. It was, Barbara sometimes thought, as if Mary Anne was instinctively or consciously trying to drive a wedge between her and her father by showing each of them a different face. That way, they'd have trouble agreeing on what she was up to.

Joe and Anne were delighted to have Mary Anne next door. She was their first granddaughter, and always special because of what they had gone through with Tommy. Joe especially loved kids. He was forever stalking them with his eight-millimeter movie camera, lumbering after them and trapping them for posterity in his blinding spotlights until they ran when they saw him coming. The grownups just shielded their faces and told him where to stick the damn thing—until the day Joe surprised them all with sound, a microphone that caught their graphic suggestions.

Joe was irrepressible, a big kid himself. Every Christmas he gathered the grandchildren—Mary Anne, and Ralph's Joey and Chris and Jimmy, Luisa's Joanna and Craigy—and took them down to Carvel on Main Street to order a cake with icing that said "Happy Birthday Jesus." It sounded corny, but Joe got a big kick out of it. It *was* His birthday, so why shouldn't they celebrate with a cake? One year Joe was crushed when the counterman asked how to spell Jesus.

Family was sacred to Joe and Anne. To the mortification of their children, Anne persisted in sending gift envelopes of cash periodically to relatives in Italy, oblivious to the fact that the war was long over and that perhaps it was the Italians, with their Fiats, Ferraris, and Olivettis, Fendi furs, and Gucci leathers, who should be sending packages to America. A few years before, Joe and Anne had made a pilgrimage to Cervinara, their first trip back in almost half a century. Near the house Pasquale had lived in, they found an old woman who had been Angelina's childhood friend. She took them to a narrow alleyway hemmed in by ancient ochre walls. "Here is where your mother and father used to come alone to talk," she confided to Joe and Anne. When they prepared to leave, she stooped down painfully and gathered a handful of dusty soil. "I am very poor," she told Joe. "I have nothing to give you, just this. Dirt from the house where you were born." Joe accepted the soil as if it were the most precious of presents, which, to him, it was. When he got home he carefully divided it into six portions, bagging one for himself, another for Antoinette, and the rest for each of their brothers and sisters.

Yet at the same time Joe and Anne were not distraught when Patty's marriage to Mary broke up. On the contrary, they said, they had never had high hopes for the union, and although they had reluctantly gone along with his folly, they could see that the couple's problems were clearly insurmountable. Notwithstanding her fealty to the church, Anne put up no obstacles to a divorce.

The business with Barbara had taken some getting used to, however. *Living together? No wedding plans?* Luisa had broken the news to them gently after Patrick had sought her services as a go-between, the return of a favor. Years before when Luisa had met a young marine corporal at a girlfriend's house and fallen madly in love, she quarreled with her parents about marrying him and following him to Okinawa. "Go with Craig," Patrick advised her. "I'll talk to Mom and Dad." He smoothed it over. Now Luisa could help him out. "Can you keep a secret?" he asked her. "I'm living with someone."

"But you're still married!" she said, scandalized.

"I'm separated," he said.

"That's not allowed," she insisted. "You can't date when you're separated."

"Says who?" he replied, and then he invited her to meet Barbara. Luisa, telling herself that she wasn't a traitor to Mary, was captivated by the slender red-haired beauty her brother had landed. "I can't believe she's a police officer!" she told him. This time she calmed Mom and Dad.

Joe and Anne also took to Barbara right away She was easy to like, they said. And they were pragmatic. What could they do anyway? They'd already gone through it with Patrick once before, and with Luisa and with Ralph.

A dozen years before they had thrown a seventeenth birthday

party at home for Ralph. They didn't know all the kids and asked his friends to invite people. One who showed up was fifteen-year-old Kathy O'Neill. A rosy, robust girl with freckles, an upturned nose, and a pealing laugh, she caught Ralph's eye immediately. Ralph asked her to go bowling, and they began dating. They had been going out a year when Joe got a call from Ralph. He sounded far away.

"Pop, we're in Richmond, Virginia," Ralph said.

Joe heard a note of anxiety in Ralph's voice. "What's wrong, son?"

Ralph hesitated. "Kathy's pregnant," he said, his voice quavering.

Joe paused only a second. "So," he said, "what're you trying to tell me?"

"I know I'm supposed to go to Manhattan College, that I have a scholarship," Ralph said.

"So what'd you run away for?"

"Well, I thought you would have wanted us to have an abortion."

Now Joe erupted. "We don't want an abortion! We want you to get married and have the child!" He was hurt. "Why didn't you discuss this with us, and if we said we wanted an abortion, *then* run away? But at least give us the option of saying no. And Ralph, no, we don't want an abortion. We want a grandchild. We want you to be happy." Joe paused. "Is this the girl you want to marry?"

"Yes."

"Come on home. Talk it over. We'll do it right."

"Okay, Pop."

Then Ralph and Kathy worried about breaking the news to her parents, but Joe mollified the O'Neills. "We either do this right," he said, "or we lose these kids forever."

Although Kathy was six months pregnant and showing, the families went ahead with plans for a full wedding and reception at the Villa Pace on Long Island, where Patrick had gotten married three years earlier. Some of Joe's relatives tried to talk him out of it. "What the hell are you doing, Joe?" one said. "You're *celebrating* this thing?"

"I'll tell you what." Joe answered heatedly. "How do you turn off love? Do you turn it off like a faucet, like a spigot—yes I love, no I don't? You either love or you hate. I love my children. I'll tell you something else. How many times when we were keeping company with our wives did we fool around and make the sign of the cross that they didn't get knocked up? I mean, who's kidding who? Am I the only one? Sure, I tried with my wife. I'm lucky, and so were a lot of you. And I'm admitting it to you."

One of Joe's relatives with a son Ralph's age asked, "Do you mind if he doesn't come to the wedding?"

"Why?" Joe asked.

"Well, I don't want him to get the wrong idea," she said.

"Sure," he said, tight-lipped. "Whatever you do is fine."

Joey was born three months later, seven weeks before his cousin Mary Anne. Over the next thirteen years Ralph and Kathy had two more sons. They were excellent parents, Joe thought, well suited to watch over Mary Anne while Patty and Barbara looked for a home in Kings Park.

The scratched school bus windows splintered the low morning sunlight, fogging everything outside. Mary Anne craned her neck anxiously for her first view of Rogers, but all she could see was the fuzzy outline of a very long building, low and long, with lots of grass. It looked creepy. What was she doing here?

It was September 1984. Her father had told her the day before—*the day before!*—that she was going to Ralph and Kathy's for a while. He must have seen her horrified face because he rushed to say it was only for a little while, until they found a place out there. She didn't want to go to school in the city, did she? Well, he said, this was what they could do: She could go to school in Kings Park if she was living with Ralph and Kathy. Then when they got their own place, they would get her. What was so bad about that?

What was so bad was she didn't want to live with her uncle Ralph and aunt Kathy. Uncle Ralph scared her. There was something about him, his strictness. He wasn't mean to her; he treated her the same as the boys; he was the same with everybody. But it wasn't like being with her father. She was living everywhere just a short time, she thought, first with her father and Barbara, and now with Ralph and Kathy. She couldn't go back to her mother. After her father took her out of there, she went back a few times for visits, but she and her mother just didn't get along. Her father had to stay there to make sure they didn't kill each other. After she moved out, her mother's mother moved in for a little while to keep her daughter company. Once her grandmother told her she was sorry. She used to think it was Mary Anne who made her mother crazy, but now she said it wasn't her fault. "I can't even live with her."

She was tired of living in places for a short time, Mary Anne thought. She wanted to live somewhere for a long time, with her father. She blamed Barbara for taking him away from her. But mostly she was mad at him. He was her father, he should know better. All she wanted was to be with him, without Barbara. But it was Barbara, she thought bitterly, who was getting rid of her. She kept hoping her father would see how much she was suffering. All he had to say was that he couldn't do it, he couldn't leave her again. She'd do anything to be with him, alone.

The bus wheezed up the driveway, and as the sun shifted she saw that the school was a redbrick building with tan windows. It had an empty, lonely look. All she could think of was that she didn't know anybody, only her cousin Joey, who sat quietly next to her, his short hair neatly brushed. She liked Joey a lot. He was two months older, and they'd played together since they were little. Joey was a good boy; he didn't get into trouble. All the boys had their own rooms, but Joey gave her his, and he went to the basement.

As they approached the school, the clamor in the bus rose, a chorus of jeers and boos. Somebody's hat was snatched and thrown back and forth to cheers. A few rows up, two boys were fighting off a third boy who was wildly trying to crush his way onto the seat next to them. They gave a sudden shove and knocked him into the aisle as other kids roared approval.

Mary Anne watched it all silently. She felt different and was sure they were looking at her, wondering who she was. She felt awkward in her new jeans and striped polo shirt that practically screamed Macy's. They looked too new, she worried. Maybe she had left a price tag on. She would just die!

Inside the school she didn't know where anything was. She just stayed next to Joey. He knew his way. Don't worry, he told her, everybody gets lost the first day. He'd show her around. Luckily, she found, they had the same homeroom with a nice man teacher. But then she had to go to her other classes, and Joey's schedule was all different. She was on her own, lost, with not even Joey to hang on to. A few kids tried to talk to her, but she didn't want to say anything. They would know she was new.

• • •

Kathy was in the kitchen making dinner, and Ralph was somewhere in the back. Mary Anne had a few cigarettes left in her purse, and she went into the downstairs bathroom for a smoke, carefully opening the window a crack first. When she finished she flushed the butt and match down the toilet and waved away the smoke. Leaving the bathroom, she nearly bumped into Ralph. His dark eyes narrowed, and he sniffed the air. "I smell smoke," he said. "No," she said, too quickly. "I do smell smoke," he said. "*You* smell like smoke." He stepped closer, sniffing her hair. "What were you doing?" he asked. "Were you smoking?"

She denied it but it was no good. He had caught her. "You're going to be punished," he said, not angrily, just kind of matter-of-factly, she thought. She reacted furiously. "You can't!" she shouted. "You can't! You have to ask my father first." At the thought of her father, her eyes stung with tears. She missed him so much. She couldn't wait for the weekend. He'd promised to come on the weekend.

When Saturday finally came, she saw his car drive up, and unexpectedly her anticipation turned to anger. She'd been waiting and waiting for him all week. She thought she'd be so happy to see him, but she was surprised to feel she wasn't. He had left her alone there. Now, *now* he was coming to visit. And with Barbara.

He gave her a big hug, sweeping her up in his arms, the way he used to when she was little. She felt the familiar tickle of his whiskers and breathed the faint smell of Canoe and tobacco and sweat, *his* smell.

She ignored Barbara, trying not to even look at her. It was her father she wanted to see. They took a little walk together, just the two of them. He showered her with eager questions: How is the new school? Did you make any new friends? Who are your teachers? What are your favorite subjects? She didn't feel like talking about it. Actually, she did want to talk to him; she was dying to talk to him. She wanted to curl up with him and tell him everything, just the two of them talking and laughing. But she had this lump in her throat and didn't want to talk, she was so mad at him. What she said in a low voice was "I'm all by myself."

She knew what he would say, that she wasn't alone, that she had her cousins and uncle Ralph and aunt Kathy and right next door Grandpa and Grandma. But she wanted him to see how sad she was. "My mother has a house," she said. "My father has a house. But I have no house." Then she said, "I feel bad about Tommy. I miss Tommy." Watching him out of the corner of her eye, she could see his face fall and his lips quiver for an instant. She had gotten to him, she knew, and she almost smiled in triumph. She had made him feel bad. Now he was the one feeling bad.

Barbara had come to dread the weekends when they visited Mary Anne at Ralph and Kathy's. One minute Mary Anne was hyper, throwing herself at her father and demanding indulgences that her stricter uncle had denied her during the week, and the next she was retreating into her sullen shell, which Barbara dreaded. A critical glance, a harsh word, and she flew into a rage, slamming doors and bursting into tears.

"I don't understand it," Kathy told them, perplexed. "All week she's fine. Then you come and there's a temper tantrum."

Barbara thought Patty might be sending Mary Anne the wrong signals, rewarding her for her petulance and encouraging her to manipulate his guilt. But Barbara realized she herself might not be the most unbiased judge. It was easy for her to say what Patty should and shouldn't do. She wasn't carrying the baggage he and Mary Anne were; it wasn't her child.

She thought Ralph had the right approach with his boys. Five years younger than his brother, with a slighter build and a thin mustache, Ralph struck her as a compressed version of Patty— tighter, less emotional, more in control. There was a strictness and a consistency about him. In his house rules were rules, and they had to be followed, by Mary Anne, too, now that she was living there. The brothers had set the ground rules for her stay. Ralph would have authority over her as if she were one of his own kids. It was the only way to do it, they had agreed. Ralph wasn't harsh and certainly not cruel. He didn't believe in hitting his kids, and he rarely raised his voice. He was clearly a loving father and deeply devoted to Kathy. But Barbara could see he was a no-nonsense type and practical. He decided something, and that was that. Maybe, she thought, he could teach Patty a thing or two.

Ralph never opened up to her much about it. She was still an outsider in the family, after all, but from the conversations she listened to when they came to visit Mary Anne, Barbara sensed that Ralph felt his brother was indulging Mary Anne too much, idealizing her. She had problems, Ralph said; she needed to be straightened out. Patty said he knew that. It was just that her brother died and her parents got divorced, so the kid needed a break.

This time Barbara couldn't blame him. They had both picked out the place. It looked acceptable at first—better than acceptable after the hovels that passed for rental housing in the Kings Park school district. What was it with real estate agents, Barbara wondered. Whatever price you gave them as your top, they always shook their heads in disbelief, saying there was simply nothing available for such a pitiable sum. She was dispirited. They weren't ready to rush into buying a house just yet; there were too many uncertainties all around. They thought they would rent at first and take their time looking. There probably wasn't much within their budget, she conceded, but $700 or $800 a month ought to find something decent. Or so she had thought before they started looking around. They were feeling pressured. They couldn't impose Mary Anne on Ralph and Kathy forever.

Then they saw the place on Grove Road. It was off 25A, a large white-shingled house with redbrick trim and, judging by the chimney, a fireplace. It wasn't the whole house; they couldn't have afforded that. It was one-third of it, one of the three separate one-family units the house had been divided into. Their apartment, with its own entrance, had a kitchen, two bedrooms, a living room, den, and enclosed porch. They could have it for $750 a month. A rookie cop lived upstairs, another family downstairs. The school bus for William T. Rogers Middle School stopped just up the block at the corner. They thought it looked fine, signed the papers, moved their things from Flushing, where DeGregorio's brother, Joey, took over the lease, and reclaimed Mary Anne.

Only then did they notice the smell that seemed to rise through the floorboards, filling the house. The smell was worse outside, and it got stronger the closer they got to the basement apartment. They discovered the true nature of their downstairs neighbors, a family of hillbillies whose mongrel crapped all over the yard and, from the smell of it, in the house as well. The wall-eyed father stumbled around in a drunken stupor, scattering his beer cans in the yard. The mother seemed to cower in the basement. They rarely saw her, but a daughter, huge and retarded, emerged periodically to address them in an odd, deep voice.

Barbara had taken the day off, a rare luxury. She had been working a lot of overtime.

She was launched on a perilous new assignment. That summer, on the strength of her solid performance in buy-bust, she had been called back to narcotics, operating out of Brooklyn South, this time long-term. After two days of orientation at headquarters and a day of brushing up with a trainer on undercover skills, she was back on the street, in sallow makeup and a kerchief, making buys. Twice a month she and hundreds of other narcotics cops blanketed different drug-plagued sections of the city for Operation Pressure Point, designed to put maximum heat on sellers and buyers, disrupting the drug traffic so that regular police patrols could reclaim the streets. She was on the Lower East Side—buying pills, red and blue Valiums, $3.00 works, dime bags of heroin, nickel and dime foil packets of coke.

One day she had made the mistake of handing over a ten too soon when she was making a buy. She realized her gaffe immediately. He didn't have the shit, he said; he'd have to get it from somebody. She demanded the money back, but he ignored her. She grabbed for his hand, and he pushed her away. No real dirtbag would ever let that pass, she knew. She'd have to fight for it. She snatched at his hand again and this time seized the bill. He pulled away, and the bill ripped in half. Disgustedly he dropped his half. She bent and scooped it up, trying pathetically to piece the halves together. He glared at her, mouthing curses. He'd get some girls from the neighborhood after her, he threatened—cut her, beat her ass up. Barbara, seething, blurted the first thing that sounded tough. "I don't give a shit. I'm from Brooklyn. What do I care about your girls from the neighborhood?"

Between Operation Pressure Point and her regular street buys, she hadn't been home much, and with Patty's case accelerating, she rarely saw him. She slept late. When she awoke, the house was empty. Patty was already gone, and Mary Anne was off at school. Barbara showered and dressed and brewed some coffee, glorying in the crisp fall sunshine that dappled the maples in the yard, turning the air golden and, she hoped, perhaps somewhat less foul. She had opened a Doris Lessing novel and was picking at some pound cake when the doorbell rang.

It puzzled her. She wasn't supposed to be home and wasn't expecting anyone. They hadn't been there long enough to attract guests. Her neighbors would hardly pay calls.

She swung open the door and stood staring at a tangle-haired boy in glasses, torn jeans, and a jeans jacket. He looked about Mary Anne's age, maybe a little older, about fourteen. "Yes?" she inquired.

"Uh, is Mary Anne here?" he asked. He seemed startled to see her.

"No," Barbara said, confused, "she's not here." She wondered, Why would she be there in the middle of the day? She goes to school.

"Oh," said the boy, backing away. He mumbled something and trudged away.

She watched him go. It left her uneasy. Who was he? Did Mary Anne know him? Obviously, because he asked for her, he knew where she lived. Didn't he go to school? Why did he think Mary Anne would be home on a school day? She wasn't supposed to have anyone over while they were out anyway, not without letting them know. It was just a coincidence that Barbara happened to be home. Had this kid shown up here before?

She thought of asking Mary Anne when she got home and then hesitated. She'd be sure to take it as an accusation. It would probably start another argument. Would Mary Anne tell her the truth anyway? Better wait, she thought, and talk to Patty about it first.

14

J OSEPH wasn't home. His wife, Linda, answered the door—at least DeGregorio assumed it was Linda. She was clearly pregnant, or fat. You had to be careful with women; you couldn't always tell. But he remembered Joseph telling him that his wife was expecting. She was an attractive woman, DeGregorio thought, with nice features and glossy black hair. It figured that Joseph would have a pretty wife; he was good-looking himself, DeGregorio thought. Actually, Federico's wife, Sara, wasn't bad-looking either. She had olive skin and short black hair. But when DeGregorio was at Federico's apartment, he had been too freaked out by the stuffed heads to notice much else. The walls were covered with hunting trophies, mounted deer and antelope heads, birds, even a bear. It gave him the creeps. Federico was obviously a fanatical hunter. DeGregorio had wondered what his own head would look like up there on Federico's wall.

Linda said Joseph was in Florida. That was strange, DeGregorio thought, looking around idly at the antiques. They had made the appointment a few days before, and Joseph hadn't said anything about Florida. Was he pulling his chain? Immediately he grew suspicious. Joseph had asked him if he was a cop. They had laughed it off, but who knew? These guys were no dummies. Maybe they had picked up on something.

The phone rang and he flinched. Linda picked it up across the room and murmured quietly into the receiver for a few minutes. Then she called him over and handed it to him. "Joseph," she said.

He picked it up, wary. How did he know where Joseph was calling from? He could be in the next room for that matter. DeGregorio acted pissed. They had an appointment. Where was he?

Joseph said he was in Florida. He was sorry. He knew they were supposed to meet, and he'd see him when he got back. DeGregorio grumbled about a wasted afternoon and hung up.

When they did meet at the Korean restaurant four days later, DeGregorio still didn't know if Joseph was playing with him. Summer was a funny time to go to Florida; wasn't it as hot as hell there?

"Awful," Joseph agreed. He said he was there on business, negotiating for a hundred kilos of coke. Was Pasquale interested at $30,000 a kilo?

DeGregorio nodded sagely, making some quick calculations. Joseph was probably getting it for $20,000, $22,000, or $25,000 a kilo. That meant laying out about two million plus. He'd sell it for three. Not bad. A million bucks profit for a couple of weeks' work at most. Could you wonder why they went into the business? He told Joseph maybe, but he was mainly interested in the other stuff.

Joseph said he had plenty of that now, too, at $180,000 a kilo, $90,000 a half.

DeGregorio said he'd see about it. He had lucked out with the Spatolas, he realized. They were obviously hooked into a major supply source or were bringing it in themselves from Sicily. And the way they were offering it to him, it didn't seem they suspected him. But he'd have to watch himself. When you got comfortable, that's when you got careless. It would take only one mistake, one slip.

DeGregorio sat at the bar of the Woo Lae Oak, sipping an Absolut gimlet. In the back the tabletop barbecues were exhaling clouds of sizzling meat smoke as the nimble Korean waitreses scurried around with trays of pickled cabbage and bottles of beer. When Joseph showed up, late as usual, he seemed distracted.

"Is a problem," he told DeGregorio. Federico, he said, was back from Italy. They wanted Pasquale for a sitdown at the Figaro. Franco would be there too. There were decisions to be made.

What kind of decisions, DeGregorio wondered. He didn't want to press Joseph or look too concerned, but these things made him nervous. He never knew what was in store. They controlled the territory, and he was on their turf. He couldn't wear a wire. The usual bureau backups outside would trail them to the Figaro, but what good were they if anything went wrong inside? How would they know?

He thought of one grim possibility: Federico could have picked up some tip on the other side. The feds, he knew, were working closely with Italian investigators, exchanging confidential information all the time. Some of it was bound to leak out—there were always leaks over there. Maybe they wanted to confront him once and for all.

They walked the few blocks through Times Square to the Figaro. When they entered the restaurant, some of the tables were still occupied, scattered with theater-goers' playbills and cups of espresso. He saw Franco, all in black as usual. Some weeks before DeGregorio had finally gotten curious enough to ask him about the outfit. It was because his father died, Franco said. DeGregorio was apologetic. When did he die? Eighteen years ago, said Franco, ending the discussion. DeGregorio also caught sight of Federico and an elusive Spatola relative, Salvatore, a cousin maybe, a tall, sour-faced man with a high forehead, bushy hair, and a close-cropped stubbly mustache. DeGregorio had seen him around a few times when he went to visit Joseph or Federico, but Salvatore seemed to prefer the background. Now they all sat around a table waiting for the last customers to leave. He waited at the bar.

It was after midnight when the place finally emptied out and they waved him over. He took a moment to light a cigarette, a subtle signal that he'd take the time he needed and wasn't totally at their beck and call, and then he wandered over.

Federico began by saying that this was to avoid any confusion, that he was here now and would go back to taking care of Pasquale, who was his customer. So that was it, DeGregorio thought with relief, which was quickly followed by annoyance. Federico was staking his claim on him. Was that why they dragged him here? What was he, some piece of shit they could trade back and forth?

But Joseph, he was glad to see, objected. Pasquale had become his customer. They were doing good business. Why should he give him up?

Because, Federico countered, he had him first.

Yeah, said Joseph with a disarming grin, but he had him last.

"When did he first go with me?" Federico asked the room. "When?" Before anyone could answer he continued, "He started with me, right? I'm asking you, am I right?"

DeGregorio just sat there watching them fight over him. Nobody was asking his opinion.

Anyway, Federico said finally, Sal could make the ruling.

DeGregorio had assumed that Salvatore was the senior Spatola here and this seemed to confirm it. He remembered that Joseph had once mentioned he got his stuff from his cousin. The bureau carried him as a heavy guy. He probably was, if he was calling the shots here.

Joseph looked disgusted. "Ah," he grumbled, looking at DeGregorio, "fuck this shit! Go back to him."

DeGregorio felt a stab of regret. He didn't want to be passed back to Federico. That wasn't taking him anywhere. Joseph operated on a higher level, along with Salvatore, who seemed too smart to open his mouth much around a stranger. The matter looked settled without Salvatore's intervention, and the meeting ended inconclusively.

Later in private DeGregorio appealed to Joseph. "Listen," he said, "I like your brother and I like you. Nothing personal. But you got better merchandise, and I get a better price. I want to keep doing business with you."

Joseph seemed flattered. "Okay," he agreed, "but I don't want you to say nothing to my brother. That's it."

Days later Joseph called with good news. He had just received five kilos from Italy, the opening installment of a huge shipment, two hundred kilos of heroin plus a hundred of cocaine.

DeGregorio worked up the numbers. Two hundred keys! That much heroin was worth $40 million. He tried to keep his voice casual. "How's it coming in?" he asked. "JFK?"

"JFK is too hot," Joseph said. "It's coming through Texas."

"I can take a pound," said DeGregorio.

This time he went to Joseph's apartment, with a slender, dark-haired FBI agent whom he introduced as his girlfriend Jane. Linda Spatola let them in. Her husband was late, she said. So what else was new? DeGregorio thought. But, said Linda, Sal was there.

DeGregorio blessed his luck. *Salvatore!* He'd been hoping to draw the elusive cousin into a hand-to-hand buy that would stand up in court.

Salvatore, cautious, had little to say. He led DeGregorio into a bedroom where he dismantled a lamp and removed a bag of white powder. He extracted a sample and passed it wordlessly to De-Gregorio who, in turn, handed it to Jane for testing. She left while he sat to wait for the results. Then Joseph walked in, apologizing for being late.

Joseph heard about the girl from Salvatore and pointedly asked who she was. "Her father's in the private sanitation business," DeGregorio said casually. "I think she's Irish or something." That seemed to dispose of it. The two cousins then stepped out for a while. Meanwhile, Jane called back with the results: only twenty-one percent pure. When Joseph and Salvatore came back, De-Gregorio told them the stuff was shit, and he wasn't interested.

Joseph apologized. "I thought it would be better," he said, adding darkly, "People will pay." He'd have some purer stuff soon, he promised.

The next batch *was* better, nearly sixty percent pure. DeGregorio felt it was time to make his move. He beeped Joseph to place a big order, half a kilo for $90,000.

But Joseph didn't call back. DeGregorio beeped him a second time, again without response. After several more tries he reluctantly gave up for the night.

He finally reached Joseph the next day. "What happened?" he demanded.

"What happened?" Joseph yelled. "There was-a ten fucking cop cars all around-a the house. That's what happened."

Shit! DeGregorio couldn't believe it. Joseph *made* them; he picked up on the fucking surveillance!

Joseph's voice was icy. "I don't know who's a cop," he said, "if you're a fucking cop. But if I go down, you're going down with me. I don't give a fuck if I got to kill a cop or any-body."

DeGregorio instinctively started yelling back. "You accusing me of being a fucking cop? You got a lot of fucking balls. How do I know who's watching you? I got more to lose than you do. You could be up to your ass in cops."

Joseph calmed down. "I'm not accusing you, okay?"

DeGregorio let his rage run on. "You know, Joe, you're a very big fucking man. I'm the one who's worried. I don't fucking want to deal with you anymore. I'm going to get fucking locked up. I don't need this bullshit."

Now Joseph tried to calm him down. They could set it up again.

"Well," said DeGregorio, pretending to be convinced, "I still need the fucking merchandise."

When they talked again a few days later, Joseph acted as if nothing had gone wrong. "Okay, how about tomorrow?"

DeGregorio played it cool. He was going to toy with Joseph. "Tomorrow for what?" As if he didn't know.

"To make the move," Joseph reminded him.

"No good tomorrow," DeGregorio said grumpily. He had already taken care of it, he said. He had done what he had to do.

Joseph sounded incredulous. "You mean you went some other place?"

What did he expect? DeGregorio said. "You didn't call me. You said you were going to call me yesterday, didn't you?"

"Well, I wasn't ready."

"No, no, no, Joe. Listen to me. You ready to do business, I'm ready. I told you the weekend I got to be ready, so I had to take care of what I had to take care of."

Joseph's tone turned mean. "You do a lot of business now, don't you?"

"I do the same as I always did. But if you can't take care of it, I got to do something, right? We've been having a lot of problems, Joe. We got to have a talk, okay?"

"Listen—you can talk?" Joseph was worried about the phone.

"Yeah, go ahead," DeGregorio said, luring him on.

"Y'see, like I say, that night something wrong. That night it went down, outside was a lot of fucking mice, a lot of them."

DeGregorio cursed the clumsiness of the surveillance agents. "Yeah," he said encouragingly, "go ahead."

"I don't know why, how, whatever. I don't want to accuse you or anybody else, okay? But y'know, anybody going to try to fuck me, they going to be fucked—badly."

DeGregorio gave it right back. "Who's trying to fuck you? You accusing me of fucking you?"

"No, no." Joseph backed off.

"That's the impression you're giving me."

"No, no. Listen. I'm not saying you. I'm saying anybody. I'm not accusing you. I'm not accusing nobody. I'm saying anybody trying to fuck me, they going to be fucked, because I don't care if somebody fucking me is undercover, is a cop, or whatever. Anybody who fucks with me is going to be fucked."

"What's that got to do with me?" DeGregorio demanded, going on the offensive.

"No, no. I'm not blaming you. I'm not accusing you. I'm only talking in general."

"But that night when you talked to me, the next day you talked to me, you were very fucking upset, like you said I did something wrong."

"What do you want me to think?"

"What am I supposed to think?" DeGregorio countered.

"I go outside and I find, you know, I had seven cars follow me. I even went up to the George Washington Bridge, all the way up there."

DeGregorio almost laughed, this was so ridiculous.

"That would fucking make me upset, too," he commiserated. "I'm not blaming you for being upset, but the only thing is, like, you're taking it out on me."

Joseph backed off. "I'm not saying it's you. Maybe somebody else.

"It's good that you—"

Joseph cut him off. "I'm only saying anybody going to fuck with me, I don't give a fuck if I'm going to do thirty years or forty years. I don't give a fuck. But if I go down, a lot of people, they're going to go down. I don't give a fuck if the Police Department next to me. I don't give a fuck because I'm not afraid to die or pay thirty years."

DeGregorio was eager to move on. "Good. Listen, I'm not afraid of that shit either. So we'd better start changing the way we do things. You calling me from a public phone?"

"Yeah."

"That's good. So am I. That's what you should be doing all the time anyway."

"We're not going to do them in my house," Joseph said.

It was the opening DeGregorio was waiting for. "No, we're going to do it in my apartment, that's where we're going to do it. I told you that a fucking month ago."

At Kearney's suggestion he had looked for an undercover apartment where buys could be easily bugged and videotaped. De-Gregorio had asked about the budget, but Kearny told him not to worry about it, that the FBI had deep pockets. "Just find a suitable location." The place he had picked was in upscale Brooklyn Heights, on a street paralleling the East River and across the elevated Brooklyn-Queens Expressway. The walkup building dead-ended on Columbia Heights, where a T intersection made surveillance relatively easy. The neighborhood had a big Italian population. De-Gregorio would fit right in. The apartment was on the ground floor, which still afforded a view of the downtown Manhattan skyline across the river. For $1,600 a month he got a hallway, a kitchenette with a window, a living room with a bar, a bathroom, and in the rear, a bedroom. He had filled the place with rented furniture, paintings, and accessories, stocked the fridge and bar, and scattered around some of Barbara's clothes, as if girlfriends sometimes stayed over. The FBI had provided the final touches: a drug scale, a Nagra recorder concealed behind a panel in the desk, and a Kel transmitter under the radiator. But it wasn't going to do them any good unless DeGregorio got Joseph over there.

"Why can't you do it on my fucking territory now?" DeGregorio demanded. "Do it my way. Try it my way. You make it sound like I just came into this fucking business last week. Maybe I seem to know what I'm doing. Why don't you give me a shot? Why don't you try it my way?"

Joseph wavered. "You're near the . . . the . . ."

"Near the bridge," he prompted. "Yeah, I'm away from nobody."

"The Brooklyn Bridge . . ." Joseph seemed to be thinking.

"The Brooklyn Bridge."

Joseph sounded skeptical. "You know the Brooklyn Bridge, you know what's out there? They got the whole fucking Port Authority there."

"There's nothing there!" DeGregorio was exasperated. The Port Authority was over in Jersey. Joseph was all screwed up. "I told you to come and see the fucking place. I said, 'Joe, come and see the fucking place.' See what you think of it, right?"

"Fine, all right."

"That's all I want you to do."

He needed to know if Joseph would bring anybody.

Just himself, Joseph said. But abruptly he seemed to have second thoughts. "Maybe me and my brother, Freddy," he said.

In that case, DeGregorio said, he might have his cousin there. He didn't want to be alone with two of them. Anyway he'd want to send a sample out for testing.

"Why don't he check the stuff right there in front of me?" Joseph asked.

"No, no. That's not the way we do things. That's not the way I do things," DeGregorio protested. He wasn't born yesterday, Joseph had to know that. "I told you how I get it checked. Didn't I tell you? He brings it to somebody who gets it checked. Remember I told you that?"

"I don't want to be fucked in front of nobody," Joseph said. "Not I don't trust you."

DeGregorio had to take issue with what he was hearing. "Joe, what you're telling me is now you don't trust me."

Joseph denied it. "No, no. I'm upset about the things, the way they're going."

"I understand," DeGregorio said. "I'm fucking upset too. I got promised certain things from you that you never delivered, right?"

Joseph was getting excited again. "You want me to get the shit when I had twenty fucking cops behind me?" He knew the risks, he admitted. "You're talking half a package, too, right?" Joseph said. "You're talking about thirty years here."

DeGregorio tried to get him to incriminate himself further. "I ain't even thinking about that. I'm thinking about a lot of money, Joe. We're talking about—"

"I'm thinking half a key here."

"Absolutely!" DeGregorio said, leading him on. "It's a lot of fucking shit, you're right. But it's also a lot of money."

"I'm just double precautious," Joseph said. "I'm glad that night I made a double check because I think I would have been fucked somewhere."

"So now we don't trust each other?"

"Wait a minute. Did I say that?"

"That's the way you sound, Joe."

"No, I'm not sound like that. I'm sound like I'm taking a lot of drugs in, that's all. Do you blame me?"

DeGregorio caught his breath over the way Joseph was hanging himself right on the phone. "No, I don't blame you," he agreed.

Once again, Joseph reflected on his close call. "I thought that night I was gonna go. That's the way I felt."

"Those things happen to me, too, once in a while," DeGregorio said manfully. "I know how you feel. It's a tough fucking business. But everything worked out right."

"I got three kids and one coming," said Joseph.

"Well, don't you think I got the same thing? You make this thing, I got no family. I got a family. We both got to be careful. Don't keep saying you, you. I got to be careful too."

"People, you know, are getting caught left and right," Joseph said.

"Joe, don't you think I'm reading the fucking paper? I know what goes on. I'm not stupid. That's why I'm out where I am. That's why I don't hang around that fucking city."

"I don't mind going for thirty, but it has to be for something good, not for—"

"Not for bullshit." DeGregorio finished Joseph's thought. "We're going to do everything Monday, guaranteed. You come and see the place, you leave. You like what you see, you call me back. We do the deal."

"Unless we get another place somewhere."

"That place is perfect," DeGregorio insisted, out of patience. "When you see the fucking place, you'll understand what I'm talking about."

15

"PATTY, do you think Mary Anne's getting high?"

"Hmmm?" DeGregorio heard the startling question but chose to ignore it as he sat at the kitchen table filling out a buy report, mumbling to himself. Mary Anne was off visiting Joe and Anne. They were only five minutes away and would drive her home later. He had a lot of government money to account for and had to reconstruct his buys. He had paid Joseph Spatola $4,400 owed. Joseph said he'd charge him only eight for the next ounce but forgive a thousand. So that meant he owed $11,400. *Fuck!* The pen stopped writing. He shook it and tried again. *Fucking out of ink!* In frustration he threw it across the room and got up to look for another.

"Patty, I asked you something."

"Ummm?" He made her repeat the question.

"I asked you, do you think Mary Anne's getting high?"

He looked up, eyes narrowing. "High? High on what? Why do you think that?"

"I don't know," he heard her say, "I don't even know if I think it. She just seems, I don't know, a little . . . *sneaky*." Her voice trailed off uncertainly.

"Sneaky?" He didn't like the sound of that. "Barbara," he said, "you're not just asking, you're asking for a reason."

"I don't know. Her behavior. . . . She seems tired all the time. And that boy . . ."

He remembered she had told him about the boy who showed up at the house one day. So what? Mary Anne had made a friend. She knew lots of kids at school now, and one came by to see her. What was so strange about that? How did that mean she was getting high, his little girl? She had lots of problems. He knew why, it was no secret. But high? High on what? He couldn't imagine it. He wouldn't imagine it. She was always a tough kid. She'd been through a lot, but she could handle it.

She was all he had left. Well, Barbara, too, of course. He loved Barbara and couldn't imagine living without her. It was so good with her. She had given him back his life, everything. He worried about her out on the street, Barbara with her red hair and green eyes out there with those *animals*. At least when he was out with the backups he could keep an eye on her, but now he didn't know who was watching out for her. But Mary Anne, she was . . . a piece of him, of his skin and blood. He looked at her and remembered everything about her from the day she was born. She was twelve years of his life, everything that happened. She was Tommy too.

"She *is* tired," DeGregorio said. "Is, not seems. Is. She does a lot, she's busy with school. Don't imagine things."

"I don't think I'm imagining, Patty. It's just that . . ."

He sucked his teeth impatiently. "Barbara," he said, "I have to finish this paperwork, okay? Can I just finish this? Lately you seem to have, I don't know, some *hard-on* for Mary Anne." That was too strong. He realized that as soon as it escaped him, but it was too late. And once words were out, you could never call them back. It didn't matter what you said afterward.

He saw Barbara's green eyes flare with a momentary fire. "What do you think, you're the only one with a case?" she rebuked him. "I've got cases too." Then she pressed her lips together, closed a book she'd been reading, and walked out of the room.

When his beeper on the table suddenly started pinging, De-Gregorio jumped up. "Great!" he said. "That could be Joe."

He heard the door click open and saw Mary Anne walk in. He called her over. "Mary Anne . . ." he began, not sure what he wanted to say. She looked at him expectantly, maybe a little apprehensively, he couldn't be sure. "Mary Anne, can you find my tape recorder? I have to tape a call." She nodded and ran off, hollering a moment later from the bedroom, "Where'd you leave it?" He tried to remember. "Somewhere in the bedroom," he shouted back. She came in with a little Sony trailing a telephone pickup mike.

"Hold it," Barbara said. "Isn't that mine?" DeGregorio looked it over. It looked like his, but she had one too. He asked Mary Anne where she had found it. On the dresser, she said. "Then it is mine," Barbara said, still clearly annoyed. "Try to find your own."

He searched and finally found his under some papers on the desk. He called the phone number on the beeper and made a face. It was Catherine.

Later, as he drove to meet Joseph at his apartment in Long Island City, DeGregorio's thoughts kept fastening on Mary Anne and Barbara. Did Barbara have it in for Mary Anne or what? He loved them both. They were both vital to him, couldn't they see that? What was this rivalry? Couldn't they get along? He pondered the mysterious ways of women. They always had to think so deeply about everything. Men didn't get hung up like that. They took things as they came, accepted things as they were. But Barbara and Mary Anne . . .

He suddenly caught himself. He was Pasquale Greco. *Pasquale Greco.* He repeated the two names urgently to himself. If he forgot who he was supposed to be, he'd fuck up big time. It was a good thing the bosses had no idea what was going on in his life, DeGregorio thought. They'd pull the plug, take down the case right now, before the risky big buy that would be his toughest test.

"Hey, Pasquale, what's-a this?" Joseph reached down between his legs into the cushion of the chair and pulled out the telltale lace strap of a black brassiere.

"Aw, shit, Joe, I'm sorry," DeGregorio said, reddening. He yanked the bra out with convincing embarrassment and kicked it under the chair. He was rewarded with Joseph's indulgent smile.

For hours before Joseph's arrival DeGregorio had paced the apartment on Columbia Heights, making sure everything was in place. Outside, four surveillance teams with views of the apartment staked out the approaches and exit routes. Inside, bureau technicians had been working since early morning, checking the Kel transmitter under the radiator and the Nagra recorder in the desk. The phone had been tapped. They had considered secretly videotaping the buy as well but decided it was unnecessary. They already had Joseph so many different ways, including the last incriminating taped conversation, which DeGregorio had made a special point of ceremoniously delivering to Inspector Brian Lavin of the Joint Organized Crime Narcotics Task Force.

With DeGregorio in the apartment, posing as his business partner, was a veteran undercover detective, Diodoro Ielardi, known as Teddy. DeGregorio had met him some weeks before, and they'd hit it off. He had introduced Teddy to the Spatolas as his money man. To make the atmosphere more homey, Teddy had begun to cook a macaroni dinner in the kitchen. What could look more authentic? But Joseph didn't show on time. What else was new? Then he called from a phone booth, saying he was lost. DeGregorio rushed out, cursing, to escort him to the apartment, but it was *them*. Joseph had come with someone, but it wasn't his brother, Federico. He was about Joseph's height, five-nine or so, but a good twenty pounds lighter and considerably more athletic. He wore tan pants, a white shirt, and a blue velvet jacket. He looked a little like an actor, DeGregorio thought. Joseph introduced him as Charlie.

When they stopped chuckling over the bra, Joseph turned serious. He was still grumbling suspiciously about the cops he'd spotted on his tail. "I don't know who's fucking me, but who's fucking me, they going get fucked," he fumed.

DeGregorio was not about to start down that road again. "You ready, Joe?" he asked curtly.

Joseph muttered assent. Then he crossed the room and turned on the TV, loud. He snapped on the radio too.

DeGregorio tried not to wince. So much for the bug, he thought; the backups wouldn't be able to hear squat. He shot Joseph a quizzical look. "What's your problem?"

Joseph didn't respond.

Why was he so paranoid? DeGregorio wondered, Did he suspect something?'

Joseph shrugged. Then he said offhandedly that to show good faith, Pasquale would have to front $30,000 of the purchase price or the half-kilo wouldn't be delivered.

DeGregorio froze. He couldn't believe what he was hearing! *Wouldn't be delivered?* Joseph didn't bring it with him? He first had to get it? And they were supposed to hand him $30,000? *Up front!* They'd have to let the money go first? No way! What if it disappeared, then what? What was this, a trick? They had him coming and going. To let the cash walk would mark them dangerously as amateurs, at worst as cops. But not to let it go, that could jeopardize the deal and the case. More to the point, regulations prohibited fronting money for drugs. They were screwed. "You got to be fucking kidding, Joe," he said. "That ain't the way we set it up."

"Got to be," Joseph said.

At least he could put up a fight. "No way, Joe. I already showed good faith. You got to trust me." He was breaking out into a sweat.

"I can't do nothing. That's the way *they* want it."

DeGregorio was almost pleading now. "Remember what we talked, Joe—the money and the goods in the apartment at the same time, remember?"

Joseph shrugged. It was out of his hands. That was the way they wanted it.

DeGregorio felt sick. He said he needed to talk to his partner alone. They huddled in the bedroom. "Teddy, you hear what's going on? What the fuck am I going to do now?"

Teddy seemed almost amused. "Well, kid," he chortled, "you just have to make a decision. You know the guy a while, right?"

DeGregorio nodded.

"Fuck it," said Teddy. "Do what you gotta do. It ain't our money. Let it go."

"Oh, shit," said DeGregorio.

Then Teddy had an inspiration. "As long as Charlie stays here." He would be the hostage for the half-kilo.

They presented it to Joseph, who grimaced. "Charlie stays here," DeGregorio insisted, "or no deal."

"Okay," Joseph said finally. "Charlie's gonna go. I'm gonna stay here."

"Fine," said DeGregorio, wondering whether it would matter. "Fine, even better."

He dug into the bedroom closet where he had stashed a green canvas duffel bag stuffed with $90,000 in hundreds. Before giving DeGregorio the money the bureau had painstakingly photocopied each of the nine hundred bills for later tracing.

He counted out $30,000, thrust it into a paper bag, and handed it to Joseph. Joseph picked up the phone, dialed, and murmured into the receiver. Then he handed the bag to Charlie and sent him off.

DeGregorio glanced at his watch. It was seven-thirty.

They settled down to wait. Teddy said he was going for a walk. DeGregorio knew he'd take the opportunity to telephone the operations center with an update. Joseph seemed untroubled. He withdrew a small foil packet, tapped out some coke on a pocket mirror, and snorted several lines through a rolled-up twenty.

Teddy came back, and two hours crawled by. DeGregorio was jumpy. "So where the fuck is he?" he demanded.

Joseph may have been wondering himself. He made another call and, a few minutes later, a third call. "He's coming soon," he said reassuringly. He looked around the apartment and beamed. "Hey, Pasquale," he said, "maybe we can share an apartment here together, huh?"

"Yeah, Joe. Let's get this settled first." He prayed Joseph wasn't screwing him.

At ten-thirty there was a knock at the door. Charlie! Finally!

He fished out a brown paper bag and handed it to Joseph, who passed it to Teddy. Teddy motioned for DeGregorio to follow him into the bathroom with the balance-beam scale. With Joseph and Charlie looking on from the doorway, they weighed the bag, confirming it was half a kilo. Teddy used a small knife to cut into the plastic and removed a few grains on a spoon. He sifted the powder into a vial of two percent formaldehyde sulfuric acid and watched the mixture turn a dark purplish blue. At least it wasn't milk powder. They couldn't know the actual purity until further tests outside.

Suddenly Joseph took the knife from Teddy and dipped it into the powder. He withdrew it, lifted it to his nose, and inhaled eagerly.

Teddy was dumbfounded. "What's the matter with you?" he blurted.

"It's good," Joseph said. "It don't bother me because I'm immune to it."

Teddy turned to Charlie. "What's wrong with your friend here?"

Charlie put a finger to his temple and described little circles.

"Okay," Teddy said, "let the money go."

DeGregorio got the green canvas bag containing the remaining $60,000 from the bedroom closet and handed it to Joseph, who counted the bundles carefully. It took several minutes. Then, with a quick good-bye, he and Charlie left.

As the door clicked shut, DeGregorio groaned and threw up on the floor.

Teddy collapsed in hysterical laughter.

"You fuck," DeGregorio said, holding his head. "If you ever tell anybody about this, I'm going to fucking kill you."

Suddenly, agents flooded into the apartment. DeGregorio watched, dazed, as they secured the half-kilo of heroin and retrieved the recorder from inside the desk, cursing as they found that it had malfunctioned and recorded not a word.

Afterward, when he had pulled himself together, DeGregorio sat down to write up the buy report. Right away he realized he had a problem. Fronting money for drugs was strictly forbidden, yet they had done it. They had had to do it. Luckily for them it had worked out, but somehow he had to fudge it. He decided just to skip over the part where they had fronted the money. The way he outlined it in his official report, Charlie had come back with the drugs and they had turned over the buy money. Nothing about fronting. Why ask for trouble?

Four days later Joseph called cautiously. "How was the dinner?" he asked.

"Not the best," DeGregorio said. "I've eaten better." The half-kilo had tested at forty percent pure, just so-so. "It was the blue plate special," DeGregorio said.

"You know," Joseph reminded him, "you didn't pay Tavern on the Green price."

Kearney said it was time to take down the case, spring the trap DeGregorio had painstakingly set and baited with thousands of dollars of marked government money. The wiretap on the phone in the undercover apartment had traced Joseph's call to the Café Mille Luci on Bensonhurst's Eighteenth Avenue, a wiseguy hangout with a long drug history. In the three months since DeGregorio's big buy, the source of the half-kilo and much other heroin smuggled in from Sicily and sold by the Spatolas had been traced to a brother-in-law of Salvatore Spatola, Ambrogio "Vito" Pipitone, an obscure Sicilian in New Jersey who was financing the traffic through American Mafia channels in Bensonhurst.

But the alliance was about to erupt into bloodshed, bureau eaves-droppers heard. The Spatolas had fallen behind in their payments. A coke deal had gone sour, and the money to pay off one set of creditors had been taken from investors who now demanded to be paid. The Spatolas were in the hole for $100,000, and Bensonhurst had run out of patience. A contract had been put out on Salvatore, who awoke one morning to find *morte* spray-painted in red on his garage door. Agents found it there before he did, and the police and FBI bosses felt compelled to head off the hit. Charlie Dean, the police sergeant who was dubious about the operation from the beginning, was especially eager to cut it short now. Some FBI agents fought to keep it going. "Fuck it," one told DeGregorio. "Let 'em kill each other." But they were overruled. The case had to be taken down sometime. This was the time. The raids were set for the next morning.

DeGregorio reached home close to midnight, quivering with tension. Barbara was waiting up. He kissed her distractedly and made for the liquor cabinet to mix himself a vodka gimlet, deciding, as he poured, to skip the ice and the lime juice as a waste of time.

Barbara hovered uncertainly behind him. She seemed to have something on her mind. "Patty," she began hesitantly. "I found a note in Mary Anne's room. "It's . . . I . . ."

He had no patience for her. Couldn't she see it was the last thing he wanted to hear right now? He hoped his catatonic stare sent the message, but Barbara seemed determined to press on. "I . . . I think," he heard her say, "it's about drugs."

"Can't it wait?" he pleaded. "I have to be up at four."

The bureau liked to strike in the hours before dawn, when even late-night carousers were home and the foulest felons snored, un-wary, dreaming dreams of a sweet *cummare*. On a dark Wednesday morning in December 1984, heavily armed police and FBI teams wielding sledgehammers and crowbars encircled the homes of twenty-two targets named in arrest warrants based on DeGregorio's sting. Within hours, without incident, nineteen were in custody, including the Guidices and the Spatolas and their major accomplices. Among the missing was Nick. DeGregorio vengefully went to Ridgewood himself to look for him, remembering the machine gun. But Nick had disappeared.

The others went quietly. Charlie, who had delivered the half-kilo of heroin that DeGregorio bought from Joseph, was identified as Calogero Davi. He told agents he worked as a busboy at the Figaro Restaurant and ran errands for the Spatolas but had no idea what he had been sent to pick up that night. They learned he was a cousin of Franco, the man in black, and a sometime professional soccer player.

The house searches of the Spatolas, Pipitone, and the others yielded a bonanza of heroin and cocaine, scales, guns, and book-keeping journals. In Pipitone's house, agents found $80,000 in the sleeve of a woman's ski jacket in the closet, as well as heroin in the bedroom of his two-year-old.

DeGregorio returned to the task force's command post in the FBI's offices over a Frank Purdue chicken restaurant on Queens Boulevard. The entire fifth floor had been cleared out to hold prisoners.

"I want to meet these people," he told Kearney. "I ain't going to hide from them. They're going to figure it out anyway. And if they don't, they're going to see me in court anyway, so what's the big deal?" DeGregorio felt he needed a way to blow off the tension and fear bottled up in him for a year.

He stopped by the room where Catherine and her daughter, Donna, were being held.

Catherine glared at him. "I knew it was you, you motherfucker," she growled.

Donna was passive, maybe strung out. "What do they want?" she asked spacily, motioning toward the agents milling around.

"They want to know what you know," DeGregorio said.

"You know everything," Donna said sullenly. "You got it all."

Outside the room where Federico Spatola sat cuffed, an agent intercepted DeGregorio. "This guy Freddy swears up and down he never sold anything to anybody," he said. "You want to confront him?"

"Bring him into the lieutenant's office in a few minutes," he said.

DeGregorio got there first and slid into a chair by the window, facing out.

Two agents brought Federico in and sat him down. "Come on," said one. "Tell the boss who you were dealing with."

"I swear to my mother, I never sell-a that shit to-a nobody."

DeGregorio slowly spun around and looked at Federico, whose mouth dropped open in amazement. "Pasquale," he blurted. "They got-a you too?"

DeGregorio tossed his police shield on the desk in front of him. "No, Freddy," he said. "I got-a you!"

Federico pulled himself together fast. He turned to the agents. "I swear," he insisted. "I only sell-a to him, nobody else."

DeGregorio went off in search of Joseph. Despite everything, he felt strangely close to him. They had spent so much time together, been through so much. Who knew, in other circumstances they might have been on the same side. He found Joseph handcuffed to a desk. "Joe," he asked gently, "you want to go to the bathroom?"

Joseph nodded, expressionless.

"It's okay, I'll take him," DeGregorio said to the agents guarding the prisoners. He could handle Joseph.

In the bathroom they stood face-to-face. Then, impulsively, DeGregorio grabbed him in a bear hug. "I'm sorry," he said.

Joseph started to cry.

"Joe," DeGregorio said, teary-eyed himself, "I'm really sorry. You're a nice guy, but you're in the wrong business."

"It's okay," Joseph said, wiping his eyes and trying to deepen his cracking voice. "Don't worry about it. I got nothing against you."

"Joe," DeGregorio said soothingly, "you got a nice wife, a nice little girl."

Joseph sniffled and broke down. "I never spent no time with her," he blubbered.

PART
Three

PART
Three

16

THE house on Grove Road gave her the creeps, especially the people downstairs. They were pigs. But she was glad to get away from Ralph. He scared her. Barbara and her father were away a lot, working. Sometimes when they weren't home she cut school, skipping the bus altogether. Some of her new friends also cut and met over at her house. They brought beer they had gotten someone to buy for them. Afterward, Mary Anne made sure to clean up the cans and bottles. Her father and Barbara, she felt sure, had no idea.

She started hanging out with a girl she met in homeroom. Chrissy had an angel's face, frosted corn-blond hair, eyes of swimming-pool blue, a pixieish nose, and a mischievous, dippy disposition. Chrissy made her laugh. Chrissy had pot. She'd been smoking it awhile, she told Mary Anne, who was impressed. Marijuana! She'd heard kids talking about it, but she'd never smoked it; she'd never even seen any.

Never seen any! Chrissy was incredulous. Outside school by the tennis courts, she opened her bag and took out her compact. The inside was packed with brownish flakes. "Cool," Mary Anne said, trying not to sound too impressed, which she was.

They found some other kids who had cigarette paper, and together they sat in the woods behind the tennis courts and rolled joints. A few times Mary Anne tore the paper, spilling the flakes to the ground. Chrissy crinkled up her nose and wheezed a zany snorting laugh, as if she were being tickled. Mary

Anne couldn't help laughing too. It was crazy, nothing made sense.

Finally she had a sloppy cylinder with twisted ends. She watched the others and lit it, inhaling the stinging, musky-perfumed vapor between coughs. She braced herself to feel an effect, but to her surprise she felt nothing.

"Hmmm," one of the kids said appreciatively. "Good weed."

"Oh, yeah!" said Mary Anne.

Chrissy leaned over and whispered to her, "You're full of shit."

"Yeah," Mary Anne said deadpan, "I'm full of shit."

They both collapsed laughing on the ground.

Many days after that she and Chrissy wandered onto the ball fields around school to smoke. Once she learned to relax and to take the smoke in deeply and hold it in her lungs, she found it did have an effect. She felt her anger kind of dissolving into laughter, especially when she was with Chrissy. Everything seemed stretched out, with no beginning or end, and so funny! She just had to get the knack of letting it happen.

Sometimes her friend Kelly, who had her license now, drove over to visit her at Grove Road. She brought pot, and they smoked in the woods around the house when her father and Barbara were away. She felt she was getting back at them somehow. Besides, she thought, her father was probably doing it himself with those hoods he was hanging around with. She knew he was buying drugs from all the times he had her get his tape recorder.

The kids from school met on Friday nights at the Superior Ice Rink on Indian Head Road. Sometimes Chrissy's mother dropped them off there, sometimes her father. First they'd hang out in the parking lot outside. Someone always had pot, and they'd smoke it there, laughing and clowning around in the darkness sliced by headlight beams of circling cars. After a while they drifted inside, taking seats in the bleachers. None of them skated. That wasn't why they were there. They came to hang out, to sit in the bleachers and pass joints back and forth, getting high to the loopy skating music and the swirls of bright skaters' outfits smeared against the creamy ice.

Mary Anne bobbed to the music, the pulsating rhythms revving up the thumping of her heart. Chrissy's blue eyes were webbed with red, roadmaps of the chemical fog Mary Anne could almost see gliding through her bloodstream. The thought struck her as funny, and she began to giggle. Chrissy looked up, surprised, and then giggled too. Soon they were laughing uproariously.

"Well, how was the skating?"

Her father was waiting in the car outside the rink as they tumbled out, still giddy.

"Good."

They scrambled into the backseat and promptly nodded off.

17

I REALLY need something today. What can you get me?

Barbara stared triumphantly at the handwritten note she had found folded in Mary Anne's pocketbook. She was snooping, she admitted it. Why not? She had her suspicions about the girl, and maybe she could lay them to rest or confirm them. Either was better than just wondering what was going on under their roof. She stared at the note again, as if to force it to yield up more of its secret. Its context eluded her, but the implications were unmistakable, ugly. Mary Anne *needed something*. Then it struck her. It wasn't Mary Anne's writing—she knew Mary Anne's cursive script, with its exaggerated, fat, curlicued letters. So whose was it? What was Mary Anne doing with it, and what did it mean?

She had searched her soul after the last confrontation, when Patty had turned on her for calling Mary Anne sneaky. She had asked herself whether she really did have it in for Mary Anne, and she became more convinced than ever that she was pure. It was Mary Anne who was giving her the cold shoulder, while Barbara wanted to be her friend. She loved Patty so much, and she wanted to be close to his daughter too. She felt bad for Mary Anne. All the things that happened to her weren't her fault: Tommy, her mother, the divorce. On the other hand, Barbara conceded, she had her own resentments. She wouldn't be human if she didn't. She missed her privacy. She was selfish and wanted him all to herself. She didn't kid herself that she was the maternal type. She didn't know how to act around a preteen-ager. But that was all a long way from making up accusations against Mary Anne.

In fact, Barbara felt guilty about her selfishness; she wished she could be more giving, more generous. Still, she thought, it wasn't her attitude that was the problem, it was Mary Anne's. And now she was beginning to realize that it was Patty's as well. At first she thought the way he had turned on her for her suspicions was crazy, but then she realized he wasn't so busy that he couldn't take five minutes to hear her out, to discuss something serious about Mary Anne. He didn't want to listen to her because he couldn't afford to. He didn't want to hear anything bad about Mary Anne. *He couldn't face the consequences.*

Maybe this would change his mind, she thought, stuffing the note into a pocket. She tried to call him, but he was always tied up somewhere on his case. She could either wait until she saw him and they had a few minutes to talk—God knew when that would be, the way he was running around now—or she could take matters into her own hands while the evidence and her resolve were still fresh.

That night, with Patty still not home, Barbara confronted Mary Anne in her room. She fished out the folded note and held it out questioningly in her open palm.

Mary Anne did not seem shocked or even surprised. She didn't seem to react at all, throwing the onus back on Barbara, who wasn't prepared to formulate an indictment. Of all reactions, Barbara hadn't expected no reaction. "What this note says to me," Barbara began tentatively, "is this kid is looking for drugs. Why is someone going to you for drugs?"

She watched Mary Anne's broad face shift from blankness to a look of puzzlement and hurt. Her brows knit in a portrait of painful confusion, filling Barbara with sudden uncertainty and embarrassment.

"No," Mary Anne said earnestly. "There's this kid no one likes, and I'm the only one he talks to. He needed something from somebody, I don't know what it was, and he asked me to pass it on, that's all. How would anyone get drugs from me?"

Barbara had to admit it was a good question, one she had asked herself. How *would* she get drugs? Barbara had no idea. She was twelve years old, new in the neighborhood, new in the school. Mary Anne had instantly put her finger on the weakest part of Barbara's case. Was the kid that clever? Or was she telling the truth? Barbara couldn't decide. She was struck by the unlikelihood of Mary Anne's explanation—it flew in the face of common sense—but Mary Anne's haunting question and her air of injured innocence were persuasive. She couldn't easily fake that, Barbara thought. Or could she? Had she genuinely maligned the girl? It was possible that Mary Anne was telling the truth. Anyway, there wasn't much more she could do. What was she supposed to do, launch an investigation of William T. Rogers Middle School?

Still, she felt she had to say something to Patty. When he finally came through the door shortly before midnight, he was so hyper that he was shaking. He went through the motions of a kiss, a dutiful peck that left her cold. His eyes were bloodshot, and his hand trembled as he poured himself a tall straight vodka.

She started to tell him about the note but stopped when she saw his blank stare. What was the point? She started again and blurted it out.

She waited for a reaction but then realized that nothing had registered. He seemed lost in himself and his case. He just wanted to go to bed, he had to be up early, he said wearily. She started to object, but then, deeply dissatisfied, let it drop.

Later that winter of 1985, Barbara was on the job, following el tracks that snaked fearsomely overhead on rusty pylons—the subway line that in a few more months would resume its transport of charged-up Mets fans to and from Shea Stadium. Now dirty snow lined the curbs, and the streets were slick with slush. She turned her old blue Chevy off Roosevelt Avenue at the edge of the stadium parking lot on One Hundred and Fourteenth Street in Corona. She parked, idling the engine to keep the heat going as long as possible. Even in her boots, her feet were freezing. She stamped them against the car floorboards to keep the circulation going and tried to raise the backups on the radio to let them know that she was leaving the car. On point-to-point, the radio had a range of only a few blocks depending on the neighborhood. She hoped they could hear her.

After eight months in Brooklyn South, Barbara had been moved again, to Queens Narcotics. Same shit, different day, the teams joked. It was the same buy-bust, but she was getting better at it and was going to move up, maybe get a real undercover case one of these days. She could remember when Patty was part of the team, and Mike too. It seemed like long ago, back before Ridgenarc.

Earlier, before they'd set out, the sergeant had outlined the targets to make sure they all knew where they were going. They used their own cars, which was as unmarked as you could get. They had many stops to make, many places to hit. This was the first.

Barbara pulled her wool hat down low over her ears and made certain her gun was securely clipped to the inside of her jeans. She didn't have to be armed, but she felt better carrying a weapon whenever she could. In summer she couldn't because there was nowhere to hide it. She checked herself in the rearview mirror to see if her lips looked bloodless, her skin sallow, her eyes sunken. Then she stepped out of the car and walked back toward Roosevelt Avenue.

Yes, she thought, they were all out. She could see them on every corner pirouetting in the cold, leaning toward passersby to hawk their wares. Every third or fourth huddle was a sale. She picked out one of them outside a bodega. He looked Spanish, she thought, a short, skinny guy with a blue hooded sweatshirt under a green Jets jacket.

She asked for coke, handed him a twenty, took the foil packet he slipped into her hand, and headed back to the car, all in the space of a minute. In the car she radioed a description of her seller; there were several guys in sweatshirt hoods, and she wanted to make sure they grabbed the right one. She was driving around to get a view of the bust when the radio traffic suddenly turned frantic. "He's making a run!" she heard, and then the signal degenerated into garbled shouts and the breathless panting of a chase. *Shit!* She screeched to a stop half a block from the corner and jumped out of the car.

He was heading her way across Roosevelt, sneakers flying, she saw with alarm. She stared for a second, paralyzed, unsure of what to do. After the buy she was supposed to stay out of sight; the sellers weren't supposed to know who fingered them. Should she get involved? She saw him racing in her direction, rapidly closing the distance. Where were the backups, how far behind? She had no idea.

She reached under her jacket to unclip her gun. When he was

about fifteen feet away, she planted herself in his path and yelled the first thing she could think of: "I'm a cop, stupid!" She started to raise the gun, but found to her horror that it was still in the holster. Somehow, in taking it out of her pants, the holster had come with it. She wondered as time seemed to crawl with agonizing slowness whether the holster was supposed to be on the gun, finally deciding no. *This whole thing is all fucked up!*

He barreled on and crashed into her. They rolled on the ground, grappling. He was weak, she told herself. He was a doper, she could take him. He snatched at her gun while she fought to keep it out of his reach. He lunged for it as she stabbed her fingers wildly into his face. Suddenly he got his hand on the gun. She kicked him in the groin. He doubled over and loosened his grip but then started grabbing for the gun again. He actually got a hand on it when she yanked it back and the holster came off in his hand! She had the gun! Stunned, he stumbled to his feet and wobbled off, still holding the holster. But by then the backups were there, wrestling him down.

"The sergeant asked for you. They need a white undercover," the lieutenant said. They had developed a white informant. The guy he was buying from was white, everyone was white. It was amazing. But there were only a couple of white undercovers around, and none were available.

It was a great opportunity, she realized. It was what she'd been hoping for.

For this job she was supposed to be from the garment district, an Irish executive doing well enough to spend hundreds, maybe even thousands, a week on coke.

Her supplier was a tall, bony Jewish guy. He looked to be in his early thirties, Barbara thought, with curly black hair and the ashen skin of a serious cokehead. After she'd met him a few times and made a few buys, he moved in close for a sudden embrace, pulling her against him and running his hands over her body.

"Whoa!" she tried to evade him, realizing abruptly what he was doing. He wasn't coming on to her, he was feeling for a wire. And she was wearing a Kel! Luckily she had wired herself. She knew enough not to run the wires down her back, which was the first place they looked. She had taped the unit under her breasts. Even lowlifes wouldn't grab a woman in front, or so she hoped. But he seemed satisfied.

She had started with a gram's "taste," enough to test whether his stuff was good. It was. She bought an eight-ball, an eighth of an ounce, and worked her way up to halves and ounces.

He never had the stuff on him. He always had her drive to a house on Woodbine Street in Ridgewood. She remembered Woodbine Street. It was like home, only a dozen blocks from her old apartment on Onderdonk. But he didn't invite her in. It wasn't his place, he said vaguely. Just wait, he'd be right back.

What he was up to was no mystery: He was ripping her off. His prices were suspiciously high. Whether or not the guy in the apartment knew it, and Barbara suspected he didn't from his sneaky way of operating, he was jacking up the price to her. That didn't especially surprise her. What ticked her off was the way he was dipping into her packets, shorting her, taking his cut on both ends. That made her look like a sucker. She couldn't afford to look stupid; she was losing face. So one day she told him she wanted to make a big buy, three ounces for $6,000, but it had to be from his source. All right, he finally said, she could meet him herself. His name was Sal.

Sal was a hunk, Barbara saw immediately, strikingly handsome, bright blue eyes, brown hair, a weightlifter's bulging pecs, and slender waist. He stepped into her car and said, "Hello, Barbara."

She almost said hello back, that's how close she came. It took a second to register. Then she froze. *BARBARA!*

"Barbara?" she managed to say with what she hoped was casual puzzlement. "It's not Barbara." That wasn't the name she'd been using. She wasn't using her own name.

Her mind raced. He must have run her plate. The last time she came she'd used her own car, the Chevy. She shouldn't have; she had gotten lazy and didn't feel like going to get the unmarked car, but figured she'd just use hers that once. It was stupid.

"You sure?" Sal asked, smiling tightly. He handed her a scrap of notebook paper. Scribbled on it was Barbara Adametz and her birth date, car license tag, and registration number. And home address.

Son of a fucking bitch! He did run my plate!

She looked up from the paper to see Sal's blue eyes drilling into her. Her seller looked nervous. If she was a cop, that made him a dead man.

She tried to make her panic erupt as anger. "Ha! That's who owns my car, my cousin," she blurted, her thoughts racing to keep up with the torrent of words spewing out. "I'm not stupid enough to have anything in my own name. If you have anything in your own name, then you're a fucking idiot. They'll take everything you have. Haven't you ever heard of RICO?"

She hoped the Kel was transmitting to the backups, who had to be wondering what was going on. She wondered if they would figure it out. Would they trust her to talk her way out of the jam, or would they come up like gangbusters? And if they did, would these humps in the car panic? Would they try to shoot their way out?

"Listen," she said, "all this is bullshit." She opened her purse to show that it was stuffed with hundreds. "You want to do business, or you don't want to do business?" She said what she could say. The money would have to start talking.

18

Barbara Adametz and Patrick DeGregorio invite you to share
with us the joy of our marriage
Saturday, the 26th of January, 1985, at 5 o'clock,
the Milleridge Inn,
Hicksville Road, Jericho, N.Y.

THERE was no one moment when they decided to marry, DeGregorio thought. The decision sort of crept up on them. It suddenly seemed like the right thing to do. He couldn't recall how it had come up, but he remembered it was nothing like the movies. No big romantic moment, no candlelit restaurant. It was kind of like when they started living together in Ridgewood. He didn't have to ask. It didn't have to be spelled out formally because there was no need; they understood each other. They would know when the time was right, and now it had come.

A few months earlier, in September 1984, just as his big buy with Joseph was going down, they had attended Mike Arnold's wedding in the elegant town house of the English-Speaking Union on Madison Avenue. They made a wonderful couple, DeGregorio thought—the tall blond Jewish groom and his sprightly Irish Catholic bride, Francine Clark. The detective and the nurse, joined in holy matrimony by a rabbi and a priest. They'd had their tough times, he knew. They'd broken up once or twice, not because they were so different but because they were so alike, sharing strong, instinctive attachments and, finally, a deep, stubborn love for each other. Mike's parents seemed delighted with Francine and ecstatic to see their son finally married. Francine said she only wished her parents could have lived to see the day. DeGregorio, who had never been to a Jewish wedding, gorged on canapés and looked on entranced as the couple exchanged vows under the chuppah, the traditional wedding canopy, after which Mike stamped on a goblet wrapped in a dinner napkin. The splintering of the glass, the rabbi explained, symbolized the irrevocability of the blessed new union. After toasting Mike and Francine, who were leaving in the morning for Hawaii, they danced the night away.

Perhaps it had left an imprint. From then on, DeGregorio thought, it was only a matter of time before they, too, would wed. One night when they were sitting in the living room of their apartment on Grove Road, with Mary Anne in her room, he said, "Barbara, we love each other. We might as well get married."

It wasn't a question as much as a statement, and as he expected, Barbara didn't seem surprised. "It would be the right thing to do," he heard her agree. For them, she said, it didn't much matter, but they had to think of Mary Anne. She deserved married parents. They lapsed into silence. It was only a formality, and yet . . .

He looked at her. She was so lovely, and he was so lucky. He was blessed beyond measure. "You nervous?" he asked her.

"A little," she confessed. "There are no guarantees."

"No," he said. "There are no guarantees with anything."

"But," she added, "if you have a good feeling, you should just go ahead and do it."

"Absolutely!" he said.

He told Mary Anne himself when they were alone. It was no big deal; they had already been living together for almost a year. But still he wanted to explain that it didn't change what he felt for her as a daughter, that nothing would ever change that, that it was in fact largely for her sake that he and Barbara were marrying. He knew she had been torn by the tumultuous changes in their lives but he was encouraged to see how well she seemed to take the news. If anything, she seemed a little dazed.

Next they told their families. DeGregorio called his parents and said he was coming over with someone to tell them something. He knew they already liked Barbara, and as he expected, Joe and Anne showered them with blessings. But he wondered what kind of reception he would get from Barbara's folks. After all, he was the one who had been married before, the one with a daughter. Although Barbara had made no secret of the fact that they were living together, he feared Grace might have found the arrangement too modern for her taste. Driving to Whitestone, he kept thinking about what he would say. But Grace and Joe also welcomed them with warm embraces. "You have the right to know about my divorce," he insisted a little stiffly, and then, over glasses of red wine, he told them his story, about Mary Anne and about Tommy. He was rewarded with one of Grace's radiant smiles.

The priest had a florid Irish face and kindly eyes creased with pained solicitude. It wasn't that he didn't want to be helpful to a faithful member of the parish, it was just that these things were difficult. Now, if DeGregorio could manage an annulment . . .

DeGregorio could see he was getting nowhere. He was disappointed but not surprised. He would have liked a church wedding, although it didn't matter much to Barbara either way. Whatever he preferred, she said. He thought that for Anne's sake, and perhaps for Grace's, a ceremony at St. Joseph's would have been nice, but he didn't underestimate the hurdle of his divorce.

The priest prompted, did DeGregorio *know* his wife had this *problem* when they married? Because, he hastened to explain, if he *had* known and married her anyway, it would indicate that he had tried to resolve a problem of the marriage. That would show strong faith and would be regarded favorably by the Church if DeGregorio now sought an annulment. But if he *hadn't* known of the problem, then he could hardly seize on it now as an escape from the marriage. It would have been his cross to bear, for better or for worse, in sickness and in health. And what was alcoholism but a sickness?

DeGregorio was getting dizzy. He thought it made more sense the other way around. If he *hadn't* known of her problem beforehand, then he had been misled or deceived and deserved an annulment. If he *had* known of it, well then, that would mean he went into the marriage with his eyes open, and how could he later claim the union was invalid? He thought longingly of Father Pizzarelli. Perhaps he should have gone to see him instead. He had once confided some of his marital problems to the Christ-like priest of

Hope House. Pizzarelli didn't lecture, he just listened sympatheti-cally. But after Tommy died, he felt funny about going back to Father Pizzarelli.

Then another thought hit him. "If I get the marriage annulled," he asked, "what would that make Mary Anne, illegitimate?"

The priest said nothing. DeGregorio had his answer.

He remembered a church near his undercover apartment in Brooklyn Heights. He had passed the First Unitarian Church on Monroe Place dozens of times. It looked comforting and old-fashioned, like something out of the Renaissance, he thought. He once knew someone who had gotten married in a Unitarian church. The service sounded a little weird, but they didn't have much time. Thanksgiving was approaching. They were thinking of a date at the end of January and had to make their plans quickly. On the first day they were off together, they drove over to visit it.

Once inside the imposing doors, he saw the nave off to the right and an office on the left. He knocked and they entered. A woman sitting at a desk looked up. She appeard to be in her late thirties, DeGregorio thought. She had striking long jet-black hair. If he didn't know he was in Brooklyn, DeGregorio thought, he might take her for an American Indian. He looked her over again. She *was* an Indian, he decided. But what was an Indian doing in Brooklyn?

"We'd like to talk to the minister," he said.

"I'm the minister," she said, flashing a warm smile. "Orlanda Brignola." She extended a hand to shake.

Orlanda Brignola! She had to be Italian, he realized. Now he was really confused. A female minister who looked Indian but was Ital-ian? Disconcerted, DeGregorio burst out, "We'd like to get married."

"That's nice," she said.

"Uh, I'm divorced," he blurted self-consciously.

"That's all right," she said easily. She said she saw no reason why two people who no longer loved each other should be forced to stay together or why two who did should be apart.

"On Long Island . . ." he stammered.

"Where on Long Island?" she asked.

"The Milleridge Inn." He finally got it out. "It's colonial," he felt compelled to explain. "We like colonial—well, not so much to live in, to visit. We like to visit colonial."

Barbara was looking at him strangely. "I like colonial style," she said.

"I'd go there," the minister said. She pulled out a brochure from a nearby stack. "Look through this," she said, "and tell me what you'd like in the service."

He leafed through it with Barbara. It looked like a book of prayers. Not the Catholic prayers he was used to—comforting Hail Marys and Our Fathers and ominously incomprehensible Latin phrases—but things about love and spirit and nature. He shrugged. Why not? he thought.

The Adametzes immediately invited the DeGregorios over so that the inlaws-to-be could get to know each other and talk about the wedding. The two Joes and their spouses quickly hit it off. Joe DeGregorio filled the room, entertaining them with stories. "I had no idea he was that big!" Grace whispered to her prospective son-in-law.

"He has a thousand stories," Joe Adametz said with a wry smile. "And," he added with a twinkle, "they're just as good the second time around."

Mary Anne seemed subdued, DeGregorio noticed. She sat quietly in front of the TV, answering when spoken to but otherwise saying little, except to Barbara's twenty-nine-year-old sister, Kathy, something of a loner herself, who seemed determined to shadow Mary Anne and sit comfortingly by her side.

They agreed on a simple wedding, just close family and friends, maybe fifty guests, no more. Barbara and Grace would send out the invitations. They could dispense with a photographer, Barbara told him. Her father had a camera. They could do without a band, too, she said. Patty's brother, Joe, could play the piano. As for the rest of it, Barbara said, she would be glad to leave it to her mother. Planning things scared her. Maybe she was still a hippie at heart. Grace smiled. She told Barbara not to worry about the cost. This, after all, was the day Grace had been praying all her life to see, her daughter happily settling down.

Barbara accompanied Grace to the Milleridge Inn where they settled on a diverse menu. Guests could choose from surf and turf, fish, beef, or chicken. Barbara picked out a traditional tiered wedding cake and California champagne.

They agreed that they deserved a honeymoon. They stopped in town at a travel agency, and after looking around at the posters, impulsively put down a $1,000 deposit for air tickets and hotel reservations for a week in Acapulco.

With the new year they began looking at houses in Kings Park. They had never liked the Grove Road apartment. Barbara and Mary Anne both said it gave them the creeps, and he also felt it was time they had a place of their own. It ought to be in Kings Park, he thought, so Mary Anne wouldn't have to change schools. She'd been through enough moving already. They spent days off going around with brokers, but nothing was right. It was the old story: The nice places were out of their range, and what was affordable was horrible. Then one night Anne called, excited. "Patty," she said, "you remember Marie, Marie Lambert?"

Of course he remembered. The Lamberts had been their neighbors when they moved to Kings Park nearly twenty years before. Jim, a carpenter, had done some nice work on the house, although DeGregorio found it a little too pseudo-colonial for his taste. He had been in their house many times before the Lamberts split; Jim left and Marie stayed. Now Marie felt the house was too much. Anne reported that she wanted to sell it and move to Florida. Wasn't that an opportunity?

"Absolutely!" he agreed. The idea of living on one side of his parents, with Ralph and Kathy on the other side, was something that would appeal to a DeGregorio, and it was surely a chance that would never come again. They could all look out for one another, and Mary Anne would have lots of family around. He checked with Barbara, who had no objection.

On their first weekend off, they drove over. He remembered the house well: a plain, weathered, cedar-shingled, two-story colonial with an adjoining one-car garage; it had a small patch of lawn and trees in front, and a backyard with a patio and a pool. On the ground floor was a beamed living/dining room—he could remember Jim lovingly working on that ceiling—with a fireplace, and a den and a large eat-in country kitchen with what Marie proudly called harvest gold appliances. Up a flight of stairs were three bedrooms, and downstairs was a finished basement with a loud tartan carpet, a bar faced in mock stone, and a laundry room. Marie wanted $130,000. On the drive home they agonized.

Barbara said she loved the beamed ceiling. But this stuff about thirty-year mortgages scared her. She wasn't exactly sure what a mortgage was anyway, and thirty years! My God, she told him, who could look ahead thirty years? She could understand rent—$500, $700 a month. You paid it to the landlord and that was that, but a *mortgage?*

Calm down, he told her. He understood mortgages. He came from the suburbs, where people knew about mortgages. They didn't scare him.

"We can't afford it," Barbara said. How were they going to afford a $130,000 house?

With a mortgage, DeGregorio countered. They would put a down payment and pay the rest over time.

Barbara asked where the down payment would come from. They had no real savings.

He tried a different tack. It would be their *home,* he said. And if worst came to worst, they could always sell it.

"I'm trying to imagine it with our own things," she said, softening.

Joe and Anne were determined not to let the opportunity pass. Joe offered to contribute $10,000 of the $13,000 down payment. Joe and Grace said they'd make up the rest as a wedding gift. That, DeGregorio explained to Barbara, would leave them a mortgage payment and taxes of $1,450 a month. It was steep but manageable. They returned to the travel agent, told him about the house, and got their honeymoon deposit back. They could use that money now. Instead of Mexico, they'd make do with the Poconos.

The wedding went by in a giddy blur of music, toasts, group photos, perfumed kisses of elderly aunts, and manly thumps on the back from inebriated uncles. In keeping with the informality of the affair, Barbara wore an off-white knee-length lace dress, and he and Ralph, his best man, wore blue suits, white shirts, and blue-striped ties. Joe Adametz, as if in tribute to his years of service with New York's Bravest, sported a jacket of fire-engine red. Mary Anne was in a gray, white, and pink dress that Barbara had bought for her at A & S in the Smithhaven mall. The frilly frock seemed to be her one grudging concession to frivolity, and Kathy Adametz, who attended her sister as the maid of honor, wore a white skirt and a blue silk blouse. Grace, in an oatmeal tweed sweater and skirt she had bought in Ireland a few years before, looked a little surprised when the female minister read the Apache blessing, but she seemed to accept the eclectic nuptials with the same resolute good humor as she did every turn in life. "I accept what is," she told DeGregorio cheerfully afterward. "The formalities of religion are not as important as a person's life."

It all seemed to flash by in a moment. One minute they were exchanging gold bands, embracing, and kissing in the blitz of Joe Adametz's camera strobe, and then suddenly it was over. They were man and wife.

They had arranged for Mary Anne to stay with Joe and Anne for a few days while they went off to the Poconos on their hastily rescheduled honeymoon. He had spent his first honeymoon in the Poconos, too, he remembered, but he had no desire to return to Mount Airy Lodge. This time they picked a small cabin colony that the travel agent had helped them find. It was rustic and secluded, with no heart-shaped tubs or Jacuzzis, no recreational facilities. Just a snug little house in the woods with a main house nearby for family-style meals. They would supply their own recreation.

They had needed to get away, he realized once they were alone. For more than half a year, since he had brought Mary Anne to live with them, they had hardly shared a private moment. He had almost forgotten what it was like and what it was about Barbara that had gripped him from the beginning: the balm of her presence, her haunting fragrance that stirred him, and her own fiery hunger for him. He could never have resisted her. He saw that now; her pull on him was too strong, and he responded to her as to no other woman. Once again they discovered their elemental attraction, and the effortless rapture he had always counted as a miracle. He was convinced that their love had lifted the curse which had shadowed his life.

He called a few times from a pay phone to see if there were any lingering questions about the undercover case. But as they gave themselves to each other and enjoyed the pleasures of an intimacy that seemed as fresh and tantalizing as their first night together, he soon forgot about the world outside.

• • •

A month after the honeymoon, while they were still waiting to move into their new house, DeGregorio, back on the job, ran into Inspector Brian Lavin of the Joint Organized Crime Narcotics Task Force. "DeGregorio, did you make detective yet?" Lavin asked.

"No, sir," he said. He'd been waiting, hoping. He figured he had a good shot at it after Ridgenarc, but he'd heard nothing.

Lavin called him into the office while he made a call. "Ray," DeGregorio heard him say, "I got a guy here who needs a gold shield." Lavin transmitted his particulars to Chief Raymond L. Jones of Organized Crime Control, the bureau in charge of narcotics, and when he hung up he assured DeGregorio it was set. Within days word came down: He was *Detective Third Grade* Patrick DeGregorio, bound for Manhattan Robbery on East Twelfth Street.

A few days later at police headquarters, in front of a beaming Joe and Anne, Barbara and Mary Anne, and some hundred other members of the force, their families, news reporters, and photographers, DeGregorio got his gold shield. It was followed shortly by a letter with the seal of the Department of Justice, Federal Bureau of Investigation:

> Dear Mr. DeGregorio:
>
> It is a pleasure to recognize your contributions as a member of the FBI/NYPD Narcotics Task Force, and particularly those in connection with RIDGENARC.
>
> We are deeply appreciative of your continuous and courageous efforts as the primary undercover officer throughout the RIDGENARC investigation. Your professional skills enabled the operation to proceed from low-level street transactions to the highest level of narcotics distribution. My colleagues in New York join me in commending you for your dedication and valor and in thanking you for the role you played in bringing this case to a successful conclusion.
>
> Sincerely yours,
> William H. Webster
> Director

They didn't do much on the house at first because they couldn't afford it. They bought new furniture and a new stove. DeGregorio had to make sure he could cook. The pool needed work, but that could wait—it was only April. They fixed up Mary Anne's room to appeal to a thirteen-year-old. They placed her bed under the window that framed the branches of a tall white birch. They arranged her collection of stuffed animals on the shelves above the bed, and on her bureau they propped up some of her favorite photographs of Tommy.

"I know what I want," Barbara told him one night. "A dog."

"A dog?" He was caught off guard. Years ago in Coram they had had a dog, Brandy. He got so wild, they finally had to get rid of him. He took Brandy to a farm out on the island and told Mary Anne he had run away.

"I always wanted a dog," Barbara said. "Now that we have a house and a yard, I want a dog."

It didn't sound like a bad idea. Mary Anne already had Pepsi, but a cat wasn't a big deal. Maybe she'd like a dog. A dog might bring them all together, like an equalizer. He mentioned it tentatively to Mary Anne, and she got all excited. She'd love another dog, she said. She seemed more excited about that than about anything in a long time. They looked in the paper and found an ad for a kennel in Smithtown that bred golden Labrador retrievers. A detective in the squad had told him how to pick a puppy: You shake your keys at it, and if it shies away, it's too timid. The first two puppies fled from his rattling keys. The third, a male, yapped playfully and wagged its tail eagerly. "We'll take this one," DeGregorio said. Mary Anne petted and hugged him most of the ride home. "I'm calling him Buddy," she anounced, " 'cause he's my buddy."

She was doing all right, he thought happily. She'd had some bad times, but she was coming along. She was on the seventh-grade basketball team, she had told him, and he was impressed. Now when she came home late from school, which seemed to happen a couple of times a week, he knew why—she was at basketball practice. It must be really knocking her out, he thought when he came home some days to find her sprawled on the living room sofa, fast asleep. Finally he got annoyed. "Why are you always sleeping, Mary Anne?" he demanded. "Get up!"

"Leave me alone," she groaned, flopping over. "I'm tired from school."

Maybe it was time she took on some more responsibility, he thought, an after-school job. To make some extra cash, he and Mike had arranged with Tony's Meat Market in Kings Park to start a weekend catering business. Mike and Francine had also moved out nearer them on Long Island. Tony supplied the meat and the two cops did the cooking. They catered a few police parties and other local functions, but the moonlighting was too demanding and they figured they couldn't keep it up for long. Meanwhile, DeGregorio thought that perhaps Tony could use somebody to help out in the store in the afternoon, and Mary Anne could do that. Tony said sure, she could clean up and maybe even help customers.

One day, after Mary Anne had started there, he and Mike were in Tony's planning an order. Mary Anne spotted Francine waiting outside in the car and stepped out to talk to her. When they finished in the store and went out to the car, Mary Anne said good-bye to Francine and returned to the store.

"Patty," Francine said, "I didn't know Mary Anne was working at Tony's!"

He told her he had gotten her the job, something to do after school.

"I just had the nicest talk with her," Francine said. "She's so mature."

"You did? What did you talk about?" He was proud of Mary Anne, and she was also impressing other people.

"I asked her how school was going, and she said fine. I asked whether they had a prom at the end of the year and if she was going. She said they didn't have a prom in the seventh grade; they had a dance. I asked her if she was going, and she said no, she wasn't. I was surprised because I always thought she was the social type. I asked her why, and she said she didn't want to be bothered because a lot of the kids are taking drugs."

"She said that? A lot of the kids are taking drugs?"

"That's what she said," Francine answered. "I was a little surprised. I asked if she knows the kids who are taking drugs and she said most of the kids are taking drugs. She found out that the guy she was supposed to go with was into drugs heavy-duty, and she couldn't be part of that. She said how rotten some of the kids were, how they thought of nothing but themselves, how they let their whole lives revolve around drugs and getting high, and how she didn't want to be associating with those people."

"Jeez, she said all that?"

"Then I said to her," Francine went on, " 'You know, Mary Anne, I used to smoke some pot, but I never really tried anything else. You ever try anything?' She shook her head and said she wouldn't even try pot. She didn't want any part of it. She saw what it did to her friends. I tell you, Patty, I was impressed."

"Yeah," he said proudly. He was impressed too. That was his girl, Mary Anne.

Mike wasn't quite so impressed. He was skeptical. He had been listening for years to Pat raving about his daughter, and he didn't buy it. It sounded phony to him. You got a sense of people over the years, and if he couldn't see when Pat was shitting him, and himself in the process, he might as well turn in his shield. He could see through her too. The kid was screwed up. It made sense after what she had been through. So when Pat told him how well Mary Anne was doing, he let him talk but he didn't believe it, not for a minute.

Ralph thought Patty was kidding himself too. From his driveway one day Ralph looked down the lane curving past his parents' house and saw kids at Patty's front door. He got home early. As an electrician with a local contractor, his jobs started early, often by seven, and ended by three. He was usually home before three-thirty. Pat and Barbara were out working. He knew they weren't home, so what were kids doing there during the day? Did school let out early? Mary Anne wasn't supposed to have anyone over when they were out. He had seen that before—kids going in and out during school hours—but he'd never wondered much about it. Now he did. He decided to go over and see for himself.

The door was locked. He rattled the knob, then pounded. No one answered. He pounded again and listened. He thought he heard voices.

The door cracked open. Mary Anne stood there, looking surprised to see her uncle.

Ralph squinted past her down the dim hall. In the back, by the kitchen, he could see a bunch of kids scurrying around. A few ran out the back door onto the patio. He walked into the kitchen and looked around. The table was clear, but the sink was full of glasses. Patty and Barbara wouldn't have left it that way. The kids must have put them there hastily. A few boys and girls he didn't recognize stood around self-consciously, shamefacedly, he thought. He had caught them at something, he was sure of it. He thought he smelled whiskey.

"What's going on here, Mary Anne?" he asked.

She looked him squarely in the eye. "Nothing."

"You know you're not supposed to have anyone here without your parents."

"We're just hanging out. We're not doing nothing."

Ralph figured she was lying. They had been drinking, he was sure of it. "I know what you're doing," he said levelly. "Stop it! You're hurting your father."

"Okay, but I wasn't doing nothing," she insisted. He couldn't decide. Did she look guilty? Or ashamed? He heard her tell the kids they had to leave.

Ralph walked back home troubled. His brother was too lax with Mary Anne, and inconsistent. He saw Pat get strict with her sometimes, but one minute he was strict and the next minute he wasn't. He was sending her confusing signals. You couldn't do that with kids, Ralph thought. Kids had to know what to expect. They needed boundaries, and you had to set them. In their house his boys always knew where they stood. No bullshit.

Now he wondered if he should tell Pat. What would that accomplish? He didn't want to mix into his brother's problems, he had enough of them. He and Barbara needed more time together. They had been married only about six months. They had a lot of adjusting to do. Maybe he should just keep his mouth shut, at least for now. Mary Anne could have learned her lesson. This could be the end of it. He'd wait and see.

19

SOMETIMES the kids came to her house, sometimes she went to their houses. Someone always had pot, and someone usually brought a six pack or two. The oldest-looking of them could usually get a storekeeper to sell to them. If they got carded, they could always stop someone on the street and get him to buy the beer for them, especially if they gave him a couple of cans. Money wasn't the problem; between them they always had enough money. When they went to Mary Anne's house, she also threw open the liquor cabinet. Some bottles were already open, and if they finished a bottle, she just chucked it in the back of her closet, along with the empty beer cans. Buddy watched everything, looking confused.

Once when kids were over partying, she smelled something burning. At first she thought it was pot, but then she thought no. This was a different smell. Something had to be on fire. Following the smell, Mary Anne lurched out of her room, bumping into kids clustered along the second-floor landing. She stopped outside the bathroom. The smell seemed to be coming from the bathroom. She fumbled with the knob and pushed the door open.

An edge of the wallpaper was on fire! She smothered it quickly with a towel, wiping away the fringe of charred ash. You couldn't really see it, she decided; she'd wash it up later. Then she saw Barbara's jewelry box on a counter and caught her breath. It was burned, all blackened. It was a cheap metal box in which Barbara kept some pins and police stuff. Fire had melted whatever was in there. Now what was she going to do? She started to throw the box in the garbage. She'd just tell Barbara it broke. She opened it again and noticed a lot of little blackened pieces inside. She picked one up between two fingers and held it close to her eyes. She couldn't make it out. It was all burnt. She brushed it off and dropped it back in the box. She'd buy a new box, she thought, and maybe Barbara wouldn't notice. She knew the kid who had been in the bathroom. What was he trying to do, burn her fucking house down? He said he didn't mean it, but she knew he did it on purpose. Asshole.

She was wrecked when they left. All she wanted to do was sleep. She made sure the place looked cleaned up, and then crashed on the couch. If her father or Barbara came home, she was tired from school, from basketball practice, whatever. She really was on the basketball team. It gave her something to say when she was late. He never really pressed her anyway, but she had a few close calls. Once she came home blasted and tried to slip in quietly. Buddy scampered to the door and slobbered over her. Her father was in the living room watching TV. "C'mere," he said. She guessed he wanted to talk, or hug her. She was sweating and shaking. She didn't want to get too close to him. "I'm cold," she said, running upstairs.

The job at Tony's was a pain. Tony spent a lot of time in the back drinking beer, leaving her to help customers. She hated cutting meat. It was disgusting. She didn't think she should be doing that. It was funny when she met Francine. She actually believed all that shit about the dance and how Mary Anne didn't want anything to do with drugs. Oh God, how pathetic! Oh, she was good, Mary Anne congratulated herself, she was real slick. She could fool anybody.

Like when Barbara found the note.

It was Chrissy's note to her. Chrissy was out of pot. Mary Anne had said she knew a kid who had some, so Chrissy had asked her to get it. She was alarmed, though, when Barbara stuck the note in her face. She had to make up a story fast. What was Barbara doing poking around in her purse? She was a sneak. Barbara had it in for her. Barbara was always trying to get her in trouble. And what was her father doing about it? He was always on Barbara's side. She didn't trust him anymore, not since he had lied to her about living with Mike, as he had lied to her about Brandy. Brandy hadn't run away; she knew her father had given him away.

She had hated it when he told her he was marrying Barbara. She knew what he was going to say as soon as he started to say it, and she wanted to put her hands over her ears. She didn't want to hear it. She was hoping they would break up, not get married. Then she could have lived with him, and it would have been just the two of them. She tried to pretend it didn't matter because she didn't want him to see how bad she felt. She set her face in what he always called a puss. When she was little he used to say, don't make a puss. She made a puss. She just sat there with a puss and didn't say anything. She wouldn't give him the satisfaction.

When he made her go to Barbara's parents' house with Grandma and Grandpa, she hated that too. All those strangers. They made a fuss over her and said to call them Grace and Uncle Joe, but she just wanted to be left alone. She ended up in the corner watching TV a lot. Barbara's sister Kathy was the only one who seemed to understand how she felt. Maybe that was because she had epilepsy; that's what her father told her. You couldn't tell from looking at her, though; she looked regular. She thought Kathy was very pretty and liked her right away, even though she didn't want to talk to Kathy much either. She didn't want to talk to anyone at the party, but she let Kathy sit with her and didn't mind when Kathy followed her around. That was probably what they told her to do. Keep an eye on Mary Anne, she's very unhappy.

Everything about that time was awful. It seemed as if Barbara was trying to be friendly, even taking her to the mall to pick out a dress for the wedding. She didn't want to go to the wedding, so why should she buy a dress? At the wedding everyone was laughing, drinking, and dancing. She just wanted to hide. She went to the bathroom and cried. When she came out she was still crying, and then she didn't care but cried in front of everybody. When her father and Barbara gave each other rings, Grandma had tears on her face. She was happy. Mary Anne just wanted to *die*.

The worst was when it was over and her father kissed Barbara and took her out to the car. They were going away. Together. Just the two of them. She was going to stay with Grandpa and Grandma. When they came back, her father said, in a few months they would move into the new house. Wouldn't that be great? She shrugged. She guessed she liked the new house, which she always thought of as Marie's house. It was better than Grove Road, but so what?

• • •

". . . getting high . . ." The words, coming from right behind her, detached themselves from the biology teacher's background drone and hung there tantalizingly. She turned her head to see a raw-boned, hard-looking boy who had been talking to someone else. She knew him slightly; she'd seen him around. He lived in her neighborhood. She'd heard that his family had moved from Queens. He was tough. "What about getting high?" she asked provocatively.

Surprised, he turned to her and said, "What do you need? I can get whatever I want."

"Me, too," she boasted. Then she said, "Where?"

He smiled crookedly. "I get it from my brother," he said. "I can get it for you too."

She was at peace, adrift, laughing with the kids at a friend's house after school. "Wan' anotha hit?" Mary Anne turned to see Chrissy offering her a burning roach end. She reached for it.

Her gaze settled on a large mirror that was lying flat on the table. She hadn't noticed it there before. It was a Budweiser mirror, and it was covered with lines of white powder. She knew right away what it was. It had to be coke. It made her a little nervous and excited. They'd often talked about it. She used to ask Chrissy if she would try coke. Chrissy didn't know. Would Mary Anne try it? No, she said, she didn't think she wanted to mess with coke.

But now, impulsively, Mary Anne fumbled in her purse for a dollar bill, rolled it the short way into a tube, poked an end into her nostril, and cautiously sniffed up a line.

It felt liquidy, as if it weren't powder that she had breathed in but some drink. She could feel it washing down her throat. It had a chemical taste, almost like medicine. She wondered how long it would take to feel anything, and suddenly she was feeling it. Everything was weird. She felt intensely happy, but she was somehow outside herself and watching herself feel it. She felt other people were watching her, too, strange eyes. She wasn't sure where she was anymore. Her body felt very strange, as if it were not her body.

• • •

Greg, the boy from biology, said he could get her whatever she needed. "What do you do?" he probed.

"Mesc, acid, pot," Mary Anne said airily. They were just hanging out near her house. She was bragging. She really hadn't done that much mescaline or acid, just a few times at the skating rink. It was a totally different sensation. Pot just made her feel kind of stretched out, relaxed, happy and giggly. And hungry, she really got the nibblies. She laughed all the time, especially with Chrissy. Chrissy was a riot. Mescaline and acid made her feel more a part of things, more intense. It was hard to explain. Acid was the strongest. She saw what was *inside* everything. It made her body feel tingly. She knew kids who had flipped out on acid, really had some nightmares. It never bothered her; she just felt strange. She really liked coke. She would've tried it again, but nobody had any.

"I can get you whatever you want," Greg said. "All you want." Then he said, "You want to sell for me in school?"

"Sure," Mary Anne agreed.

"I'll introduce you to my brother, Vic," Greg said. "Maybe you could work something out. You know where I live?"

Mary Anne nodded. It was a large redbrick house not far from hers.

"Come by sometime," Greg said.

The brothers were across the street from their house when Mary Anne walked over later. Vic was much older than them. She guessed he was in his early twenties, maybe twenty-three. He was very good-looking, really handsome in a mean-looking way, with blue-blue eyes, one earring, and lots of tattoos on his arms. He had a Harley motorcycle, she saw with admiration, but he didn't look like a biker with studs and leather, just nice clothes, short dark hair, and some expensive gold.

"Vic just got out of jail," Greg said as if reading her mind.

She wondered what he did to go to jail, kill somebody? But she thought it wouldn't be cool to ask.

"You ever hear of Fat Tony?" Greg asked.

She had read about Fat Tony in the newspapers, a gangster who had just gotten sentenced to about three hundred years in jail. "Yeah," she said. "I know who that is."

"That's my uncle," Greg said, looking proud.

"You want to sell," Vic said—a statement, not a question.

"Yeah," Mary Anne said.

"That's good," he said. "You look innocent. No one would suspect you."

She guessed that was a compliment.

"I got people working for me in the city," Vic said, as if to reassure her of his experience. "I want to get something going out here." He gave her an appraising look. "Can you be ready in a couple of days?"

Mary Anne shrugged. "Sure."

"I'll give you my beeper number," he said, digging out a scrap of paper from his jeans pocket and scribbling on it. "You beep me, I'll call you back. Give me your number, I'll call you first."

Greg said something to Vic and Vic's face hardened. "Your father's a cop?"

"Yeah," she said. So what? What did that matter? "Don't worry about it," she said. "He don't know you."

A few days later he called her, and they arranged to meet in the park between their houses. Vic, tattooed arms folded, was waiting by his Harley when she walked up. There was a paper bag by his feet, and he reached down and handed it to her.

She didn't bother to open it. He scared her a little. Greg told her he had gone to jail for beating up his girlfriend.

"Put it away," he said. He told her what was there: ten-dollar bags of pot called dimes, ounces for twenty, eighths of a pound for thirty, mescaline at $5.00 a hit (a hundred were rolled up in a newspaper), acid, also at $5.00 a hit (there were five sheets, which she should keep flat, unrolled).

"How much is here?" she asked, stuffing the bag into her big black purse.

He said about $500 worth. It should last her three or four days. When she sold that, she should beep him and he'd get her more. He climbed on his bike and kick-started it.

She sold everything at school in less than a week and beeped Vic.

When he roared up on his Harley, she had the money ready. He counted it and handed three tens back to her. "That's for you. This you sell," he said, handing her another paper bag. And this"—he gave her a smaller paper bag—"is for you."

She looked at the smaller bag. "This is mine?"

"That's for you," he confirmed.

Later in her room, propped up on the bed, she opened the bag he had given her free and sorted out the stuff: the mesc, which looked like Nerds, little purple candies; a sheet of acid covered with cartoon decals; and a bag of pot. She got up, pushed the door firmly closed, and opened the window. When she smoked pot in the room she made sure the window was open or the air-conditioner was on. Or sometimes she sprayed perfume around to mask the smell. Not that she really gave a shit. Barbara was in the bedroom next door, but so what. *Airhead.* She flipped on her TV, rolled a joint, and lit up, sucking in the sweet, musky smoke and letting her mind drift.

20

"**Y**OUR Honor, the Government calls *Detective Patrick DeGregorio.*"

He gulped at the sound of his name echoing in the crowded courtroom. This was it. Compulsively adjusting his loosely knotted blue-striped tie, he stepped up to the witness chair and raised his right hand to be sworn in.

In April 1987, more than two years after his undercover case was busted, the Ridgenarc defendants—what was left of them—were coming to trial in Brooklyn Federal Court. For DeGregorio it was almost sadly anticlimactic. Most of those he had nailed, seventeen of the original twenty-two defendants, had taken pleas. It was hardly surprising, given the evidence he had amassed. The Guidices, the Spatolas and their wives, and Franco Davi, the man in black, had decided not to risk trial and had pleaded to scaled-down charges carrying substantial prison terms. Now only three defendants remained: the accused importer Giuseppe Ambrogio "Vito" Pipitone, one of his associates, Matteo Concordia, and Calogero "Charlie" Davi, charged with delivering the half-kilo of heroin to DeGregorio in his undercover apartment.

Behind him, on the raised bench, hunched a wizened figure in black, Judge John R. Bartels, at eighty-nine the oldest working federal judge in the country, or so DeGregorio heard. To his left in a gated corral of leather chairs sat the jury, twelve men and women whose gazes swung curiously from DeGregorio to the defendants, to their lawyers, to the judge, and back again. Behind the defendants stretched rows of pews filled with relatives and associates, spectators, and a few news reporters. DeGregorio could imagine the curses, the *malocchi,* being hurled his way, but he shrugged them off. He had been through it before. When Frankie's partner had gone to trial in the smoke-shop gun and bribery case, he repeatedly mouthed "white devil" and gave him the finger in court. DeGregorio had started to protest, but the judge ordered him to keep quiet. In chambers he said, "Detective, do you think I'm blind? I know what's going on. But if you make a fuss, we're going to have a mistrial. Do you want a mistrial?" So he kept quiet, and the jury quickly returned convictions. He hoped it would be that simple here, but he had his doubts. He figured the defense would try to put him on trial. Lawyers were wily bastards.

In his opening to the jury, Vito Pipitone's lawyer, Steven Scaring, had shrewdly chosen not to attack the government's case head-on. "We don't contend that there was not a conspiracy involved in this case," Scaring conceded. In fact, he acknowledged, "the evidence will show that this was a big conspiracy. A lot of people were involved. And because of that, and the largeness of this investigation, some innocent people got caught up in the presumptions, in the speculation, in the surmise of the government."

DeGregorio remembered his first case that went to trial, the mutt he had grabbed with drugs on patrol with Doyle in the one-oh-nine. He'd had to testify there too. During a recess the defense lawyer came over to him in the corridor to share a smoke and some remarks about the weather. Back in court during cross-examination, the lawyer turned on him. "Officer DeGregorio," he thundered, "is it or is it not a fact that we just had a conversation in the corridor?" Taken aback, he panicked. Had he broken some rule? Should he be denying it? The lawyer, the jury, and the judge were waiting for his answer. "We did," DeGregorio agreed. "Thank you," said the lawyer. "No further questions." Later the lawyer explained to the shaken rookie that if he had denied it, he would have opened the way to an attack on his credibility. The lawyer had no hard feelings. "Welcome to the world, son," he said.

DeGregorio nodded to the assistant U.S. attorney, Greg O'Connell, huge at six-feet-four with wavy hair and a mustache who would lead him in friendly questioning through the prosecution case.

"Approximately how many undercover assignments have you engaged in in the course of your duties?" O'Connell asked.

"Several hundred." He tried to remember to keep his answers short. No speeches.

"Have your undercover assignments also included narcotics un-dercover assignments?"

"Yes."

"During the course of your experience as an undercover officer and detective, have you learned the manner in which narcotics traf-fickers conduct their affairs?"

"Yes."

He was led through his bona fides and an outline of the inves-tigation, and through all his buys and the big half-kilo deal that capped the case. Then Scaring got his shot at cross-examination. DeGregorio could see what was coming as Scaring turned to the $90,000 buy and the $30,000 DeGregorio had paid up front. The lawyer was trying to poke holes in his account, trying to create doubts in the minds of the jurors.

DeGregorio felt a flutter of nervousness. He knew fronting money for drugs was against departmental rules. He had done it because he had to, but he had left it out of the buy report. Was it coming back to haunt him?

"Now the backup people would be concerned about thirty thou-sand dollars of city money, is that right?" the lawyer probed.

"Federal money," DeGregorio corrected him, glad to have a factual misstatement to attack. "I'm sure they would have been, yes."

And, Scaring continued, wouldn't it have been nerve-racking to surrender all that money and wait for three hours for the drugs to show up?

DeGregorio nodded. "First of all," he said, "I threw up, if you want to know the truth." The confession drew sympathetic chuckles from the jurors and spectators.

Now Davi's lawyer, Joel M. Lutwin, took over the attack. He waved the buy report in which DeGregorio had fudged the payment of front money. "By the way," he asked offhandedly, "in the report now in evidence as defendant's exhibit A, is there any mention of you giving Mr. Davi thirty thousand dollars, sir? Is there any men-tion?"

"No," DeGregorio admitted.

Lutwin drilled the point home. "Take a look. None at all?"

He asked about DeGregorio's assertion that Davi went to pick up a package.

DeGregorio saw a chance to reinforce his point. "He was first given thirty thousand dollars, and then he went to pick up the package."

Lutwin would not let that pass. "That's the thirty thousand that's not in your report, is that correct?"

"Right," DeGregorio acknowledged.

Lutwin pretended not to hear. "Is that right?"

"Yes," he had to repeat.

During a recess, DeGregorio ran into another of the defense lawyers, who clapped him familiarly on the back. "We're all Italians here," he confided.

DeGregorio, incensed, shook off his hand. "*I'm* an Italian," he snapped. "You're a *guinea*. And so are the people you represent."

"You'll really enjoy the trial," he told Mary Anne. "You'll see how the justice system works." There was a message he could send her, he thought, as he did when she and Tommy were little and he took them to the eight-three station house, put them in a cell, and pretended to lock the door. A cop he knew had actually taken his daughter to the morgue to scare her straight. He drew the line there. That was a little much, he thought. But he did need to spend some time with Mary Anne, he decided. There was something going on with her. She would come to court with him for a day even if she had to miss a day of school. It would give them a chance to talk. She'd be fifteen in a few weeks, deep into adolescence with all the strange moods and conflicts the teen years bring—especially, he thought, to girls. With all his cases, he knew he'd been out a lot and had kind of lost touch with her. They needed to get close again.

It was a while since Ralph had asked him what he was doing about Mary Anne. It was back in the fall, he realized, because they were raking leaves on Ralph's lawn. It took him by surprise. Doing about what? he asked his brother. The kids she had coming over, Ralph said. She had kids coming over after school when no one was home, even sometimes in the daytime. Did that surprise him? DeGregorio said no slowly; he knew she was popular. So she sometimes had kids over. There was nothing so terrible about that.

He wasn't even surprised they were drinking. He had once gotten an outraged call from the father of one of Mary Anne's schoolmates. Beth had come home drunk from Mary Anne's house, the father raged. What did DeGregorio know about that? DeGregorio didn't know what to say but said he'd look into it. Later he asked Mary Anne about it, and she told him Beth hadn't been there. Maybe she had lied to cover up where she had been. He didn't know what to say to that. He had put it out of his mind and never mentioned it to Barbara. But maybe Ralph was right and he should look into it. Ralph said it was none of his business—he knew what they had all been through—but he thought Pat should make a policy and stick to it. That was his suggestion. DeGregorio nodded. Ralph was right.

Mary Anne had been acting strange lately, he realized. She was tired a lot and snappish. It was clear she was going through a difficult stage, but he told himself it would pass. He wondered if she had a boyfriend, someone named Vic. A boy called sometimes at night. A few times he answered and heard Mary Anne say on her extension, "Hi, Vic," before he hung up.

She seemed cheerful on the ride into Brooklyn. She chattered away, but not about anything important. She's a chameleon, he thought. You never know what to expect with her. Still, he was happy she seemed happy.

Court had already started as he pushed open the heavy oak door and led her down the center aisle to a seat. She seemed aloof, he thought, kind of arrogant, detached. But maybe she was just trying to cover up her embarrassment when people turned to stare. They looked amused, and that probably rattled her, he thought. The detective and his daughter.

"See," he whispered to her, pointing to the defendants in the front, "that short one with the black hair is Vito Pipitone. Remember I told you about him?"

She nodded. For once she seemed to be paying attention.

"They gave me creepy looks," she whispered back. "They're scary."

"Don't worry," he reassured her. "They're the ones with the problem, not you."

Scaring called Pipitone as a witness in his own defense. That showed how desperate they were, DeGregorio thought. He nudged Mary Anne to pay attention and turned his attention to the stand.

Under Scaring's gentle prodding, Pipitone told of coming to America with his family from Sicily at the age of fourteen, working at a relative's meat market in Brooklyn, with his brothers and brother-in-law, Salvatore Spatola, opening a café and a pizzeria. He admitted that he hadn't paid income tax and that the $80,000 the FBI searchers had found in the sleeve of a woman's ski jacket in his home was his.

"What about the guns, Vito? Were they your guns?" Scaring asked gently.

"Yes," he said.

"Why did you have guns?"

"To protect myself."

"You heard the government agent say they found some heroin on top of a bed in the room where you had your two-and-a-half-year-old," the lawyer went on. "Do you know anything about the heroin?"

"Nothing about it."

"Was that your heroin?"

"No."

DeGregorio wanted to snicker. This was funny stuff. Triumphantly, he turned to look at Mary Anne. She was sitting stony-faced, watching something else, obviously not concentrating on the testimony.

Finally it was the prosecutor's turn.

"Didn't you call Joseph Spatola on his beeper from time to time?" O'Connell asked.

"I don't remember."

O'Connell turned to the money found in Pipitone's house. "But eighty thousand dollars in cash, you would agree, is a lot of money."

"It is not a lot of money."

DeGregorio smiled, thinking how the jury was likely to feel about a pizza man who shrugged off $80,000.

Now it was Calogero Davi's turn. His lawyer tried to humanize "Charlie," calling him "a schlep in the Figaro Restaurant." Davi, also taking the stand, said he was thirty-seven, a hairdresser, born in Toretto, where he met Pipitone. He came to America in 1972. Yes, he allowed, he was arrested once. One of his customers at the hair salon had a fight with a meter maid. He was hauled in as a witness and ended up accused of chasing the meter maid with a scissor.

The charge was later dropped. Members of the jury giggled. A schlep.

Lutwin led him through the $90,000 half-kilo sale in the undercover apartment.

"Well, that day Joseph told me to go with him," Davi said. "I ask no question. You know, you not allowed to ask questions of the boss. He approach me and say, 'Charlie, come with me.' Okay. I went with him." It was Spatola's car, Davi said, not his; he didn't own a car. He didn't own a house. He had nothing.

Spatola, he said, gave him a key and sent him to an address on East Seventieth Street in Manhattan to pick up a package. He got lost. He finally found the place and the package, a taped brown bag, very full, on the kitchen table. Then he got lost driving back to Brooklyn. He delivered the package to Spatola and was told to wait on the couch. When Joe Spatola asked him to count a big bundle of money, he related, "I start to understand something was going wrong. But I can't say anything because I was afraid they would kill me."

"You were given thirty thousand dollars, were you not?" the prosecutor pressed.

Davi denied getting any money up front. "They probably made a mistake," he insisted, contradicting the detectives.

"Well," he asked excitedly, as they were driving home after the trial adjourned for the day, "how did you like it?"

"Okay," Mary Anne said. He waited for more, but that was it. She lapsed into silence. Then she said, "I can't believe they kept it in the kid's room."

"What?" he said. He didn't understand what she meant.

"The drugs," she said disgustedly. "Keeping them in a kid's room. Ugh!"

"Oh," he said, excited to see an opening. "You thought that was terrible, huh?"

He waited for an answer, but she seemed distracted. "Barbara never says anything to me," she said. "She always tells you."

Her shift caught DeGregorio off guard. "What do you mean?"

"Why can't she tell me to my face? She has to go crying to you? I think she's a little sneaky."

"Aw, Barbara's not like that," he protested. "She cares for you a lot, honey, she does. It's hard for her too. She's going through a lot."

"Well, why is she always trying to get me in trouble?"

"She's not trying to get you in trouble. But why don't I talk to her?"

Mary Anne pouted. "It won't do any good."

"I'll talk to her," DeGregorio repeated quietly, as if to himself.

"I have a note from the jury."

Judge Bartels' announcement electrified the courtroom, interrupting DeGregorio and Jim Kearney, who were chatting in the empty jury box, and drawing lawyers and spectators in from the corridor.

The judge looked puzzled. He read the note: " 'We have reached a verdict on all three counts.' " He frowned. "I don't know three counts."

"I'm sure they meant the three defendants," a lawyer said.

Everyone scrambled for seats as the jury was led in. DeGregorio clenched his fists, clammy with anticipation.

"Have you agreed upon a verdict?" the clerk asked.

"We have," the foreman said.

"How do you find the defendant Giuseppe Ambrogio Pipitone on count one of the superseding indictment?"

DeGregorio closed his eyes.

"Guilty."

Matteo Concordia?

"Guilty."

Cologero Davi? Counts one and two?

The answer was swallowed by mayhem, with family members shouting and weeping. Kearney and DeGregorio thumped each other on the back. Judge Bartels thanked the jurors and released them. Then he paused. "Did I hear right? Was the defendant Davi *not guilty*?"

"Not guilty," affirmed his lawyer.

The clerk took issue. "Guilty on count one. Guilty," he said.

"That's not what I heard," Scaring said.

The judge ordered the jurors recalled, but they had already filed out of the courtroom.

"Everybody's recollection is not guilty, Judge," O'Connell said.

"Maybe I'm wrong," the clerk said.

Suddenly the marshals returned with the jurors, who had been intercepted before leaving the building.

The foreman cleared it up quickly. "Not guilty on both charges."

"My error. I apologize," said the clerk.

21

SHE saw right away that it wasn't her jewelry box. It looked like hers, it was on the bathroom counter where she always kept it, but it wasn't hers. The metal was too shiny. Hers had been old; this one was new. It was meant to trick her. She didn't want to know about this, she told herself. She seriously considered not opening it. Maybe she should forget about it, she thought, not get entangled with this. It was too weird. Either way, she was not going to be happy. Whatever this was, she felt sure, it could only point in one direction: Mary Anne.

Had she made a mistake with her life, Barbara wondered, a terrible mistake? How did she get into this? She loved Patty and couldn't imagine life without him. She had been so happy at the wedding. They were so right for each other. But she didn't bargain on Mary Anne. Somehow Mary Anne was just suddenly there. Barbara thought she understood Mary Anne. She had tried to be motherly, or at least *step*motherly, and understanding, but she didn't know how to deal with an angry teenager, a jealous, confused, rebellious girl doing God-knows-what while having an answer, it seemed, for everything.

They were arguing more now, she and Patty, over inconsequential things, but why kid herself? The problem wasn't them, it was Mary Anne. It was as if Mary Anne had taken over the household. They had virtually stopped answering the phone. Almost all the calls were for Mary Anne anyway.

Barbara had tried to transfer out of narcotics. She and Patty needed steady tours opposite each other so one of them would always be around to keep an eye on Mary Anne. She appealed to her lieutenant.

"Personal problem?"

"I think my daughter's getting into drugs, Lieu. When Patty works nights, I have to be home."

He nodded sympathetically. Barbara figured she wasn't the first with a family addiction problem. Usually it was the cops themselves. The department was good with alcoholic cops. They were sent to the farm for drying out. They dried out and went back on the job. If they fell off the wagon, they were sent back to the farm. There seemed to be no limit to the times they could fuck up. As long as it was drink. Drugs, forget it. They were out of there.

The lieutenant approved her transfer and sent her to the captain. The captain had no problem. Next, they told her, she had to run it past Chief Ray Jones of Organized Crime Control. But Jones wouldn't see her.

She was stunned. She felt like Dorothy in the land of Oz. The wizard wouldn't see her. She didn't know what to do—throw herself on her knees and beg? Jones sent word via a detective that if she wanted steady tours, she could go back to patrol.

She gave up. Narcotics was her best shot at a gold shield. She couldn't pay that price. Still, she did what she could to arrange her hours so that as often as possible one of them was home. But that meant they hardly saw each other. She blamed Mary Anne for that, for accomplishing what she'd obviously set out to do from the beginning—undermine their marriage. And *he,* in his misguided way, was letting her get away with it. She was running out of patience. She had a life too. Did anybody care about her life?

Six months later, in August 1986, she made detective, but the long-anticipated promotion further complicated her life. She was transferred to the six-seven squad in East Flatbush, Brooklyn, a longer commute from the island. And they were locked into the house. A thirty-year mortgage. She had never planned anything a week in advance, and now she was supposed to look thirty years ahead.

What was it with Patty? she often asked herself. He refused to open his eyes to what was happening with Mary Anne. Clearly, she realized, he was so afraid of losing her that he was living in a dream world. But she wasn't sure how far she could go to wake him up.

Mary Anne wasn't her daughter, she was his, and there was something unfathomable between the two of them, something she was afraid to tamper with.

She opened the jewelry box. She had kept her police name tag there and a spare black rubber backing for her shield. She saw right away that the rubber was melted and burned, and her nametag was blackened. She couldn't even read her name. She poked around and pricked her finger on a pin, a pin from some raggy piece of cloth. She picked it up. It was charred, a little burned stripey thing— *her medals!* Her police ribbons! They had been *roasted.* She tried to figure out how her jewelry box could have been incinerated but couldn't imagine. And what would she get if she asked Mary Anne? Another bullshit story? Barbara couldn't stomach the thought of confronting her and the lies that would surely follow. She would just put it out of her mind, just forget it.

A beer can! What was a Budweiser can doing in Mary Anne's closet? She was rummaging again. Whatever this kid was up to, Barbara resolved, she was going to get to the bottom of it. If it meant going through Mary Anne's room when she was out, well, she was going to do that. And now, she thought with a triumph, she had found a beer can.

She reached in through piles of shoes and sneakers and plucked it out. It was light, obviously empty. Were there more? She groped deeper through the mess and hit another object, something glassy smooth and hard. She pulled out a Jack Daniel's bottle! Also empty. She scrabbled furiously through the shoes and found yet another bottle—Gilbey's vodka. Empty too. She fought off a black rage and tossed the bottles and can back into the closet.

When Patty came home, she sat him down in the bedroom, closed the door, and told him the story.

He said she was overreacting. "Come on," he said. "Have we ever seen her drunk?"

No, she admitted, they hadn't *seen* her drunk.

Well, he told her, it would be pretty hard to hide. Maybe kids had partied there, like Ralph had said. There would be some bottles. She'd be afraid to put them in the trash and would toss them into her closet. Barbara herself said they looked old. Two old bottles and an old beer can didn't amount to much. Maybe that's all there was to it.

Barbara felt like screaming. Maybe anything. But she could see what she could see, even if he refused to. She didn't know how much she wanted to say to him, whether this was the time to have it out. She clamped her jaw shut and stamped out.

"Oh, Barbara! How nice!" Grace said, beaming, as she swung open the door to her daughter's unexpected visit. Then her mother read her face and looked stricken. Grace's open mouth framed a question, but she left it unasked when Barbara could no longer contain herself and collapsed into sobs.

Grace eased her into a chair in the sunny kitchen. Breezes from Little Neck Bay fluttered the flocked curtains. Barbara felt so protected here, like a little girl again. She had so many happy memories of the house, and she knew the story behind each and every object.

Joe heard the commotion and came in, also first grinning with delight, then suddenly looking pained as her anguish drawned on him. "Honey . . ." he said, perplexed.

She didn't know how much to say. She didn't want to say much at all, just be comforted. It was Mary Anne, she blurted. She just couldn't take it anymore. She knew how Mary Anne should be raised, she said, the way she had been raised here in Whitestone.

"Are . . . you leaving Patty?" Joe asked hesitantly. Barbara imagined how this was hurting them. She knew how much they loved Patty. She shook her head.

They let her cry, not interrupting her with questions. Barbara knew what her mother would say. She had said it before. Barbara, too, had gone through a "Bohemian phase," as Grace called it, walking around in sandals the year round, even in the snow; the awful places she had lived in; her motorcycle phase; even, Grace sometimes dared to mention, the drugs. What they had to go through with her, Grace used to tell her much later, when she was grown. They didn't know what to do. Did she want to know what they did? They did nothing. They prayed, and waited until it passed. With God's help, it did.

Grace stroked her hair. "Patience, Barbara," she said. "Patience."

"You have to stay together," Joe said.

· · ·

Now she had found it, Barbara thought. This was finally it, the *evidence* she had been waiting for. It was sitting right there in Mary Anne's room, so blatant it seemed like an added insult. She hadn't even bothered to hide it. It was a *fuck you* sign.

Frenzied, she snatched the crushed joint from the ashtray and cupped it in her palm, rushing it next door to their room. She wrapped it in a tissue and stuffed it in the corner of a dresser drawer. Then she grabbed the phone and dialed Patty at the squad. Good, she thought when she heard him called to the phone. Good, he was there.

"I found a roach in her room!" she shouted before she said hello.

She heard him exhale with annoyance. "What can I do?" he said.

"What can you do? You can come home."

"Barbara," he said with a tone she found infuriatingly patronizing, "I can't come home now."

"Oh no?"

"No," he said adamantly. "What do you want me to do?"

"I don't know!" she was yelling now. "I don't know what I want you to do. I know I want you to deal with your daughter."

"So what the fuck can I do about it now?" he growled into the phone. "I'm here. I'll talk to you later."

His peremptory tone enraged her. She resented being put off. "Would I make this up?" she demanded. "Would I? Why are you closing your eyes to this?" She was almost in tears now.

"What the fuck am I supposed to do?" DeGregorio asked. "Search her room?"

"Yes," she said. "I did."

"Barbara," he said icily, "I can't talk to you now." There was a click and she was holding a dead line.

He looked angry when he finally came home. All right, he said gruffly, he would talk to Mary Anne. Where was she, upstairs?

When he came down, he sat heavily in a chair at the kitchen table. "I showed it to her," he said.

"And?"

"I said, 'Do you know what this is?' "

"Yes?" Barbara was riveted.

"She said, 'Sure, it's Chrissy's.' "

"It's Chrissy's! She said it was *Chrissy's!*" Barbara could not believe this.

"Let me finish. She said it was Chrissy's. Someone gave it to Chrissy, and she had smoked it in her room. What was so bad about that?"

"What's so bad about that?" Barbara screeched.

"Barbara! For Chrissake, will you let me finish? Then she said something like, 'Get real. If I was going to smoke pot, would I do it in my own room?' "

"What did *you* say?"

"I . . . I . . . said yeah—no, I didn't think she would."

"That's what you said? And that was it?" She was incredulous.

"Well," he said, "what was I supposed to say? I mean, Barbara, what the fuck do you want me to do? Can I prove she's lying? Maybe it was Chrissy's. Maybe it's a stage. It'll pass."

"Yeah," Barbara said angrily, walking out of the kitchen. "It's a stage. Smoking dope in your room is a fucking stage."

Voices. She heard voices in the house and stiffened. A moment ago she was abuzz with wine and laughter. Now she tensed. Something was wrong. It was Patty's fortieth birthday. As a surprise she had taken him out to celebrate at the Fifty-sixth Fighter Group, the restaurant at Republic Airport, with Ralph and Kathy, Mike and Francine, and her old partner Carmine Napolitano and his wife, Fran. They'd had a few drinks, a lot of wine. The others had driven home, and they were going back for a nightcap around the fire with Ralph and Kathy. But as soon as Barbara opened the door, she froze in mid-laugh.

The voices were coming from the kitchen. There wasn't supposed to be anyone there besides Mary Anne.

Barbara's eyes locked on three pairs of sneakers strewn in the hall. She peered into the living room and saw Mary Anne sprawled on the couch, snoring. Ralph and Kathy, sensing the imminent onset of an embarrassing family blowup, offered a hasty good night and slipped away.

Barbara stalked into the kitchen.

There was a stranger sitting at the table, a girl she had never seen before. "Hi!" she said brightly to Barbara.

"Hello," Barbara said deadpan, her eyes narrowing with anger.

From the bathroom by the den came the sound of retching.

She tried the bathroom door, and it opened. A second girl was bent over the toilet, heaving and vomiting. She looked up, terrified.

In the living room, Mary Anne stirred drunkenly, then staggered unsteadily to her feet and, reeking from whiskey, made her zombielike way to the staircase. Patty just stood there, watching her.

"What are these kids doing here?" Barbara screamed. "You know there's never supposed to be anyone here when we're not here."

Mary Anne seemed ready to say something, then closed her mouth and just stared blankly, even defiantly. Somehow it was worse than any lie. Then Mary Anne heavily mounted the stairs to her room.

"Get out of here!" Barbara shouted at the two flustered girls, who gathered up their sneakers and fled.

She didn't trust herself to say anything to Mary Anne. Patty, she saw, started uneasily up the stairs after her.

Later in their bedroom, still beside herself with rage, Barbara paced in circles, cursing to herself. She was so keyed up and angry, she couldn't sit down. "I'm out of here," she mumbled, not caring whether or not he heard. "I'm out of here. I can't take this shit."

He looked at her defiantly. "Is it her fault her brother died and her parents got divorced?" he said.

"For Chrissake, Patty!" Barbara exploded. "Stop making excuses for her! I don't know whose fault it is, but as sure as shit it's not mine!"

She was cracking up. It was a two-hour commute to the six-seven, and one night a week—for the turnaround, an early tour on top of a late tour—she stayed overnight in Brooklyn. She wasn't getting much sleep and was exhausted all the time now, even sometimes nodding off at the wheel. A few days before she had embarrassingly dozed off in the middle of a DA's interrogation of one of her witnesses. She was getting migraines and taking too much Tylenol with codeine. She was vomiting. Her hands were shaking, and her face was breaking out.

When Barbara got home the next day, she was surprised to find no sign of Mary Anne. Her books were there. She had obviously come home from school and gone out again. She was supposed to be grounded. They were running out of punishments. They had already taken out her telephone extension after Barbara heard her talking on the phone at two o'clock in the morning.

Barbara called Joe and Anne next door. No, Joe said, Mary Anne wasn't there.

She strolled in a few hours later.

"Where were you?" Barbara raged. "Who said you could go out?"

Mary Anne gazed back with a trace of defiance, a look that infuriated Barbara. "Daddy said it was okay," she said.

That did it. "Nobody tells me anything!" Barbara screamed. "Who needs it? Who needs this shit?" She tore upstairs, threw some clothes and toiletries into a suitcase, flung the suitcase into the trunk of her car, screeched out of the driveway and drove to her parents' home.

She fell, sobbing, into Joe's arms. He held her awkwardly, trying to calm her. "Mom will be home soon," he said comfortingly. "She'll be home in a few minutes."

She was incoherent, she realized, but she couldn't bother to make sense. "A fire!" she muttered. "It could have been a big fire. I'll come home one day, and the house will be burned down." She saw that her father was looking at her strangely. He had been a firefighter. He knew how fires could start, how they burned up people, whole families in their beds. Didn't he understand? He looked at her blankly, tears clouding his eyes. When Grace came in, Barbara threw herself into her mother's embrace. "I can't take it anymore!" she wept. "I have to stay here for a while."

"Of course," Grace soothed.

"Is it . . . drugs?" Joe asked.

Barbara blew her nose. "Yes," she said, "I think so."

The next morning she went to work straight from her parents' house and, after her tour, returned there. The thought of going home made her head throb. It was peaceful in her parents' house, and she felt like a child again.

When the phone rang that night, Grace answered. She spoke for a moment, then put down the receiver. "It's Patty, Barbara," she whispered. "Are you home?"

"No," Barbara said. Then she said, "Wait. I'll talk to him." She picked up the phone, not sure what she wanted.

"Barbara," he said softly, "let's talk. Can we meet for dinner?"

She dropped her voice so low that it was almost inaudible.

"You know the Rafters?" he asked. "Cross Island and One Forty-ninth? How about if we meet there at eight?"

He was already at a table when she entered. He stood up and hugged her, a long, warm, loving hug that brought tears to her eyes.

"I love you so much," he said. "We have to stay together, we have to. We have to work it out. Come home. Please, Barbara. Things will be different."

She filled out a UF 57, a request to transfer. She hadn't been able to get out of narcotics, but now that she was in the squad maybe she'd have better luck. If she could get a detail where she did days when Patty did nights, one of them would always be around to watch Mary Anne. They'd agreed to speak with one voice. Mary Anne couldn't play one against the other. She turned in the form and crossed her fingers, but the request came back rejected. They needed her where she was.

"Where are you going?" Barbara looked up to see Mary Anne descending the stairs, dressed to go out. Black jeans, a black T-shirt, earrings, bright lipstick, and lots of makeup. Her bleached hair was teased into a soft blond cloud. But she was still grounded. So where did she think she was going?

"Daddy said I could go out!" She was so vehement that Barbara wondered if he had again softened his edict without telling her. It wouldn't surprise her.

"Where?"

Mary Anne's face bore a look of frosty superiority, as if she had triumphed once again. "Just next door."

Well, Barbara thought, Mary Anne could visit her grandparents. There'd be no harm in that. "Don't be late," she warned.

It bothered her. Was Patty crumbling again? They had been through this before. They were supposed to stick together.

She hadn't come back by eleven-thirty. Annoyed, Barbara called next door.

Joe sounded surprised. "Mary Anne's not here," he said.

Shit! Furious, Barbara dialed Patty at the squad. "It's eleven-thirty, and we don't know where she is!" she screamed. "I'm going to look for her."

She snatched her keys off the hook by the kitchen table and ran out to the car. Racing the engine, she slammed into gear, leaving a film of rubber tread in the driveway. She zigzagged through the subdivision, barely slowing at stop signs, shot west toward the high school, and then had a better idea. She spun in a U-turn and headed for the stores by the Getty station and the 7-Eleven where she often saw kids hanging out.

Sure enough, there was a mob of kids just past the gas station. She braked by the side of the road and watched for a while, searching the faces. When she spotted Mary Anne, she veered across the road into the crowd, scattering the kids in panic. She nosed the car right up to Mary Anne. "Get in here!" she screamed.

Mary Anne looked shocked. She probably thought Barbara was losing it. Well, she was right, she was cracking up. Mary Anne was probably embarrassed, too, embarrassed that Barbara was making a scene here with all her friends. Good, Barbara thought. She'd fucking make a scene. She'd make a big fucking scene and embarrass her in front of everybody. She'd embarrass the shit out of her.

"What's the matter?" Mary Anne asked.

The feigned innocence drove Barbara berserk. "Get in the car," she ordered tight-lipped. "Get in and don't say anything. If—you— say—anything—I'm—going—to—kill—you."

"You're not my mother!"

Barbara lashed out, smacking Mary Anne stingingly on the cheek, raising a red welt. Mary Anne got into the car.

She drove home grimly. Mary Anne seemed about to say something a few times, but Barbara cut her off. "Don't talk," she said. "Don't say anything. Don't even talk to me." Barbara was afraid of what she would say or do. When Barbara opened the door, Buddy scrambled up eagerly, only to slink back, insulted, when Mary Anne rushed past him and ran upstairs to her room.

Barbara, cursing to herself, grabbed the phone and angrily stabbed out Patty's number. "Come home!" was all she could bear to say. She stomped around the house in circles, cursing.

Overhead, she could hear Mary Anne also pacing and muttering.

When he came home, she turned on him. "Make up your mind, Patty," she warned. "It's down to this. It's me or Mary Anne."

She saw him slump down on the couch and bury his face in his hands. When he raised his head, his eyes glistened like wet raw meat. She cringed looking at him.

"Look, Barbara," he said haltingly, "Mary Anne . . . is my daughter. After Tommy, she's . . . all . . . I . . . have . . . left."

She knew all that. They were beyond that now. "I know, Patty, but—"

He waved an arm, cutting her off. "But," he said hoarsely, "I am not going to let her take me away from you."

It was before noon, but it was already hot. Downstairs, the July sun sliced wickedly off the rectangular blue mirror of the pool. Maybe, Barbara thought, she'd go down and sit on the patio. It was her day off. No one else was home. Patty had left early. Mary Anne was in summer school. She had failed most of her subjects in Kings Park High School and had a lot of work to make up if she was ever going to graduate. The phone rang, and she picked it up in the bedroom.

A husky voice said hello, it was Officer something—she couldn't catch the name—from the Fourth Precinct, Suffolk County Police. "Is this Mrs. DeGregorio?" It startled her. She usually went by Barbara Adametz. "Yes." She stiffened. A paralysis gripped her stomach. She felt faint and started shaking. The phone was bouncing against her cheek. She realized she had been dreading a call from the police, this call, these words.

"I'm calling about Mary Anne's accident," she heard him say.

"Accident!"

"Driving the van?" He said it like a question.

What accident? What van? Mary Anne didn't have a van. She didn't even have a license. Barbara realized suddenly that she was reacting like every parent who hears about trouble with a kid. No parent was ever prepared, ever ready. It always came as a surprise.

It was a hit-and-run the day before in the Waldbaum's parking lot, the officer said. Nobody was killed or hurt, but there was some property damage. She had to be issued a summons, and they'd have to bring her in. "Have a good day, ma'am."

"Oh, my God!" Barbara said. None of it made any sense. But wasn't that what parents always said?

She knew it would come to this, she knew it. It was starting, she thought. What she had feared for so long was starting. With trembling fingers Barbara dialed Patty at the one-oh-nine. He'd just been moved from Manhattan Robbery to Queens Robbery, back where he had started in Flushing. Now her mind raced, her thoughts tumbling in panic as she waited for him to pick up. They were going to need a lawyer. They could be sued. *They could lose the house!* When she heard his voice, all her restraint crumbled. "The police called!" she shrieked. Disjointedly, she related the conversation.

He promised to leave immediately.

She paced through the house in a daze. They had just finished repainting Mary Anne's room peppermint pink. Paint cans and rollers were still in the hall. Mary Anne always complained about her room, and they had not redone it in the three years they had lived there. The wallpaper was still left over from Marie, and the furniture was Mary Anne's old children's set. They had some over-time money now, so they were fixing up the house step by step. Mary Anne's bedroom was the smallest and was the easiest to redo. It had sounded like a good idea, Barbara thought. A paint job and some white curtains with a bold design, something with flowers— Mary Anne liked flowers—a pink lampshade to match the walls, some new furniture, and a dressing table. She and Mary Anne were always competing for the bathroom, and with a vanity Mary Anne could put on makeup in her own room. It could be therapeutic.

The new vanity had come, but it had been delivered with a chip. They had called the store many times to pick it up, but they were still waiting. Now, impulsively, Barbara grabbed the damaged piece and violently shoved it to the door. Buddy, terrified by the noise, cowered in the kitchen, whimpering. She dragged it down the drive-way, scraping it along the asphalt, and flung it down by the trash bags waiting by the curb. Get it the fuck out of here, she thought. Let the garbage men pick it up.

22

SHE could give a shit. What was she supposed to be, afraid of Barbara? Who the fuck was Barbara? Barbara was no one to her. So she found some old bottles in her closet, so what? What could she do? Who was she? Mary Anne didn't come out of her room now if she thought she'd run into Barbara, and Barbara had to be doing the same thing. Mary Anne waited in her room until she heard the door slam, so she knew Barbara had left. They never crossed paths.

Her father was her father, but what did he know? He didn't know anything. He worked late a lot and was never home. She could even get high in her room. She could say it was Chrissy's, she could say it was anybody's. Prove something. She was getting over on him like she was getting over on everyone else. She was good, Mary Anne told herself, she was very good. She was sixteen and didn't give a fuck.

She remembered when her father was working with the drug dealers. She always wondered if he had to take drugs with them. She asked him once. He said no, but she wasn't so sure. He probably did it with them. He had lied to her before, and he probably lied then too. Well, she thought, he did what he did, and she did what she did. She knew he was trying to get closer to her, to see what was going on. She knew that. Part of her wanted to respond to him, run into his arms like when she was little, feel his big hands hugging her, his whiskery cheek. But she was angry at him, what he did to her. Screw him too.

Taking her to that trial. What was she supposed to do there? She could have died from embarrassment just walking into that big room with the chandeliers and the American flag, bigger than a church. She didn't want to go. She wondered what she was doing there. She fingered the hem of the brown sports jacket she had thrown on over her jeans and looked down at her feet so that she didn't have to see all the people staring at her. The old bald man in the black smock, was *he* the judge? He looked a hundred, and asleep. Everybody gave her creepy looks. She didn't see why she had to be there. It was about drugs. That was how drugs got into the country. So what? They got caught, too bad for them. She didn't give a shit. It was boring. Stupid thing. She couldn't wait until she got out of there.

School sucked. She had flunked most of her subjects, so they put her in skills classes. Positive Attitudes Toward School, PATS. Smaller classes, one-on-one with teachers. It meant she couldn't sleep in school. She used to be able to, which was why she flunked everything. She was always so tired. The teachers were so boring, it made her tired, and she just liked to put her head down on her arms in the back and sleep. She thought some of the teachers might complain to her father, but no, nobody ever said anything; at least he never said anything to her. One even put her in the back, doing her a favor so she could sleep. If she had to meet Vic, she just beeped him from the school phone and went outside to wait for him. High school was different from Rogers. They left her alone a lot. If she wanted to go out for a cigarette between classes, she just went.

She got high a lot with Chrissy. They still went to the skating rink on Friday nights. Everybody met in the parking lot and got high, and then they went inside, up into the bleachers. She didn't bother with pot much now. Pot was boring; all she got was hungry and giggly. Pot was for parties or when she was in her room watching TV and just wanted to relax. With the other kids she usually took mescaline or acid. She tore one of the little pictures off a sheet and popped it into her mouth. It tasted bitter, like rubber or carbon paper, she thought. She licked off the design, her tongue tingling slightly, and then swallowed the little wad of paper.

Some of the kids did three tabs at a time; the most she ever did was two. Acid made her feel so . . . *alive*. She could feel the lives inside things. Her eyes got wide. She felt waves of paranoia. She was sure people were watching her. Her whole body felt tingly and weird, as if she were someone else. It went on for hours and hours. Later she felt like crap, but she didn't mind it, so she'd do it again. If a bunch of them chipped in, they could get some coke. Coke really sent her flying. But somehow it was never like the first time, which was the best; she never came up to that level again.

While she was in summer school she took a part-time job at Lenny's Clam Bar in Smithtown. She worked the front desk, she was the cashier, and she also waited tables and the counter. She didn't have her driver's license yet. Her father or someone else had to take her there and pick her up.

She noticed right away the guy in the kitchen. God, was he hot! Everyone called him Chuck; he was a cook. From the front desk she could look through the window into the kitchen and see him cooking. He was big, he had to be six feet, with a good build, brown hair, and deep blue eyes. He was older, maybe nineteen or twenty, she thought. He had a great car, a silver Firebird.

She smiled at him a few times when they passed each other. He smiled back, thrilling her. One day he was standing outside, waiting for Lenny's to open, when she drove up with her father. She was so embarrassed. Her father had to be bringing her! He must think she was some little baby. She prayed her father wouldn't wait with her. What if he started talking to Chuck? She would *die*. Thank God, she thought, he was late for work and drove off. She gave Chuck a weak smile while they waited together.

"That your father?" he asked.

"Yeah," she said self-consciously. "He has to come this way anyway." She lapsed into awkward silence, wishing she could think of something good to say.

"If they ever get here with the key," he said.

"Yeah," she said, grateful for a new opening. "They're late a lot, huh?"

"Sometimes," Chuck said. "You look like a nice Italian girl," he said.

She flushed with embarrassment. How did he know she was Italian? Because her father drove her?

"Are you nice?" he teased.

"Sometimes," she said, desperately trying to turn her embarrassment into charm.

"You want to go out sometime?" he asked.

Go out? With him? She couldn't believe it. He was actually asking her out! "Uh, sure," she said, ". . . if I'm free." She'd be free, she told herself. She'd be sure to be free anytime he asked.

"Next Saturday?"

"Ummm, sure," she said.

They went to a movie. He had flunked out of high school and gone to cooking school, he told her. He was really rich. His father owned laundromats. He asked her out again, and then again.

One night in Port Jefferson he bought a six pack, and in the car she started chug-a-lugging them. He looked on, surprised. "I didn't know you drank beer," he said.

"Why?" she said, teasing him this time, " 'Cause I'm a nice Italian girl?" It was his turn, she saw, to be flustered.

On their next date he took her to Whitaker's in Smithtown. He was old enough to get in, but she had to sneak in a side door. They met at the bar. "You want sex on the beach?" he asked her.

"Huh?" She reddened.

He waved over the bartender. "Sex on the beach," he said. It was a drink. She didn't know what was in it—vodka and something that gave it a color, and then it was set on fire so it burned. You had to wait for the fire to go out to drink it. By the second one she was wasted; she tried to pick it up when it was still on fire and burned her finger. But she hardly felt it.

"Want a beer?"

They were in his house in Smithtown. It was a big, modern house. In the living room she noticed a big-screen TV and a spiral staircase up to a loft.

"Is . . . isn't anyone home?" she asked.

No. His parents were away on a trip. They were never home, he said. His brother and sisters were away. He showed her the basement where they had a big bar and a Jacuzzi. He handed her a beer, and then they went upstairs to his room. It was a real boy's room, she thought, with sports stuff, school banners, and weights. There were two beds in the room. She eyed them uncertainly.

"That's my brother's," Chuck said. "He doesn't live home anymore." He kissed her.

She thought she had never loved anyone like Chuck. She had gone out with several guys and had kissed some of them, but Chuck was the most gorgeous guy she had ever dated. She couldn't believe he loved her too. He could have anyone, she thought, but he wanted her. She was overcome by desire for him.

"Are you on the pill?" he asked.

She shook her head.

"That's okay," he said, leading her gently, unresisting, to his bed. "I'll use something."

"Who wants to smoke?"

They were doubling, she, Chuck, Chuck's friend, and his girl-friend, driving in Chuck's car. She took a lit joint from Chuck's friend and sucked in the smoke. Chuck looked surprised. "You smoke?" he said.

"Yeah," she said.

They went back to Chuck's house, the four of them. He asked what she did, coke? She did coke, she said, mesc, acid. Chuck said he did coke himself on and off but had stopped for a while. He had some coke, he said. They did some coke, everyone but the other girl who didn't want to. She just drank and got ripped drinking. Mary Anne felt the powder rise in her nostrils like silvery liquid and glide coolly down her throat like medicine syrup. She felt deliciously tingly.

Chuck said he could get whatever he wanted because he had a friend who was big-time. He could get heroin; did she ever try heroin? *Heroin!* No, she said, a little nervous. She had never done heroin. She didn't know what kind of high it gave and didn't like needles, but she might want to try it sometime.

The house was quiet. It was after midnight. Her father and Barbara had to be asleep. She tiptoed out of bed and listened at their door for sounds. Nothing. She slipped on a T-shirt and jeans in the dark and crept downstairs, ruffling Buddy's shaggy neck to reassure and quiet him. Then she slipped open the door and stepped outside.

He was there where he said he'd be, waiting in the Firebird in the street off her driveway. Just seeing his lean form outlined behind the wheel made her heart jump with excitement. He loved *her!* The warm night air misted delicately under the car headlights. She slipped in next to him, snuggled close, and they drove off.

They stopped at Whitaker's for a drink and then drove to his house. They did some coke, their bodies melted together, then they sat in the Jacuzzi. Before dawn she dressed quickly and he drove her back. She slipped into the house and into her room unnoticed. She woke up when her father was hammering on the door; she was late for summer school.

A few nights later she sneaked out again. This time she was surprised to see that Chuck was driving a brown Ford van with some writing on it. There were tools in the back. She looked at him quizzically. "My father's," he said. She didn't care. It was Chuck, he was there. They stopped at Whitaker's and drank. When it was time to go, Chuck stumbled. He was totally blasted, Mary Anne realized. She was high, but not like him. He couldn't even drive—he could hardly walk. She helped him out to the van and then, shrugging, shoved him into the passenger seat. She went around to the driver's side and got behind the wheel. He slumped, sleeping, as she searched his pockets for the key. She didn't have a driver's license, only her permit. But her friends had been letting her drive illegally for a while. She had never driven a van before, but how difficult could it be? She lurched erratically out of the parking lot, figuring it out as she went. She drove to Chuck's house, where they went down to the basement and ended up asleep in each other's arms.

It was already light when she cracked open her eyes. *Day!* Too late to sneak home. Fuck it. She didn't know what she'd tell her father, but she'd make up something—say she had stayed at Chrissy's or something. Who gave a shit? She closed her eyes and slipped back into a comalike sleep. It was midday when she stirred again. She had to get home, she thought dazedly. *Ugh!* Her clothes smelled gross. She asked Chuck if he had something she could wear. He gave her a shirt and some jeans. She had to roll up the cuffs several times.

From then on she didn't care. She made up her mind that she just didn't give a fuck. They could ask her all they wanted, yell all they wanted, she would do what was good for her. She didn't have to explain anything to her father, certainly not to Barbara. Barbara was nobody. If they stopped her, she'd leave anyway. It was her fucking life. Who were they, who was anyone, to tell her what to do?

One night they met Chrissy in Whitaker's. Chrissy was a drinker even more than a dopehead. She made Mary Anne laugh, she was crazy. They drank Seagram's with Chrissy and invited her over to Chuck's. She ended up in Chuck's room with them. She slept in Chuck's brother's bed while they slept in Chuck's bed. Chrissy didn't bother them; they did what they wanted to anyway. Chrissy was cool.

A while later, her father said he and Barbara would be away overnight. He told her where they would be, but she forgot. And she didn't give a shit where they went. He said Grandma and Grandpa would look in on her.

She didn't care whether they did or didn't. She invited Chuck to stay over at her house, which they had never done before. It would be great.

They did coke and got really wasted. It was funny when she woke up: She was in her own room at home, and *he* was there with her in her bed. She looked from his sleeping face to her new white curtains flocked with pink and black blossoms, to the birch tree outside, and back to his face. It was so weird. Everything was the same, but everything was different. She was still fucked up and felt like someone else. She wanted to lie with him there forever, she felt so close to him. When she tried to get up, her head throbbed. She had to get up, she thought. She wanted to do something nice for him—make him some breakfast. He'd like that.

She went down to the kitchen and opened the refrigerator. Nothing. Old leftovers in Saran Wrap. God! What did they do? Didn't they ever *eat*? She'd go to the supermarket and buy stuff for breakfast, that's what she'd do. She'd take the van. She fished through his pants for the keys and slipped out.

The morning sun felt like a hammer pounding nails into her eyeballs. She nearly passed out from the agony. She was so fucked up, she thought, she could hardly *see*. She tried to fit his key into the ignition and couldn't find the slot, her hand was shaking so much. Finally she got the van started and lurched off. Shopping, she thought obsessively. She needed to go shopping. She needed things to cook for breakfast, she'd go to Waldbaum's.

She was in a sweat. She was crashing. The coke had worn off, and she was coming down fast, too fast. She had a splitting headache and a deep hunger. She *needed* something fast. Where? Who did she know? She thought of her friend John; he was always good. She could get from him, and he was close by. Trembling, she drove to his house.

John didn't have anything. Shit! He said he knew where they could get. There was this guy in Fort Salonga. She told him to jump in the van quick and lead her there.

They did some coke with the guy and bought some to take with them. They did it in the car. Powder like cool silken liquid flowed up her nose and down her throat, pumping delicious energy and joy through her body. Everything looked different, strange; she was outside herself. She was soaring.

She lost track of time. Suddenly she remembered: *Chuck!* He was home waiting for her. Waldbaum's, she had to get to fucking Waldbaum's. She started up the van, with John next to her, and sailed down 25A. She saw the parking lot at the last minute and veered sharply right, speeding into the entrance past astonished shoppers. She could see their faces as she flashed by. She passed a spot and slammed on the brakes, backed up, and nosed in.

She pushed a cart down the aisles. She wondered for a moment: Was she moving or was the food moving past her? She couldn't tell. She felt people watching her, spying. She grabbed some milk, eggs, bacon, and orange juice, and wheeled it to the checkout and out of the store, and climbed back into the van.

John was sitting there with a half-smile, out of it. She started up, swerved to miss one of those long yellow bumpy things they put in parking lots to make you slow down, and smacked into another car. *Shit!*

She was out of there, she thought. No way they were going to catch her. She didn't see anyone in the car. Maybe nobody saw it. She stamped down on the gas and peeled away.

"Mary Anne, your father's here."

She saw him at the same minute, pushing through the front door of Lenny's and heading for her at the register. He looked angry. She felt a spasm of fear, then defiance.

"You didn't tell me about your accident, Mary Anne," he said. "Why didn't you tell me?"

"No," she said. She shrugged. She didn't feel like saying any more than she had to. How did he hear about it? she wondered. It had only happened yesterday morning.

"Now we have to go down to the police," he said.

Somebody must have seen her, she thought, and traced the plate. Did Chuck give her up?

She told the manager she had to leave for a while and followed her father out to the car. *Oh fuck!* Barbara was there too. She climbed in, not saying anything. Barbara stared out the window, ignoring her. Good, she figured; she'd ignore Barbara back.

At the police station in Hauppauge she waited alone while her father and Barbara talked by themselves at a desk with someone not in a uniform, probably a detective. Then they called her over. "Tell him what happened," her father said.

She tried to calculate how much they already knew and how much she should say about Chuck. They probably didn't know she was high. How could they know? The detective had a report form. "I hit the car by accident. It wasn't my van, and I left," she said.

"You don't have a license, is that right?" the detective asked.

"No," she whispered.

The detective said something about going to court and paying a fine. Then they left.

A few days later her father said they were going to see the man whose car she hit. She quailed. She actually had to meet him? Face-to-face? She had to, he said. But first, they were going to stop at her bank to make a withdrawal from her savings account. Then they drove to Waldbaum's. She wondered why it had to be in the same place. Did they have to meet exactly there? she asked. They had to, he said.

They pulled up in the lot by a car where a man was waiting. A middle-aged guy, she thought. She didn't recognize him or the car, but obviously he had seen her or the van.

"Oh, she's young," the man said. He seemed surprised. Her father took him aside and they talked. Then she saw her father give him her money, $1,000. She felt sick. It had taken her so long to save it. But she just wanted to get out of there, she told herself.

She needed a ride to Coram. Who had a car? Kelly! Maybe Kelly could pick her up. She called her and said she had to get some money from her mother. Could Kelly give her a lift?

Mary Anne was on the outs with Chuck. They had called him about the accident, and he was totally pissed. Maybe Chuck blamed her. She didn't know. She hadn't seen him lately. Anyway they could only have gotten her name from him.

She wanted to get her own apartment, she told Kelly. She couldn't stand it at home anymore. She needed more money so she could get an apartment. Kelly pulled into the driveway of her mother's house. Mary Anne was glad to see there was no sign of her mother's car. She must be out working, she thought.

She didn't have a key but knew which window latch was broken. She looked around quickly to see if anyone was watching, then pushed up on the wood. As she expected, the window yielded, opening the width of her body. With another quick look around, Mary Anne hoisted herself up and through, tumbling to the bedroom floor. Kelly squirmed in after her.

She knew exactly where to look. She crouched under the gold couch, searching for the hiding place. Ah, she found it! Her hand closed around a fistful of bills, and she withdrew the wad. Tens and twenties. She flipped through them quickly, counting about $500. She stuffed the money into her jeans and climbed back through the window, waiting for Kelly behind her. Then they got back into the car, and Kelly drove her home to Kings Park.

A few hours later she was at home when the phone rang. "Yeah?" she answered. There was no reply at first. "Hello?" she prompted.

"Mary Anne?"

The familiar voice shot her back to a bad time. Involuntarily, she grabbed a lock of her hair and began twirling it nervously.

"Did you come in here?"

"No." She tried to sound puzzled.

"I know you did because people saw you."

"No, I didn't," she insisted.

"I know you did it, but I'm not going to do anything."

•   •   •

They were stopping her all over school. Did she have anything, they wanted to know, did she have stuff?

"Don't worry," she told them all. "After school, meet me behind the stores."

She went to the pay phone and beeped Vic. He got back to her in a few minutes. She wandered outside and settled herself on a stone block in front of the school and lit a joint. Who gave a shit if anyone saw her? *Airheads*.

She heard the distant buzzing before she saw anything. It became a roar and Vic rumbled up on the big Harley. As always she noticed his tattoos and his deep blue eyes. *A real Guido*. Dynamite-looking, she thought. Balancing on his idling bike, he handed her a paper bag, and she stuffed it into her purse. She didn't bother to open it. She was sure he was keeping count.

Later, after school let out, she walked along the road with a bunch of the kids, heading for the 7-Eleven. She passed the light and turnoff into her subdivision and kept walking. The store was just beyond, almost in sight.

They crossed over at a break in the traffic and milled around the video store. She ducked behind the building, opened her purse and the paper bag, and pulled out a packet of folded-up newspaper. She unfolded it and picked out three lumpy little purple mescaline tablets. *Nerds*. They looked just like the candy. She popped them into her mouth, sucking away the acidic, slightly bitter aftertaste that always made her think of carbon paper.

She stood on the side of Ivy Lane, surrounded by eager buyers. She tore tabs of acid off the sheets, measured out palmfuls of mesc, and handed out dimes and eighths of grass, sweeping up the money as fast as she could stuff it into her purse. She was wired, hyper, adrenaline pumping. She *heard* colors and felt in her soul the humming of green trees and the popping blue of the sky smoking with clouds. Everything was watching her; there were eyes everywhere.

A tall boy shouldered in. "I want to check the counts," he said challengingly.

Mary Anne gave him a disgusted look but reached into her pocketbook and extracted a large Ziploc bag. Still holding on to it, she let him finger an eighth of a pound of pot through the plastic, checking the seeds and stalks, evaluating the quality with a con-noisseur's eye. Only then did he hand Mary Anne three tens and she relinquished her grip on the bag.

A girl wanted two dimes but had no money for her. Could she pay later? Mary Anne's saucerlike eyes fastened on the girl's gold bracelet, a slim twisted rope. "I'll hold that," she said.

The girl pried it off her arm. Mary Anne dropped it into her purse and handed over the bags.

A gray van screeched up. "Hey, Mary Anne, what you got?" yelled the driver, a boy she knew from school.

"What you want?" she countered. She felt like laughing. Every-thing seemed silly and funny.

"I was passing by. I seen you here," the driver said. "What do you got?"

"What do you need?" she repeated. That, too, struck her as ri-diculous, and she began to giggle.

She didn't immediately see the little lox-colored Chevy Nova make the turn across the road and into the dead-end street.

23

He glared at her over the kitchen table. He had seen what was in the paper bag that fell to her feet, the pot and purple mescaline tablets, sheets of acid, and God knows what other shit. He had kicked it away, afraid somehow to pick it up, as if handling it would have meant he'd have to take the next step. Which was what? Arresting her? That was unthinkable. He wasn't a cop here. He was her father.

Now he was looking at what had spilled out of her purse, all those bracelets and rings. Where did she get all that gold, DeGregorio wondered. How *could* she have betrayed him like this? He had closed his eyes to a lot. That was the problem, he now realized. And she had laughed at him. She must have thought he was a fucking idiot.

He was afraid to open his mouth to speak. He didn't know what would pour out. Thank God that Barbara wasn't there. She'd had it with Mary Anne. The next move would have been out of the house for one of them. Or they would have murdered each other. If Barbara found out about this, he could imagine her reaction. Barbara had been right all along, he thought. She had tried to tell him, but he wouldn't listen. Ralph had figured it out. And Mike. Everyone, he guessed, had seen it before he did. He didn't want to see it. It would have meant losing Mary Anne after he had already lost so much. But now he probably was going to lose her anyway.

She hadn't betrayed him. He had betrayed himself. She hadn't gotten over on him any more than he had wanted to be gotten over on. He had sent her all the wrong signals. She had been out in the open. She had practically advertised it. He could have seen it happening, he *did* see it happening, but he just ignored it. He hadn't gotten fucked. He had fucked himself.

"What's it going to be, Mary Anne?"

She played with a salt shaker. "It wasn't mine," she said sullenly.

He lost it. "Don't bullshit me!" he shouted, slamming his fist on the table, sending dishes jumping. "It was yours! Do you think I'm a fucking moron?"

"It wasn't," she said, pouting.

He paused to get a grip. All the things he had ignored or brushed over—her overnight absences, the bottles in the closet, the note, the roach in the ashtray, all her lies—they mocked him now. And there was something he still struggled to deny, although the evidence was inescapable: She was *selling* too. Selling and using.

"Mary Anne," he began again, "you have to get help, you know that. There's a place called Apple. . . ." Her friend Joanna's mother had mentioned it once.

"I know Apple," Mary Anne said.

"You do?" It caught him by surprise. "You know about it? How do you know about it?"

"Kids talk about it," she said. "They shave your head and everything. They abuse you. I'm not going there."

"You have to go for treatment somewhere."

"I'm not going. I don't need to go."

His rage boiled over, and for a moment he thought he might jump over the table and strangle her. He could just kill her, she was so fucking stubborn. In his anger and frustration he burst out crying. "You're killing me!" he wailed, his big shoulders heaving. "You're killing Barbara! You're killing my whole life!" He smeared away his tears with his hands.

She was looking away, not meeting his eyes.

This was it, he told himself. If he didn't make up his mind now, Barbara would make it up for him. If Mary Anne agreed she needed help, he'd get her help, and she could stay. But she was refusing. He had no choice. "You have to go," he said, forcing himself to say the words. "You—can't—live—here—anymore."

She stared at him blankly, then shrugged. "Good," she said. "I'll leave."

"Good," he said. "Get out."

She got up from the table and went into the bathroom off the kitchen. He could hear her running the water and blowing her nose. She came out looking composed, picked up her pocketbook, dropped in her wallet, keys, and change, and started toward the door.

"Wait," he said.

She hesitated and turned. For a moment, he thought, she let down her guard. She looked like a little girl again, his little girl, confused and vulnerable. But then quickly her expression hardened.

"Keys," he said.

She looked back, puzzled.

"Your house keys." He held out his hand.

She rummaged through her purse and found them. She dropped them into his open palm and walked out.

He was in shock. He just sat there in the kitchen. Then suddenly he ran to the door and double-bolted it as if to strengthen his resolve. In a burst of rage he snatched some black plastic lawn bags from under the sink, tore upstairs to her room, and stuffed the bags with clothes from her closet and drawers. Her shit was out of here too. He dumped the bags in the garage.

He didn't know how long he sat alone in the kitchen, oblivious to the hours sweeping by on the clock over the sink. He was still there when Barbara came home after eleven, looking surprised to see him just sitting there, staring, in the greenish glow from the pool lights outside.

"What happened?"

He didn't know what to say. "I threw her out," he finally said. He didn't say why. He was afraid if he told her the story, she might get angry enough to leave too. He couldn't lose both of them.

She didn't question him, which relieved him until he realized how disgusted she must have been not to say anything. It was as if it was not a surprise to her; it should have happened long ago.

He slept fitfully, straining for the sound of the door, jerking awake, remembering that she didn't have a key and would have to knock or ring. Would he hear her? Once he thought he heard something and sat up, listening. But it was only Barbara breathing.

He awoke at daybreak queasy with guilt and worry. Had she come home? Was she asleep in her bed? He crept to her room to look. Her bed was still made and empty. She was gone.

Oh, God, had he done the right thing? He needed advice. He

remembered hearing about a group called Tough Love. Had a cop whose kid was in trouble told him about it? He couldn't remember. He looked up the number in the phone book.

The woman who answered sounded friendly. He wondered if she was a volunteer, another parent. He told her that he had thrown his daughter out over drugs.

"Did you tell her she could come back if she goes into treatment?"

"Yes."

"And?"

"She won't go."

"Then you were right," said the woman. "You have to wait. You have no choice. Be strong." She told him about an upcoming meeting and invited him and his wife. He could call anytime he needed reinforcement.

"Dad?"

It was Mary Anne! DeGregorio went weak in the knees. He couldn't believe it! She was calling home, reaching out to him. Since she had walked out the night before, he had thought of nothing else.

"Mary Anne! Where are you?"

There was a pause. "At Chrissy's."

He was so relieved, he started babbling. "Oh, you're at Chrissy's. That's good, I'm glad. I didn't know where you were, I had no idea, I was worried. I'm glad you called, sweetheart. Are you ready to come home?"

"No."

"No?"

"No. I need my clothes."

She needed her clothes. She was calling for her clothes. "Okay," he said quietly. "They're in the garage."

He left the garage open when he went to work that day, but when he came home, the clothes were still there. They were still there the next day too.

The day after that she called home again. "Dad," she said curtly, "can you meet me by the bank?"

"The bank?"

"I need my money."

He tried to stall. "Come to the house, Mary Anne," he said. "I'll meet you here." If only he could get her back to talk, he thought.

She said she'd meet him outside the house in an hour, but she wasn't coming in.

He kept peering out. Finally he saw her walking up the drive. She was wearing different clothes, clothes he had never seen before—Chrissy's, he guessed. How did she get there, he wondered? If she came from Chrissy's, she might have walked. He met her in the driveway. "You want to come in?" he asked. "Sit down, talk?"

She ignored the question. "I can't get any money without your signature," she said. "It's my money. I earned it."

"It is your money," he agreed, "it's definitely your money." He touched her arm. She pulled away. "Mary Anne," he said, "you're making a mistake. I love you, sweetheart. Let's get help."

"I'm okay," she said, turning away.

"You're not okay. You need help. Come here." He reached for her again.

She took a step back, evading him. "I need money for an apartment. You're not helping me. You're not helping me at all!"

Before he could stop her, she turned and walked off. He watched her shrinking figure disappear around the corner of the park.

Later, passing Ralph's house down the street, DeGregorio spotted his nephew, Joey, on the lawn and stopped, then waved him over. Joey was a star on the varsity baseball team, with possible professional prospects. They talked about how the season had gone.

"Joey," he said then, "you knew what was going on?"

Joey nodded tentatively.

"You knew she was selling?"

"Yeah," Joey said. "Everyone did."

Everyone! Was he, DeGregorio wondered, the only one who didn't know? "You knew who she was buying off?" he persisted.

"Yeah." Joey stared at his sneakers and toed the grass. He looked uncomfortable.

"Did you ever talk to her, Joey, try to straighten her out?"

"I tried, Uncle Pat. She wouldn't listen to me."

"But you never told your father? You never told me."

Joey's voice dropped to an almost inaudible level. "No."

•   •   •

"Barbara . . ."

He had been trying to think of a way to tell her, to break the news about how he had caught Mary Anne selling. He had been consumed by the guilty secret. The longer he had waited, the more difficult it became to explain why he had kept this from her for almost two weeks.

She was reading, distracted. Since Mary Anne left she had withdrawn into herself, clearly drained and eager to reclaim her solitude.

"Barbara . . . I . . ."

At the break in his voice, she looked up sharply.

Before he could organize his thoughts, the story tumbled out. He watched intently for her reaction. She looked at him with what he took for disgust and pity, maybe even contempt. "I figured something like that," she said.

"You *figured?*" He was astonished. "But you never . . . said . . ."

"No," she said.

So she, too, had figured it out, he realized.

The basement light was on, he saw. It was strange; he usually remembered to shut it off. Barbara didn't usually leave it on.

He had just stepped out the door but stopped before making a run through the pelting rain to his car. He saw it out of the corner of his eye, through the ground-level window. He debated whether to go back in and turn it off or just leave it. He could leave it, it wouldn't matter; it could burn until he got home. But he couldn't forget it, he couldn't let it go. Okay, he'd shut it off.

He went back in and clambered down the stairs to the basement. He was reaching to snap off the switch when he glanced down and recoiled in horror.

A human form lay crumpled behind the bar.

It—she—was a sodden mess, retracted into a fetal crouch.

Mary Anne!

He dropped to one knee and bent over her.

She was asleep—or had passed out. He smelled the sour reek of alcohol. Her matted hair was pasted to her scalp, and her dripping clothes had left puddles on the tartan carpet. She looked, he thought, like a pile of rags or a bag lady, a beggar, a bum.

She must have sneaked in the open patio door. But how long had she been down here?

He thought a moment, had an idea, and tiptoed out, leaving her sleeping. He left the house, got into his car, and drove to work. Then he called home.

The phone rang and rang. He thought she might have left again until he heard a click, a clatter, and a thud. She must have dropped the phone.

"Hello?"

She sounded numb, listless. He pictured her in her sopping clothes and felt sick.

"Mary Anne?" He tried to sound amazed.

"Ummm."

"Oh, you're there," he said. "*Now* do you want help?"

"I want help," she mumbled.

In the squad room DeGregorio held the receiver away from his ear and stared at it for a moment, speechless. Then he replaced it almost reverentially and looked around. Suddenly, as it all dawned on him, he spun into frantic motion. Who was around? Who was in charge? *Lieutenant Tom Houston!*

"Lieu," he shouted, "sign my twenty-eight!" The department had a form for everything. A UF 28 was for emergency time off.

When he arrived at the house, she was sitting at the kitchen table. Her clothes were still wrinkled and musty, but she had dried out, washed her face, and combed her hair.

"So," he asked gently, "you want help?"

"Yeah," she said.

"Great!" he said.

She hesitated. "After a while."

"That," he said, "is the wrong attitude. You need it now."

She shrugged.

"I spoke to a woman in the Suffolk County DA's office about Apple," he said.

"Only for, like, thirty days," Mary Anne said.

"That's not up to you," DeGregorio said.

She thought for a minute. "I don't want to go there."

"Then I told you, you're not living here anymore."

PART
Four

·

24

TH E fact that Logan Lewis, the founder and director of Apple, was even alive was something of a miracle, for which he came to credit Jehovah. "Jehovah always thought I was worth something," he said, himself the image of a black Jehovah, stern-visaged and formal with a penetrating gaze and a thin mustache. He and Jehovah had triumphed over the degradation of crime and drugs. Others, he felt certain, could do so too. He could show them the way.

Born in 1943, he grew up with two sisters in Harlem, children of a striving postal bookkeeper and his wife who seemed constantly on the move. When he was six the family relocated to Brownsville, Brooklyn, and two years later, by which time Logan had two more sisters and a brother, to the Bronx. A tough, angry youth, he was expelled from three high schools before being sent to stay with relatives in Babylon, Long Island, where he was expelled from a fourth. Logan returned home and fell in with a violent black gang, the Egyptian Crowns, that rumbled with homemade zip guns and chains. His idol was his uncle, a street hustler and drug seller who wore sharp clothes and carried a gun. By fourteen Logan was drinking and smoking dope. At seventeen he stabbed a milkman during an abortive robbery. He was prosecuted as a juvenile offender and given three years probation. It only made him wilder. He drank more, tried more drugs, and became a militant racist, targeting Jews, Italians, and other whites. In desperation his father tried beating him into submission, to no avail.

Logan left home and actually landed a good job as a file clerk in a large Manhattan law firm. At twenty he married a childhood sweetheart who bore him a daughter and two sons. It looked as if his life had finally straightened out, and then he was arrested again in a burglary. This time he did six months in the Bronx and a year on Rikers Island. By the time he got out in 1966, his wife, kids, and job had vanished. He found work with a rug importer on lower Fifth Avenue, where he quickly worked his way up to manager of the import department, while shooting heroin supplied by his uncle and living a wild life in Greenwich Village, experimenting with opiate hash, acid, crystal methamphetamine, and Thorazine.

Many lunchtimes Logan left the rug office for a quick subway run to Brook Avenue in the Bronx, where he copped his drugs before returning to his office to doze the afternoon away. His boss finally caught on and fired him. But then, needing him, he lured Logan back with a raise that came in handy not only for drugs but also for his new family. He had met another junkie, and they had a daughter. But soon that marriage also dissolved. He slept in door-ways and supported his habit by robbing numbers runners. In 1970, at twenty-seven, with his dark skin glowing yellow and his fingers bloated from shooting dope, he wound up in Lincoln Hospital with hepatitis. But as soon as he was out, he started again.

One night while he and some relatives were getting high in the Bronx, his baby niece picked up a foil packet of crystal meth and, taking it for candy, swallowed it. The child soon went into convulsions. The six stoned adults could barely call an ambulance. On the way to Jacobi Hospital, Logan tried to blow into the baby's mouth to keep her breathing. After she was rushed into the emergency room, he and the others milled around in the corridor, still in drug stupors. A psychiatrist came out and motioned Logan aside. "I know you're high on something," he said. Logan nodded gravely. The psychiatrist leaned forward conspiratorially and whispered urgently, "I want some!" Logan traded him some crystal meth for Thorazine. Afterward, outside, he shook his head. Damn, he thought, he had almost killed his niece.

In his younger years, feeling his habit raging out of control, Logan had learned to detox himself. He'd buy some black market methadone from addicts on the street and wean himself off heroin. But that no longer worked; he was too far gone. He had been shooting twenty-five bags a day and gobbling barbiturates. He was strung out. He applied for admission to a drug program on Houston Street. They made him sit in a chair and wait for hours. He grew sicker and sicker and finally fled.

He was at rock bottom, his jaw wired from a fracture and an abscessed arm wrapped in filthy bandages. An aunt was on the board of a drug treatment program on Long Island, and after talking to his mother, she offered to bring him there and he submitted. It was a struggling communal program called Deter in a small office over a delicatessen in Patchogue. He was put to work with twenty others renovating a warehouse. Each day a different church donated food, and each night neighbors opened their homes to provide beds. A benefactor gave Deter a bungalow colony in the Catskills, and Logan moved up there to work on the place.

Three months later, by Labor Day, 1970, Logan went back to the Patchogue office as a staffer to supervise intake. No one was paid; it was still a communal operation. Whatever money was raised was divided for the group's upkeep. There was no public support. Members raised funds by making and selling ashtrays and other handicrafts. By early 1971, Logan was co-director of Deter's Patchogue program, now grown to one hundred residents and staff. Patchogue became the intake center and Bloomingburg in the Catskills the residential treatment facility. Logan slept in the Deter office in Patchogue or went home to his aunt in Deer Park. He did some speaking in Amityville, where there had been a number of drug overdose deaths, and drew the interest of benefactors who offered to stake him in his own program.

In July 1971, a year after joining Deter, Logan started a new program with a $37,000 grant. Operating under the Amityville, Copiague, East Farmingdale Opportunity Center, he took these initials and called it the Ace Drug Rehabilitation Program. Modeling Ace after Deter, he set up a communal home in a rented house in Amityville. Later he purchased a building nearby on Albany Avenue and Great Neck Road and changed the name of Ace to Alba-Neck. But local opposition blocked the occupancy, and the program remained where it was.

Lacking a high school diploma himself, Logan recruited a behavioral psychologist, Chester Copeman, of the State University at Stony Brook, who had been testing drug desensitization on rats. Copeman introduced Logan to the theories of Albert Ellis and his

Guide to Rational Living, a handbook of cognitive therapy. As Logan understood Ellis, people were not disturbed by things but by the views they took of things. Thinking produced feelings, which generated actions. If you understood and changed the *thinking,* you could change the *action.*

Logan saw it as an effort to break away from the brutal screaming therapies of Synanon and other early antidrug programs based on demolition of the so-called addictive personality. That, to Logan's way of thinking, was like going to a doctor with a headache and getting punched in the face. Instead, he thought, addicts should be welcomed into a family, the therapeutic community, where self-destructive patterns could be exposed and corrected. He believed that although a wide variety of factors, including genetics, led people to drugs, most behaviors were learned, and therefore they could be unlearned as well.

Looking for ways to reverse behavior, Logan experimented with aversive therapy, so-called counter-conditioning, featuring a device called a shock box. The eight-inch cube, a "stimulus generator" made by a Nebraska company, cost just over $200 and ran on eight flashlight batteries. Metal plates were wired to the arm of a patient, who was then asked to recall certain experiences with drugs. There followed an unpleasant but nonhazardous electrical shock. Patients determined their own thresholds of discomfort. Alba-Neck also adopted some other harsh measures, including sleep deprivation and humiliating punishments. If you acted like a whore, you had to go around dressed like one.

By 1980, Logan adjusted the therapeutic mix once more. The shock box was out, along with humiliation. That couldn't have been right, he reasoned. No other affliction was treated by degrading the victim. Why substance abuse? Even the Marines had moved away from humiliation as a training tool. And why, for that matter, did ex-addicts always have to put themselves down? It rankled him. "I am not recover*ing,*" Logan insisted, "I am recover*ed.*"

The Alba-Neck program grew, and Logan rented larger quarters in Melville. Once again local opposition sparked a bitter court fight, and once again Logan was driven away. Next he found a vacant nursing home on Veterans Highway in Hauppauge. It smelled of old bedpans, but he received a $50,000 grant from the state to renovate it. A sympathetic reporter wrote a favorable story in the local paper, but the town of Islip rose in opposition, winning a court injunction until Logan finally prevailed. The new facility, rechristened Apple—A Program Planned for Life Enrichment—opened in 1980.

Logan had turned his life around. In 1974 he had married one of Ace's first graduates. He had also been introduced to the Jehovah's Witnesses and become a believer. Jehovah had parted the waters and led him safely through, Logan believed. "He always sent me what I needed," he said.

If anyone was destined to test Apple's new program, it was Bobby Alberti. A cocky little bantamweight, Bobby grew up in Long Island's Five Towns, where his father was in the tire business. He played football and ran track at Lawrence High School, where the yearbook coyly listed his affiliations as the "shooting club" and the "flying club"—sly allusions to his fondness for drugs. Bobby had been shooting heroin since junior high, a secret he kept from his parents until one of his friends died of an overdose. He tried to kick his habit alone in three days via cold-turkey withdrawal. He sweated and vomited and went into convulsions. His parents exiled him to Synanon in 1971.

At the time, Synanon was widely regarded as the country's pioneering drug treatment program. It had been founded on $33 in Santa Monica in 1958 by Charles E. Dederich, an alcoholic, who took the name from an addict's mangling of the word seminar. Dederich had been through Alcoholics Anonymous and felt it did not address drug addiction. In his therapy addicts were stripped of their self-esteem in harsh encounter groups and criticism sessions, and then taught to rebuild their identity in relation to the group. It was a form of brainwashing, Dederich readily acknowledged. "We try to wash all the things out of a person's brain that got him into trouble and clean him up nice and shiny, like any school does," he once explained.

Dropouts from the drug scene in the sixties flocked to Synanon, drawing tremendous national publicity and millions of dollars in contributions from major American corporations. At its peak Synanon had assets of some $30 million, including antiques and other valuables collected by Dederich and his family. But Dederich grew

increasingly authoritarian. When he decided to stop smoking, he
decreed that all Synanon members quit too. He ordered men at
Synanon to undergo vasectomies, divorce their wives, and change
sexual partners. He bought guns for his security force, called the
Imperial Marines. He sued reporters who began exposing his cult
and put out death contracts on defectors and other critics. In 1978,
at Dederich's behest, two of his security guards put a live rattlesnake
in the mailbox of a lawyer who was suing Synanon on behalf of
former members. The lawyer, Paul Morantz, was bitten and hospitalized, but survived. Dederich, in deteriorating health, pleaded
no contest to the charges in 1980 and was placed on five years
probation and fined $5,000 for his part in the conspiracy.

Bobby Alberti watched Synanon self-destruct. Lured to the program by idyllic photos of horseback rides in the California hills, he
was met at Los Angeles Airport by two Synanon goons in a van.
They sped him to the compound, shaved his head, and threw him
on a couch in a closed room. "When you've kicked," they said, "come
out." He saw hundreds of residents listening mesmerized to the
piped-in words of Dederich, who, Bobby found, also bugged their
rooms so he could listen to them in intimate moments. After four
months Bobby was fed up. He insisted he was cured and wanted to
leave. The leaders wouldn't release him. It was, they said, a lifetime
program. Bobby finally talked his way out and began walking from
Santa Monica to Albuquerque, where he had an uncle. He hooked
up with another drifter, who stole his savings and driver's license.
Bobby begged a bed in Fort Apache and kept on walking.

When he reached Albuquerque, he scored some heroin and was
hooked again. He linked up with another pusher and peddled drugs
out of a green Fido's Ice Cream truck in the southern New Mexico
town of Truth or Consequences. Then Bobby stole his partner's
stash of five pounds of pot and fled east. Back in New York, he and
a partner were selling the pot when customers tried to rob them.
The two sellers fought back, and the attackers were beaten off.
Unaccountably, they filed a complaint, putting the police on Bobby's
trail. He was being tailed one day in Cedarhurst, Long Island, when
he tried to escape. The police gave chase, and Bobby bailed out,
abandoning the car and diving into Reynolds Channel where he hid
under the swampy water and tried to breathe through a reed, as
he had seen in the movies. It worked. The police brought in a

helicopter to search for him, but Bobby escaped in the back of a pickup truck. The next day, however, realizing the game was up, he surrendered, with a lawyer. On the way to booking he was treated to a dose of street justice—a swift beating by officers exacting revenge for their fruitless chase the day before. Bobby ended up with a five-year sentence, but even in Sing Sing he found that getting high was easy; smuggled drugs were plentiful.

In 1975 he was paroled and returned to selling drugs. He beat some suppliers out of a debt and was repaid with vinegar forcibly poured down his throat, burning his membranes, damaging his lungs, and sending him into an eighteen-day coma. In the hospital doctors had to cut open his throat to treat him. In the agonies of cocaine and heroin withdrawal, he repeatedly ripped out his intravenous tubes and shriveled to a hundred pounds. He filched bottles of codeine from hospital supply cabinets to stay high. Released, he went back to drugs. Then he overdosed on heroin. A companion dropped him on the lawn of Logan Lewis's Ace center in Amityville.

Even in Ace, Bobby continued to get high on smuggled drugs. Once he loaded the program's TV set into a van and sold it to a pusher for some heroin. When the set was discovered missing, Bobby blamed it on the staff. The scheme came to light seven months later when the dealer himself entered treatment at Ace and, asked routinely if he knew anyone there, pointed to Bobby. "I bought a TV set off him once." Bobby was busted to entry level and humiliated with punishing work contracts. Then an old deal came back to haunt him. One of his former Demerol customers flipped and became a police informant. Now, five years later, they dusted off an old warrant for violation of parole. Pressured by the police to turn, too, Bobby refused, went to trial, and was convicted. As a prior offender he was sentenced to three and a half years. He did some of his time, then won parole on a work-release program. He went back to drugs, switching from expensive cocaine to cheaper heroin, and hid out in Astoria, dodging both his parole officer and dealers out to kill him for previous swindles.

Desperate for money, he was eyeing an old woman on the street one day and was about to mug her for her pocketbook when something stopped him. He told himself that this was it; he had reached rock bottom. He made his way back to what he remembered as Ace, found it had become Apple, and begged Logan Lewis for readmission. Logan agreed and became Bobby's personal counselor. Somehow this time the treatment stuck. Bobby not only made it through the program and married a fellow graduate, but he also rose in the ranks to become Logan's vice president. He particularly came to treasure the most tangible symbol of his rehabilitation: his very own eye-popping red Porsche, which he had saved for and parked ostentatiously in the middle of the Apple parking lot.

"See this?" Bobby liked to tell frightened new arrivals, gesturing at the Porsche. "If I can do it, you can too."

25

"I DON'T want to go," Mary Anne said.

She sat behind Barbara, scrunched up in the narrow backseat of the Nova, glowering out the window at the turning leaves. It was the first full day of fall, 1988. Kids were back in school. *Other* kids. Next to her lay two black plastic bags of clothes and toiletries, all she was allowed to bring with her. This was bullshit, she thought. She had made a mistake to agree. Maybe she could still get out of it.

She had an idea what to expect, and it only unsettled her more. A few days before, her father had taken her to see the place, just a quick look from the outside. Crossing Veterans Highway in Hauppauge, she caught a glimpse of a sign, **a p p l e,** in small red letters, and then they pulled into a parking lot. The first thing she thought was that it looked like a regular house. Are you kidding, *a hundred people* live here, in this old house? Then she thought that it looked weird, like a haunted house. She didn't like the look of it. They drove away before anyone could ask them what they were doing there.

"I can't force you," her father said, "but you're going." So he *was* forcing her, she thought. He had made up his mind. She might have had a chance alone with her father—she knew how to get over on him—but not with Barbara there. She was like the enforcer.

She still didn't know why she had gone home that rainy night and sneaked back, wasted, into the house. All she knew was that she had gotten bad, and there was nowhere else to go. What her father and Barbara still didn't know was that she had been living next door at Grandma and Grandpa's. They were away on a cross-country trip. Her uncle Louis was staying there, her father's young-est brother. He was only nine years older than her, and they got along. Louis was cool. He had fooled around with drugs—she'd seen a scale in his room once. And he had seen her smoking a joint in the backyard. She told him she did coke too. She was sure he wouldn't give her up. Before that she had lived at Chrissy's for a few days and then with some other friends. She didn't know when Grandma and Grandpa would be coming home, but it was probably any time. There was nowhere else to go. She couldn't stand her life.

She had agreed to what her father said, but now she didn't know. She was scared. He had taken her to sign up. It was just an office off the highway, not the house where you stayed. They didn't even know when they'd have a bed. She had to sit in a blue plastic chair and fill out a long form. The clipboard kept slipping off her lap. She didn't want to sign up, she didn't want to go there. She couldn't see where her father was; they must have made him wait outside. He had talked her into it. Why had she let him? She knew she had to do something. She had gotten bad, she knew that. But she didn't think she had to be stuck away in boot camp or whatever Apple was. The stories about the head-shaving scared her. She didn't need that. She could straighten herself out. Maybe she needed a little help, but not this much.

The questions on the form jumped out scarily at her: *Have you ever been arrested for rape? Assault? Homicide? Child molesting? Does any member of your family use illegal drugs? Do you have any of these com-municable diseases? Are you pregnant? Were you ever admitted to a psy-chiatric hospital or psychiatric ward? Have you ever attempted suicide? How many times? Date of last attempt and outcome?* Are you kidding? she thought. Who does these things? Child molesting? These are the people they get here? From a psychiatric hospital? Rapists? People who try to kill themselves? This is where they want her to go?

She had to check off all the drugs she had ever tried and the ones she used most. It told her what she had to bring. It was so *exact,* she thought: *five* blouses, *seven* bras, *seven* pairs of underwear, *two* blankets, *three* pillow cases, *two* towels. God, it sounded like the army! There were pages of rules: *No getting high. No physical violence. No stealing. No hookups (emotional or physical). No negative rapping. Residents are not allowed to leave the property without permission. You must be searched every time you come back into the house. You must submit a urine analysis whenever asked for one. You must take a Breathalyzer test for alcohol whenever asked for one. Residents' letters are screened coming in or out. You should follow your last directive given. . . .* God, it sounded awful!

Then they told her to leave. They would call when they had a bed. She hoped they never did.

Her father was waiting downstairs by the car. "From now on," he said, "you're staying with me. I'm not letting you out of my sight."

He made her ride to work with him and wait in the car while he went up to the squad. She waited for three hours. She was so angry. There was nothing to do. The radio wouldn't even turn on, he had taken the keys. Was he afraid to leave her the keys? When he came out he said he had an idea. He drove into Manhattan to a strange part of the city where the streets just had letters—A, B, C, D—and really low numbers, the Lower East Side. She looked around, surprised. There were huge bunches of bummy-looking people standing around burned-out buildings. It looked all bombed out. Was he trying to scare her? She looked, but all she did was nod and mumble, "Yeah, whatever." She didn't want to let him think he was impressing her. She wouldn't give him the satisfaction.

The next day he drove her to the doctor. She needed some medication for a urinary tract infection she had picked up in her last weeks of drifting around. On the way her father said to her, "You had better get on the pill, Mary Anne. The only thing you haven't done yet is get pregnant."

Three days later someone from Apple called and talked to her father. A bed had opened up suddenly. Was she ready to come in? She thought about home and her friends and school. Not that she loved school that much, but still it was where she knew everyone. Why should she change her whole life? "No," she told her father, "I'm not going."

9-19-88

Maryanne,

Hey, babe, how's it going? I guess it's just about time for you to go now. But don't worry about it. Just think about what you have to come back to when you get out. You have all your friends, your family & your most favorite, your very own bed. You know something?

I am upset that you are leaving for a while, but I am also glad because you are gonna be helping yourself get rid of some of you bad habits you have & you are gonna be making your father happy. And I know that as much as you think your father & Barbera are pain in the ass. You are gonna do this to help him & Barbara & yourself at the same time. I am gonna call & visit you as much as possible. But please try and stay out of trouble while you are their. Just think how much cleaner and better you are gonna feel about yourself when you get home. I know you can do it, just if you would try: And while your gone I'm gonna straighten my ass up a little bit too. We have been through so much shit together in these last 5 years. And I am very glad that we have stuck together. And what ever you do. Don't think that anything between us will be changed, when your back, because it's not. I'm gonna think of it as. You are away on vacation. And I am just gonna wait for you to come home. The good part about this whole deal is that you admitted that you have problems. And you want to straighten everything right? right. And Don't think about [Chuck]. Because he is a dick & there will be plenty of other guys. You are gonna meet so many other guys. You are only 16. I hope that you will bring this note with you to Apple, so if you feel lonely or anything you can read it again to see how much I care about you & how much I want you to get the help you want. And Don't forget I ♡ ya. You also better bring that picture of us together, when you look at it just think of all the stupid & burnt things I have said. ha! ha! ha! ha! ho! Well I do have more to write but my hand hurts. So I write it another time. OK? OK. Before you leave try to re-member to give me your address. Well honey got to go now see ya later sis.

   I ♡ ya.
   Chrissy

"She doesn't want to be here," her father said to a guy who came up to the car at the intake center, where she had filled out the forms a few days before. He was short and skinny, thirtyish, with a feathery mustache. She didn't want to talk to him, she didn't want to talk to anyone.

He said his name was Tom, and he worked there. "Who you bullshitting?" he said to her. "You have a problem."

She felt like punching him. She was pissed. Who did he think he was talking to?

"You know, Mary Anne," he said, "the streets will always be there if that's what you want. They're not going anywhere."

She looked away. *Asshole.*

Her father asked when he should drive her to the Apple residence.

Tom shook his head. "We take her there," he said. He looked impatient. "Let's go," he said to Mary Anne.

It dawned on her that this was really going to happen. She felt scared. She didn't say anything but put on a puss and sulked. She felt sick to her stomach.

"When can we see her?" her father asked.

"We'll let you know," Tom said.

Her father got out and started to pull her two plastic bags out of the backseat.

"No." Tom blocked him. "She carries them herself." He pointed to a waiting van.

She struggled out with the bags, dropped them by the car, and threw her arms around her father. "Good-bye," she said, burying her face in his shoulder. She kissed his neck and felt her eyes streaming with tears.

"Good-bye, sweetheart," he said huskily, hugging her. "Talk to you soon."

She turned to Barbara and hugged her quickly. "Good-bye," Barbara said.

"Good-bye," Mary Anne said. She noticed, surprised, that Barbara was also crying. She's really happy, Mary Anne thought. She's happy I'm out.

She dragged her bags to the van without looking back. The driver, a heavy guy who said his name was Lou, motioned her into the passenger seat, and they started off, driving down Veterans Highway. Five minutes later the van turned left across the highway and bounced up the driveway she remembered from the time her father took her there to look around. The house looked the same—creepy, like from the Munsters.

The porch was full of people standing around smoking cigarettes. She carried her bags through the crowd, trying to ignore the searching eyes. She didn't like the looks of some of them. They looked wild, like street people. They scared her.

Inside the door she saw that she was in a big living room with worn-out furniture and stairs to a second floor. It looked incredibly busy, with people running around, up and down the stairs, back and forth, and phones ringing off the hook. It was making her dizzy just to see all the frantic activity. In the corner a tall boy was shadowboxing with one hand held behind his back. God, that was weird! She tried not to stare.

"Sit here at the ric desk."

She sank into a wooden chair, not sure what a ric was. She turned around and could see a kind of cafeteria or dining room with a sign, IN A SITUATION WHICH IS NOT NORMAL, DO NOT LOOK FOR NORMAL. She wondered what that meant.

At the desk a dark-haired boy with a mustache said he was the resident in charge, and he had to get some information. He opened a spiral notebook and painstakingly entered Mary Anne's name, address, Social Security number, and date of arrival. He looked up. "I need two female searchers. Susan and Eleanor"—he waved over two girls standing nearby—"bag search." Before she could say anything, her things had been carried off.

"Do you think I'm bringing in drugs?" she asked.

"You could have a roach in a pocket," the boy said levelly. "Even a seed could be planted."

Eleanor, a thin, reserved black woman in her twenties, led her down a hallway where Mary Anne saw a boy on his hands and knees scrubbing the floor with a Brillo pad the size of a penny. There was something repulsive about the sight, Mary Anne thought. Then she realized it was that the boy was the only one working; everyone else was just passing by. Why, she wondered, was he cleaning and the others weren't?

Eleanor motioned her into a room with bunk beds where the other girl, Susan, friendlier and pretty with glossy black hair, was waiting with her bags. She had to strip and open her mouth and hands, pull back her ears, lift the soles of her feet, and squat to show them she wasn't sneaking anything in. They seemed to be going down a checklist, examining the linings, cuffs, and collars of her clothes, the insides of her shoes. They opened up a can of baby powder, removed a bottle of rubbing alcohol, and opened and sniffed all her cosmetics. They opened an envelope of photos and tossed them aside.

"Hey!" said Mary Anne, seeing Tommy's picture drop on the floor.

"No family pictures," said Eleanor.

"Here," Susan said a little more sympathetically, "take a shower and shampoo with this." She handed Mary Anne a small plastic bottle.

Mary Anne regarded it suspiciously. "What's this?" she asked.

"Kwell," said Susan. "It kills lice and crabs."

Ugh! People came in with crabs? She didn't have bugs, and the thought of other people there with bugs disgusted her.

After her shower she returned to the big living room. This place was freaky, confusing. Everything had a funny name. Half the time she didn't know what anyone was talking about. Susan said this was rap, that was rap. Finally she asked, what's rap? Rap was her group, Susan said, resident adolescent program. A supervisor came out of an office behind the ric desk, a tall guy who called over a chunky girl. "This is Laura," he said. "Laura's your housemate. She'll hang out with you in the beginning while you're in orientation, show you around."

Mary Anne eyed Laura warily. She didn't look too friendly, Mary Anne thought. What the hell was she doing with this Laura? "You'll be in room one," he said. "Who's in room one?" A big number of hands shot up, maybe ten. Mary Anne was surprised. Some of them looked old, too, and kind of tough. "You'll be on bathroom crew," he said.

She walked around with Laura, who told her she'd been there six months. She'd been probated there by the court. She had done all kinds of shit. Her room was full of bunk beds. She was on the bottom. She stuck her head in the bathroom. Nasty. It looked old and rusty.

People were shouting, and everyone was moving. She heard the banging of metal chairs being unfolded and the scraping of running feet. *House meeting! House meeting!* She followed the noise to the dining room where chairs were being set up in rows. Reddening with embarrassment, she was motioned to a seat in the front, along with some other kids also in orientation. Laura sat behind her.

A guy people called Ned, short and muscular with a round, kind face, waited at the front. He must have been there a long time, Mary Anne thought, everybody knew him. Suddenly he yelled, "How's everybody doing?" The answer came roaring back. "OKAY!" Then a thin woman with dark hair, very pretty, took over. The kids cheered; they seemed to really like her, Mary Anne thought. She leaned back to Laura. "Who's that?"

"Londi Alberti," Laura whispered. "Bobby's wife."

Londi looked out over the assembled house. "John," she asked, "how does the program work, daily routine?"

A tall boy near the back stood up and spoke in a monotone. "Basically the general concept is the same as other TC's. We see each other as brothers and sisters. We change through peer pressure. It's very structured. We get up at six-thirty. Breakfast is six-thirty to seven-fifteen. After breakfast, seven-fifteen to seven forty-five, we clean our rooms. Seven forty-five to eight-thirty, clean-up crews. Everybody has a crew. We have a concept here. No free lunch. Everybody pulls their weight. You can't just hang out and eat your food. You gotta earn. You start here with no privileges. You work very hard to gain your privileges. Out there, things came easy through stealing. After the morning meeting we go to school or staff-run groups to lunchtime. Lunch is twelve to twelve forty-five. After lunch, you tighten up your crew again for about fifteen minutes. Then you have school or another house meeting or go to another group. There are all kinds of groups. There's an orientation group, females group, C of A group. We have AA on Monday nights. In the afternoon there is study time for about two hours unless you're on contract. Dinner is four-thirty to five-fifteen. If you're in orientation, it's your time unless you're on contract. Sometimes during the week there's another house meeting at night. Ten, lights out. We have rec on Friday and Saturday nights. Sundays are basically not therapeutic days."

Londi nodded. "What are contracts?" she asked. "Mike?"

Mary Anne leaned back again. "C of A?" she whispered.

"Children of Alcoholics," Laura said.

She heard a boy's voice from the back. She was embarrassed to turn around. "We have a contracts program based on contracts and rewards. For negative behavior you receive negative consequences. For positive behavior, positive consequences."

A boy in a red sweatshirt said he was sent to bring toilet paper up to the bathrooms but instead of doing it right away, he decided to bring it up later at noontime when he was upstairs anyway. "I procrastinated," he said. "It was a laxed attitude, part of my image, having a laxed attitude. It was procrastination. Procrastination can hurt me on the outside too."

"How can it hurt you on the outside?" Londi pressed.

"Procrastination can hurt me on the outside as far as on the job. Procrastination on getting a job done for my boss. Him by telling me, listen I need this done. The consequences could be me losing my job."

Another boy in a plaid shirt rose. "We're going to have to pay bills, gas bills, telephone bills, and stuff like that. When we get that money to pay that, we can't hold on to that money. We got to pay those bills right away. We can't procrastinate. We can't fall back on old ways of belief and get high."

"The house accepts?"

"Yes!"

A boy in an orange shirt stood up. "I'm a baby. I want what I want when I want it. I'm into deceiving, lying, manipulating." He sat down.

Londi shouted, "We're going to have some MOVE UPS! Okay?"

The room erupted into bedlam.

"Everybody want to play?"

"Yeah! YEAH!"

One by one, to cheers and applause, beaming residents were called up to the front for what looked like promotions. "There was a time when I never thought I would reach this point," an older black man said. "I had a lot of setbacks, I was fighting many things. I was here for months and months. Every time I reached a point, I would always come back down. So I thought this was unreachable, and as you can see, it's not. When you think you're losing it, hold on to it!"

"How does it feel?" Londi asked.

"It feels fantastic!" he said.

Londi called another three residents up, introducing them, to loud applause, as the new house coordinators. "What did you change about yourself, Artie?" she asked a heavyset older man with glasses.

"Old . . . beliefs," he stammered.

"What old beliefs?"

Artie looked painfully uncomfortable. His eyes darted around as if searching for a way to escape. "Feeling that I'm different, that I'm better . . . I'm worse than other people," he said, groping for words.

"How are you a more responsible person?" Londi pressed.

"To my children."

"How?"

"Writing them, calling them."

"How to yourself?"

"Feeling good."

"How are you a responsible person to yourself? Since you've been here, how have you worked toward being a responsible person to yourself?"

There was a long pause.

Londi raised her eyebrows. "Is that a hard question?"

"I guess by feeling comfortable, not manipulating anymore. Not lying?" Artie made it a question.

"By being more truthful and honest?" Londi prompted.

"Yeah."

"Okay." Londi let him off the hook.

A woman with long coiling black hair was called up next. Mary Anne recognized her from the search.

"Susan has taken a very, very, very long time," Londi said. "Today's her birthday. You're on CU to reentry!"

The residents cheered.

"What's CU?" Mary Anne asked Laura.

"Consideration up. Reentry means you're out of here."

Susan wiped away tears. "There's nothing better than being straight on your birthday," she said. "I feel so good, I just hope that everyone else can feel this way when they get to the stage I'm at and that you can push yourselves to get to the stage I'm at. It takes a long hard road. You can't do it alone. You think you can, but you can't. I thought I could, but I needed help. That's the help, these people here." Her arm swept the room.

Londi brought out a cake and everyone sang happy birthday. Susan opened a small package and took out a stuffed teddy bear.

Londi muttered something and seized it, trying furiously to scratch off the price with a fingernail.

"Londi," someone yelled from the audience, "you remind me of my mom."

She looked up and grimaced. "I remind you of your mom. Thanks a lot."

Londi said something about the new residents, and Mary Anne froze. She prayed they wouldn't make her get up in front of everybody and say something. She would *die*.

But all Londi said was, "Greeting of the house?"

There was a patter of applause, a stamping of feet and a rhythmic chant: "HUH-HUH-HUH-HUH-HUH-HUH-HUH!"

26

"OH, I can't wait to see her!" Anne said eagerly, for what DeGregorio figured must be the tenth time. He shook his head and looked at his mother in the rearview mirror. His father was next to her, staring silently out the window. DeGregorio had taken the bigger car, the Chevy Celebrity. Joe wouldn't have fit in the Nova, not with Barbara there, too, sitting wordlessly in the passenger seat. "Ma," he said, "I told you, we're not going to see her."

It was no use. He sighed. His mother wasn't getting it. Mary Anne had entered Apple just six days ago and wouldn't be allowed a visit for a long time. She had to earn a visit. How many times had they told him that? This was just their family orientation night. Later, every other Wednesday night, the families of the kids in rap would meet to talk among themselves. Everybody had a different story, DeGregorio was sure, but probably when you got down to it, they were all the same. Kids who fooled their parents. Parents who fooled themselves. "So, Patty," Anne said, "you don't think we'll be able to see her?"

It had been a bad week. Now that he'd had time to think a little, long-repressed feelings finally broke through, plunging him from hopefulness to despair. He was consumed by guilt, then resentment. Why should he feel guilty? It wasn't his fault. Everyone knew right from wrong. It didn't matter how old you were, you were free to make your own choices. Mary Anne knew what she was doing. She could have *not* done it. Kids were always doing things that their parents then blamed themselves for. Why was this? But it was his fault, wasn't it? Would it have happened it he'd been watching out?

He was amazed at how one person's acts could touch so many others. Their whole family was in turmoil. One kid fucks up and the effects ripple out. Twenty people suffer the consequences. There must be millions of kids like Mary Anne, DeGregorio thought. No wonder the world was such a fucked-up place.

The odds were against her, he knew. He hated to think of that, but it was true. He'd had a depressing talk at intake with Tom, who had his own grim tale to tell: smuggling coke in Florida, locked up eighteen times, shot seven times. Jesus Christ, he thought, these were the people he was leaving Mary Anne with! Tom had told him that only fifteen percent of those who came in to Apple ever graduated. Of those who left, half or close to it left within the first month. And of those who finished the whole program, only seventy-five percent stayed clean through aftercare.

Fifteen percent, he kept thinking, fifteen percent, that was her chance.

The day he brought her in, seeing her walk away from him across the parking lot to the Apple van was like feeling his heart walk away, walk away and get drilled with a shot, clean through. The pain was excruciating; he felt his life draining away. She was all he had left of his own blood after Tommy. Now he was losing her too. He told himself she had to do this, that this wasn't her death, it was her chance at life. But Tommy had had a chance, too, and Tommy was snatched away. His eyes stung with tears. He turned away so that if she looked around, she wouldn't see.

DeGregorio parked the car, and they walked across the lot to the Apple residence, with Anne oohing and aahing over the grounds and the sight of the spotlit building through the trees. "It's so nice here!" she kept saying. "It's a house. It's like a home." DeGregorio looked at his father. He was taking it all in, looking around, saying nothing. Barbara was quiet too.

"Mr. DeGregorio!"

He turned around and tried to place the huge black man with the bulging physique of a bodybuilder.

"Johnny Knight," the man prompted, encasing DeGregorio's hand in a bone-crushing shake. "I met you at intake."

"Of course." Now he remembered. He was one of Mary Anne's counselors. "How's she doing?" DeGregorio asked.

"As well as she can," Johnny said. "She's scared but trying hard."

Scared! His little girl was scared! The thought panicked him. What was happening with her? Johnny's report was hardly comforting. She was in the care of ex-junkies, hopheads.

The staffer taking them around only heightened his anxieties. He was strikingly handsome with a glowing tan and mesmerizing crystal blue eyes. He introduced himself as Mark Howard, Apple's director of communications, and like Bobby and other senior staff, he told them, an Apple graduate. He must have heard it before, that he didn't *look* like a junkie, because he told them no, actually, the Leave It to Beaver look was misleading. He'd started drinking at thirteen and moved on to pot, hash, Quaaludes, barbiturates, coke, heroin, and speed. It landed him in the Pennsylvania Railroad Station, where he lived as a bum until, having hit rock bottom, he found his way to Apple.

The story was meant to be inspirational, but DeGregorio grew more morose. "You know," he said belligerently, "the only time I ever met someone like you was when I was putting cuffs on him."

During the few minutes before the orientation meeting was set to start, they were free to wander through the house. Anne exclaimed over the neatness and order, the feeling of discipline and structure, the signing in and signing out everywhere. She liked that, she said. That would be good for Mary Anne.

Suddenly Anne stopped and gasped. "Look at this!"

They came back to where she stood in front of a bathroom, staring at a signup sheet on the door. On the last line was an unmistakable scrawl, a familiar signature in plump, looped letters: *Mary Anne DeGregorio.*

"She's really here," Anne said.

"Yep," DeGregorio said. "She really is."

They gathered in front of the bathroom, letting it sink in.

Suddenly Anne banged on the door.

DeGregorio rushed to grab her arm. "Ma, what are you doing?" he asked, startled.

No one answered, so she banged again.

It opened a crack. The face inside registered shock.

"Mary Anne!" shouted Anne. "It's Grandma!"

The door slammed shut. They stood there stunned.

DeGregorio guided his mother away. "Maybe we should wait for her outside," he said.

It was time for the meeting, so they had to go. Anne kept looking back, but Mary Anne didn't come out.

The TV room was already filling with parents when they entered. They took seats together on a threadbare tweed couch. Mark Howard gave a little talk. All DeGregorio could think of was Mary Anne, scared, in the hands of a bunch of junkies. Had he made a mistake putting her here? He looked up sharply when he heard Mark say that in New York State, possession of an ounce of narcotics sufficed for a felony conviction.

"No," DeGregorio corrected him loudly. "It's two ounces."

He saw all eyes in the room travel to him. He didn't give a shit.

Barbara poked him sharply in the ribs. "Shhh," she whispered. "What are you doing? Nobody cares."

Mark paused at the rude interruption. "This meeting is not about technicalities of the law," he said dryly. "Now," he said, sensing DeGregorio's antagonism, "what's your story?"

He told them haltingly about Mary Anne and his anguish. They didn't seem too surprised to hear he was a cop, DeGregorio noticed. He realized that probably nothing would surprise anyone there.

Other parents started talking. A heavy woman said, "We didn't know in the beginning that he was into drugs. The older son, we knew right away. Two Thanksgivings before he came here he'd disappear. I'd drive around. His room became a mess. We convinced him to go into Brunswick for thirty days, but after the insurance was gone, he was out. He'd be out for a while, then he'd go back again, until the insurance ran out."

Her husband cut in. "I remember a neighbor came. James had passed out in the parking lot. We didn't know he drank that much. My wife thought he was dead. Later we knew he was doing crack. He stole some things. We told him, 'Get help or go to jail.' " He paused to collect his thoughts. "I've been there myself. I'm a recovering alcoholic. My life is an open book. I know what he's going through. I've gone through it myself."

He had a message for his son, he said. "It doesn't get any better out there. He knows my history. He's seen me clean. He's seen me go through three detoxes. Hopefully I have everything under control—just for today." He paused again. "It takes work. You get into the drug groove, you don't know how to get out of it. He was on his way out. We saw walking death for him."

His wife interrupted. "Every time the phone rang, my heart stopped."

The father resumed, lost in his own recollections. "I had my own ass to save. I was trying to recover."

His wife said, "Our other son has been in jail because of drugs. We were relieved he was in jail. At least he wasn't dead."

"I don't know," the father said, shaking his head. "We're doing something wrong."

DeGregorio felt better when the meeting ended. He wondered why it was comforting to hear other people's problems. It should make you sad, he thought, not happy. But somehow he felt better. All these pathetic people had started out trying to do the right thing, and then something happened.

He chatted with a few of the older residents on the way out. He was struck by their courtesy and politeness. These weren't street junkies, not anymore, not like the ones he knew. They didn't look like sorry shufflers and shirkers. They looked him in the eye and called him sir. He was impressed. They didn't all belong in jail. They were human beings.

On the ride home he tried to sort out his thoughts, but his mother kept up a rat-a-tat conversation. She liked what she saw, she was so impressed. That was the right thing for Mary Anne, she said, just a place like that. DeGregorio smiled wearily. It was just like his mother. You never had to wonder what she was thinking, she was glad to tell you. His father was different. A silent thinker. DeGregorio realized that more than anything he wanted to know what his father thought. He trusted his father's opinion more than anyone's. He always had, since he was a kid. But it would be better not to ask him, not now. They'd find a quiet time in the next few days.

When they got home, he and Barbara sat up, talking. They had started to communicate again, although he realized it would be a long time before they could reestablish the trust, the closeness that years of turmoil had shredded. They would have to go easy with each other, be gentle, piece their intimacy back together little by little. They couldn't rush into it; it would have to happen naturally. You couldn't forget the bitter things once said, but with time, he hoped, the pain would fade. She was starting to come around. She'd been transferred to sex crimes. It was interesting work, she'd told him, more structured than just being in a squad. She needed that. She needed structure now, he thought. The Hundred and Twelfth was also a shorter commute; she needed that too.

He realized that he didn't know what she thought about the visit either. She was a little like Joe, she kept things inside of her. He asked her what she thought.

"For the first time," she said, "we know where she is. We know what she's doing."

He went over to see his father the next day. Joe decided he liked Apple too. It was a good thing she was there, it was right for her, for all of them. Maybe it was no one's fault, but Patty hadn't supervised her properly. He never clamped down on her when he should have. Now Apple was doing it for him.

The following Sunday, DeGregorio got up early, before eight. Barbara stayed in bed. He brewed some coffee and sat at the kitchen table, thinking. He stared at a legal white-lined pad. At the top he had carefully written the date, *10-2-88,* and on the same line, to the left, had begun, *Dear Mary-Anne,* hyphenating her name the way he had always done it, for reasons he had never examined. No one else in the family wrote her name that way. She herself always wrote it Mary Anne, the way it was supposed to be.

He knew what he wanted to say, what was in his heart, but it had never been easy for him to express himself on paper. His father, Barbara, almost everyone he knew was better at it. In person was one story, but putting it down was the hard part. When it came to Mary Anne in general, he now conceded, he had trouble seeing straight. He had been so fearful of losing her, and then, he realized despairingly, he had lost her anyway.

He sat for a long time, chewing on the pen, staring at the page, not knowing how to go on. It was hard enough communicating with Mary Anne when she was standing there in front of him, but at least her presence offered him some feedback. This was impossible. It was like talking to an empty room.

Finally he began writing hesitantly in a well-formed, almost child-like script:

"Me, too," Maxine said. "I saw you at intake when you came in. Was that your father?"

Mary Anne nodded again. "Yeah."

Maxine leaned forward conspiratorially. "Wanna come to South-ampton?"

"Huh?" Mary Anne was confused. "You can go to Southampton?"

"Shhh," Maxine said. "Split, get high? I know a guy there."

Was she wacko? Mary Anne wondered. She just got there. She had been there, what, two days? This other one was still in orientation too, like her. Couldn't she at least wait until she was on level one? She didn't even know this girl. Why should she run away with her? This was too crazy. Mary Anne shook her head. "No," she said. Maxine shrugged. It didn't matter.

She was already exhausted. She had to get up by four-thirty in the morning to shower, and she couldn't put her head on the pillow again until after ten o'clock at night. They had already served pizza bagels twice. Going through the food line, she blew: "I'm sick of pizza bagels!" she announced.

A girl behind her on the line said, "You haven't been here long enough to be sick of anything."

Mary Anne turned slowly and raised her right middle finger.

She got pulled out of line. "If you weren't still on housemate, I'd write you a contract," an upper-level boy she didn't know said, "for functioning off your image, doing what you want when you want."

Later Londi needed her Social Security number for a form in the office. Mary Anne couldn't remember it. Londi wrote her a contract for "blowing on the tool of responsibility." To make sure that she memorized it, Londi had her write the number five hundred times. She felt so stupid and told some boys, "I feel like a dick." That was overheard, "an inappropriate statement in front of two males," an upper-level said, and got her another contract. She got three more contracts the next day: for forgetting to sign the shower sheet on the door of the bathroom, for complaining about it—what a supervisor called "dribbling on the floor"—and for telling some boys kiddingly, "I have a tattoo on my ass." She spent a lot of extra time on her hands and knees, cleaning.

When she went into the living room the next day, she stopped, frozen in mid-step. There was Maxine, her head down, sitting on a stool in the middle of the room. Residents walked around her as if she weren't there. No one looked at her. There was something sickening about it, as if she had been turned into stone.

"What happened to Maxine?" she asked Laura.

"She split," Laura said. "She sneaked out, hitched to Southampton, met her fiancé, and got high."

"Why'd she come back?" Mary Anne asked.

"I guess she had to. She got probated here by the court."

"What are they doing to her?"

"She's on isolation ban now," Laura said. "No one can acknowledge her, say her name, or be alone in a room with her."

Later, at a splitee group meeting, everybody had to talk about Maxine and give up their guilt, admitting anything they'd done wrong and hadn't been caught at. Mary Anne confessed that Maxine had told her she was going to split and that she had kept the secret. For that they both got put on isolation. Even when Maxine's contract was over, neither of them could talk to each other. Mary Anne was also ordered to serve two extra hours of inspection duty and write a five-page composition on the theme, "What's on my mind that is causing me to blow."

She removed a cigarette from the pack she had marked with her name; otherwise she would have gotten another contract. She was on the porch lighting up—smoking in the house was a heavy contract—when a thin teenage girl with a sassy turned-up nose, ice-blue eyes, and a mane of frosted blond hair materialized and, dreamlike, walked past her into the house.

Mary Anne's heart flip-flopped. She thought she was hallucinating.

Chrissy!

She resisted the urge to cry out. Chrissy had to be coming to get screened so she could visit her.

She followed Chrissy into the house, gaping when she saw her drop into a chair at the ric desk.

Chrissy was signing herself in! Chrissy was coming into Apple!

She knew what she had to do. She told an upper-level that she knew Chrissy from the outside. They were immediately put on

isolation ban. No contact. But Mary Anne was thrilled. Finally someone she knew was there. Not just someone, Chrissy! At least they
could see each other.

She watched achingly as they led Chrissy away with her bags. She
heard someone shout, "Female searchers!"

"Bunch of animals," Mary Anne muttered.

An upper-level overheard her. "What'd you say?" she demanded.
She made Mary Anne stand in front of the house and apologize to
everyone. And on a behavior sheet she wrote, "Isolation with
Chrissy."

She was finally allowed to get mail and was given two letters from
her father. She felt all mixed up. Holding the envelopes, just thinking about her father, made her nervous. She was still angry at him.
He was out there, home. She was in here, having to deal with all
this alone. But she felt a pang reading his words: *I know I have said
this to you before. I will always be here for you. . . . I would give my life for
you if it would make things easier for you. But I'm learning that there is
only one person who can make things better for you. That person is you.*
Just seeing his writing, she could hear him saying it, it was so real
to her. She couldn't help it, she started to cry.

There was also a letter from Aunt Luisa in Florida. She said that
for Halloween she and Craig were thinking of going to a costume
party as Wilma and Fred Flintstone. Did Mary Anne think that was
a good idea?

There was a letter from Grandpa too. He sounded a little angry
at first:

> There's no reason to discuss why you're with Apple—you're
> last four years were not the best insofar as family love and unity
> is concerned. Nevertheless this is a new beginning and still time
> for my beautiful granddaughter to be crowned Miss America—so
> hang in there baby—make us all proud! . . . Do me a favor—
> tonight just before you close your eyes to sleep, look upward to
> God and just say, Thanks, God, for helping me.

"Mary Anne, your father's here!"

She knew she had a visit coming—after a month you could have
a visitor—but she wasn't sure how she felt about it. She was eager

to see him, but she was nervous and wasn't sure what would come out.

She walked into the living room.

He was standing by the ric desk with Barbara, holding a big pot and arguing that it was just macaroni and what was wrong with that. It was macaroni for his daughter, and there'd be plenty left over for the house. He had cooked enough for about fifty people. She saw the resident in charge stir and sniff it to make sure it was okay. There was a bag of rolls and pastries, too, and she saw that being checked. Finally her father was waved through.

She hugged him and Barbara too. She was surprised how good it felt. They went for a walk outside. Buddy was there in the car! She couldn't believe it. They had brought Buddy! She ran to the slightly opened window to reach a hand in, and Buddy in his frenzy nearly crashed through. She leashed him, and they took him for a walk around the parking lot.

He asked her how she was doing. She said she was okay. She suddenly felt awkward, as if he were a stranger. She thought she had so much to tell him, but something held her back. She still resented him, she realized. There was this lump in her throat.

He didn't seem to notice. He was beaming, peppering her with questions: How was the food? How was school? Was she learning a lot? How were the kids? Had she made any friends? She couldn't start to answer a question before he bombarded her with three more. Then he seemed to realize it and stopped himself, grinning.

She began slowly. School was good, harder than Kings Park, and better. She was learning more and getting good marks. Then she said, "I belong here. I had a drug problem. It's hard to be here, but I'm glad I'm here."

He looked down at her, proudly, she thought. "You *should* be here, Mary Anne," he said. "You're going to be okay."

"I know," she said. She felt like crying.

Janice, Beth, and Kelly all wrote her letters. She didn't know whether she was happy to know what was going on or depressed about how much she was missing. Everyone was going to a new disco, Danielle's in Farmingdale. Chuck wasn't going out with anybody—*shocked or what?!* Janice had almost no classes that semester: *The only one's I have are English and Social Studies to graduate.* Kelly and Phil were arguing but were still together. He bought her a gold birthstone ring that she picked out: *He's not too good with jewelry, so I pick my own stuff. . . . Oh yeah—are you ready to get shocked—Robert killed himself in the garage with the car running. . . . He was found on the garage floor, so they think he tried maybe to get out & he left a note saying he wanted his parents back together. . . . So how do you like the weather? . . . My car sucks on snow and ice. . . .*

"I still want it," Mary Anne admitted to Chrissy. The ban was still on, but they conspired to meet and talk secretly. She hadn't gotten high in a couple of months, since coming to Apple, but to her surprise, she wasn't over it. If someone had something, she would have eagerly taken it. Did the desire ever go away? Sometimes she missed it so much. She wouldn't admit it to anyone else but Chrissy. She didn't even have to say it for Chrissy to know. They could read each other's minds.

They recalled the times they got high together. They had to talk about it secretly because negative rapping carried heavy contracts. They were crimeys, breaking the rules together. When the ban was lifted they stuck to themselves, just the two of them, even wearing each other's clothes. They were like one person.

Then she got caught wearing Chrissy's belt.

"You're blowing on the tool of responsibility," Bobby Jo, a plumpish, dark-haired staff counselor scolded her. "Do you remember the five tools?"

Mary Anne struggled to remember: "Honesty, humility, sincerity, responsibility . . . *Shit,* she was blocking. What was the fifth one?

"Truthfulness?" Bobby Jo prompted.

"Truthfulness!"

"And the three D's?"

"Determination . . . direction . . . discipline," Mary Anne recited.

Bobby Jo reinstated the ban with Chrissy. "You're negatively reinforcing each other," she said.

Mary Anne was furious. She got up and moped outside by the parking lot, but Kevin, an upper-level, ordered her back on the porch. Residents couldn't just wander around.

"Fuck off," she said under her breath. She strolled back to the house with deliberate slowness and made a show of spitting on the ground.

Shit! Bobby Jo had spotted her and changed direction toward her. *Now what?* She spit on the ground again.

She already had one of the biggest contract folders. She practically collected behavior slips. She got them for talking about people behind their backs, negative rapping, singing forbidden acid rock songs, refusing to constructively criticize fellow residents in group, leaving a hot curling iron in her room, and telling a chief coordinator in front of the whole house to fuck off.

She looked and looked again. The boy was *cute!* She hadn't seen him before. Did he just come in? He was shortish, with a round pleasant face, deep-sunken brown eyes, and a spikey fuzzball crewcut. Sometimes they cut your hair when you got there, she knew. She took in his jeans, T-shirt, and leather jacket. There was something about him; she almost wanted to cuddle him. He was on the porch with some other kids, and she placed herself near him, guaranteeing they'd get into a conversation. "Hi," she said, "did you just get here?"

No, he said, he got there yesterday; he signed himself in . . . again. He'd been there before, spring of last year. He'd stayed six months. "Name's Alex," he said. He sounded a little pissed that he was back, she thought.

"I'm Mary Anne," she said. "You split?" she asked, curious.

Yeah, he said, a few times.

"A few times?"

"Three times," he said.

Three times! He had split three times? In six months?

No, he said, four times, actually. The fourth time they didn't take him back.

How'd he get back this time? she wanted to know.

He looked at her—why was she so curious?—but then he shrugged and said, "I don't know. I begged Bobby Jo." It embarrassed him to admit it, she thought. He had an attitude, like her.

"This your first time here?" he asked her.

"Yeah," she admitted, wondering if it sounded too nerdy. It would be better if she had split a few times, like him.

"What was your choice of drug?" he asked.

She shrugged. "I did blow," she said, "and other shit."

He nodded knowingly.

Bobby Jo seemed to come out of nowhere. "What's going on here?" she asked sharply. She pulled Mary Anne aside. "You're talking too much," she said. "Stay away from him." When she got back to the porch, he was gone.

She learned a little more about him in group: He grew up not far from her on the island, his parents were separated, he was smoking pot in the fifth grade, he dropped out of school in the ninth grade, he started tripping out on mesc, and then he free-based coke. He got all screwed up, then did crack in the city, stole stuff, lived on the street, and sold drugs in Brentwood. He told his mother he would either kill her or himself, and she called the cocaine hotline.

Crack! Crack hadn't been around when she started. She heard it really wasted you. It was just getting going when she got bad, and she never got into it. A little longer on the street, though, and she might have tried heroin.

"Hey, babes!"

It was a few days before Christmas when Chrissy caught up with her on the porch and slapped her on the back.

Mary Anne turned away. She didn't feel like talking.

"Hey, babes!" Chrissy said again. Mary Anne shielded a letter she was reading.

"Whatcha got?" Chrissy persisted. She walked around to see what she was holding, and Mary Anne pivoted numbly to block her.

"Hey, whatsa matter?"

Mary Anne walked away. She didn't feel like talking. Now now. Grandpa had sent her a poem.

Grandpa, what do you want for Christmas?
What do I want for Christmas, Please let me explain!
First and always you should never suffer any pain.
Always smile and stay as beautiful as you are right now!
Help those who need you, teach them, show them how.

Always be honest, never an untruth, not even a little lie—
And please let me be with you, if for some reason you
should cry!
Be fair and just to all your friends,
Believe in magic, talk to animals, and it's nice to pretend!
Love your father, it will last forever.
He'll always be there in good or bad weather!
Love Your God and pray to Him every night,
Because whatever is wrong, He'll make it right!
What I want for Christmas, that's easy to see—
Just love me Mary Anne, that's good enough for me.

It was the first Christmas she could ever remember not being
home.

"Make a run for Chrissy! All upper levels, make a run for Chrissy!"

It was a few days after Christmas. She was in the dining room,
suddenly aware of shouts and running feet. It made no sense to
her. She looked at Laura blankly across the lunch table. "What?"
she asked.

"It means look for Chrissy. Chrissy's missing."

Mary Anne slumped back hard against the metal folding chair.
Chrissy! But she had never said anything!

Mary Anne could follow the news bouncing through the dining
room.

"Chrissy split!"

"Who split?"

"Chrissy!"

"Chrissy? Chrissy split?"

28

T H E Y had failed, Barbara kept thinking after Mary Anne left for Apple. They had failed because they couldn't solve their own problem. They had to send Mary Anne away. They had to turn her over to *strangers*. It shamed her. As bad as it had gotten at home, she thought they'd be able to regain control. They were two adults, two *cops,* for God's sake. She was one teenage girl. How could they not be stronger than Mary Anne? But they hadn't been, she conceded wearily. They'd lost, Mary Anne had beaten them. And for that she felt guilty. They'd had to abandon her.

At the same time she felt relief, and guilt, too, over her relief. Of course she was relieved—the daily torture was over. Mary Anne was finally someplace where she couldn't hurt herself and the people around her. Barbara didn't have to stew, her stomach tense and sour, waiting for Mary Anne to burst in or sneak in, and for the battle to begin. They wouldn't have to lie awake nights wondering when the call from the police would come—a *final* call.

When exactly did it go wrong? she wondered. Was there a particular moment? Could they have done anything differently? At what point? Did it have anything to do with logic? Grace and Joe told her they were glad Mary Anne was getting help, she needed it. They didn't have to blame themselves, she and Patty, they'd done the right thing.

She wondered about the therapy. She wasn't a big believer in shrinks and counseling. Basically, people were what they were. You couldn't make them over. Not that she distrusted Apple. She liked the looks of it, and it had lots of spirit. But seeing all the wounded, desperate, eagerly hopeful families there made her want to cry. All those fucked-up kids and all those guilt-ridden parents, all whipping themselves with the same questions: How did it happen? Why did I fail?

Patty was manic. He raved to her about Apple, how good the place was. After the first visit he eagerly signed up to volunteer as a fund-raiser at Apple bingo games. He offered to donate the TV when Apple moved Mary Anne's adolescent program to a new residence that had been renovated nearby, on Lake Ronkonkoma. And he pledged the DeGregorios—all of them, his parents, his brother Ralph—to buying ads in the Apple magazine. But then, she saw, he tormented himself with doubts. Did he do the right thing? he asked her. Could they have done anything else? How could she answer him? She didn't know in her own mind.

The damage to their relationship had been done, she thought, and she wasn't sure it could ever be properly repaired. They had said terrible things to each other that would take a long time to forget. But they had to go on with their lives. They still loved each other. It would just take time to learn to respond tenderly to each other again; they'd almost forgotten how.

After Mary Anne was at Apple a few months, Family Court in Hauppauge called them in to set their contribution to her care. Mary was called in too. Shortly before, DeGregorio had phoned to tell her that Mary Anne had gone into treatment. She seemed to take the news with mild surprise but little other emotion, DeGregorio thought. Later, Mary wrote her daughter a short letter saying she was happy that Mary Anne had gone for help and that she had confidence Mary Anne would make it through fine, that she knew Mary Anne loved life too much to destroy herself. She wanted Mary Anne to know that she loved her, too, and missed her.

Mary Anne was escorted to the hearing in Family Court. They were just able to smile and say a quick hello. She looked good, Barbara thought, maybe a little better rested than on their first visit. They put them in different rooms—she and Patty in one room, Mary in another way down at the end of the corridor, and Mary

Anne somewhere else. They saw Mary in the distance, but she made no move toward them. Patty was just as glad. He had nothing to say to her.

A caseworker shuttling between the two rooms examined their pay stubs, W-2 forms, and estimates of their monthly expenses. Then they met with the hearing officer who found they could afford $250 a week toward Mary Anne's care.

Barbara was outraged. They couldn't afford a thousand a month, it would bankrupt them. They showed the hearing officer that the caseworker must have been looking at their gross pay, not their take-home. The hearing officer agreed, and he lowered the payment to $100 a week. Mary, who drove a school bus, was assessed $25. They got a book of coupons to send in with the weekly check. Together their contributions didn't cover the whole cost of keeping Mary Anne there, probably less than half. Apple would raise some of its own money, and the state would pay the difference.

Barbara knew they had to do it, but still, she thought, $400 would sting, it would be tight. That was money they couldn't use to go out, get their lives back together.

Patty was glum too. They'd be living from paycheck to paycheck. But, he reasoned, it would be easier knowing they were paying for Mary Anne to get well. He said he had read that it cost $40,000 to keep an inmate in state prison for a year. If Mary Anne weren't in Apple, that's where she'd be sooner or later. Apple, the alternative, was a lot cheaper. The government was getting a bargain.

Thanksgiving, 1988, came and went. It was a difficult time and the roughest on Patty, Barbara thought. They went to Joe and Anne's, as they usually did. Joe raised his glass in a poignant toast to his missing granddaughter. Patty kept saying it was just another day, that the celebration was only a custom, nothing special, as if to convince himself that Mary Anne's absence didn't hurt as much as it did. There had been no chance of getting her home for the holiday; home visits weren't allowed so soon. They'd heard almost nothing from her. She had sent only a few lines, to ask for a curling iron and some toiletries. Either they weren't allowing her to write, or she was finding it too difficult. Either way, it was torturing Patty,

Barbara knew, although she could see he tried to keep his own letters upbeat. They all ended similarly: *I hope to see you soon Sweetheart. Your still my little girl and always will be.*

She noticed that Patty had dug his barbells and dumbbells out of the basement and created a workout schedule with Ralph. Barbara wondered how long it would last this time. Men were always dead serious about building up their bodies—at least for a few weeks. Patty seemed to get interested in bodybuilding every year around the holidays, as if in penance. Then right after New Year's he promptly forgot about it again. There was one thing he didn't forget: He went regularly to the cemetery to visit Tommy's grave. He talked to Tommy all the time, Barbara knew.

December brought Mary Anne's first report card in the mail. It showed solid B-level work, a big improvement over her failing grades in Kings Park. Then a week before Christmas an envelope arrived with Mary Anne's familiar script. It was a silly card with a mocking rhyme and just a few scrawled words of greeting, but to Patty it was an eloquent affirmation: She was reaching out to them. He carried the card reverently next door where he and his mother oohed and aahed over it. Louis had dropped by, and after Patty showed it off to him, they sat in the living room talking about Mary Anne. For the first time Louis confessed that he had known Mary Anne took drugs; he had even been there when she'd gotten high.

"I don't know," Louis murmured. "I feel so guilty about everything."

Patty waved it off. What was past was past.

"I'm going to get screened, Patty," Louis said. "Who do I have to see there so I can visit her?"

Joe busied himself writing a poem to send to Mary Anne. He called it "Grandpa, What Do You Want for Christmas?" When he finished it, he read it to them before sealing the envelope.

On Christmas Eve the whole family reassembled as usual at Joe and Anne's for the traditional Italian feast, including seven kinds of seafood—flounder, shrimp, eel, scallops, octopus, squid, and bluefish. As was his custom, Joe preceded the meal with grace and a recitation of family events throughout the year just ending. He saluted his son Louis's success as a car salesman, his son Joey's househunting in Florida, and his grandson Joey's achievements on the baseball diamond. When he got to Mary Anne, tears glistened in his eyes. "Mary Anne is doing great," he said hoarsely. "We're so proud of her. The whole family is behind her."

DeGregorio thought of their little Christmas tree next door. He hadn't been sure he wanted a tree this year. It had been mainly for Tommy and Mary Anne, and now both of them were gone. But in the end he and Barbara agreed they'd get a small tree. Under it they put a few wrapped gifts for Mary Anne—a new pair of jeans, a sweater, and a jar of strawberry preserves.

Barbara couldn't help it, it was a reflex. She thought of Mary Anne back in the house and she tensed, her temples began to throb. It was a nippy Saturday morning in February 1989, nearly five months after Mary Anne entered Apple. She was coming back for her first home visit. Patty had driven to pick up her and her escort. Barbara wandered through the house, idly straightening up, moving things around that didn't need to be moved. She was jumpy.

Buddy sensed her first, scampering wildly to the door. She opened it and the furious tan whirlwind hurled himself at her, nearly bowling her over before streaking around and around her, legs pawing the air, tail thumping the ground, tongue slobbering. "Buddy! Buddy!" Mary Anne said. "Did you miss me, Buddy?" Barbara saw her ruffle his furry head, instinctively feeling for the hard, bony knob above his eyes.

"Hi," she said to Barbara, subdued, distant but polite. She walked over and gave Barbara a quick hug, brushing her cheek for a kiss. Barbara told herself to smile and hugged her back. The escort, a stunning, mocca-skinned girl, hung back self-consciously until Mary Anne introduced her. She was Gina, an upper-level.

Mary Anne said she'd show Gina the house, and Barbara watched Patty trail them, as if afraid to let Mary Anne out of his sight for even an instant. He was all over her, Barbara thought, too much.

They went next door for breakfast. Barbara was amazed to see that Anne had set out her finest china. The table was piled with sweet rolls and cheeses, salami, and loaves of crusty semolina bread. Joe and Anne made a huge fuss over Mary Anne, squeezing her cheeks and hugging and kissing her, until Barbara could see it was making her uncomfortable. When Ralph and Kathy came in, the hugging started all over.

"You're treating me like a guest," Mary Anne mumbled. "I'm not a guest, I live here."

After breakfast she ducked away. Mary Anne wanted to be by herself, Barbara thought. Everyone was all over her, and she needed some time alone in her old surroundings. And then the visit was over; it was only a few hours the first time. Patty drove Mary Anne and Gina to the Kings Park Plaza mall to pick out some candy and a can of Chock Full o'Nuts coffee to take back with her, symbols of her rising status at Apple.

Barbara was relieved when they left. Nobody had been relaxed because it was too artificial. There was too much to deal with, unfinished business from years of conflict. One visit wouldn't break the ice.

The day after the visit she and Patty drove down to Florida to visit Luisa. Patty did most of the driving, saying time and again how nice it was going to be when Mary Anne was out and had her license and they could take long trips together and share the driving. Barbara kept her skeptical thoughts to herself. Mary Anne still had an open charge on her record of driving without a license. That would have to be resolved first. It might be dropped if she completed the Apple program. *If.* Barbara had her doubts.

They found Luisa starved for news of the family. With the DeGregorio clan centered fifteen hundred miles north, she complained of feeling cut off and isolated. She was particularly hungry for news of Mary Anne.

Patty radiantly described her progress, her excellent grades, her joyous home visit.

Barbara wondered if he was deluding himself again. Was he in for another fall? But she allowed him his illusions, if that's what they were. She was hoping that he was right this time.

They drove back to New York in time to make their regular Wednesday family group. She and Patty took seats together on the couch in the TV room. Mary Anne stood at the far end with some of the other kids.

Bobby Jo, the dark-haired counselor with the no-nonsense air, picked out a small, skinny boy across the room to start the discussion.

"I've been here ten months," the boy said. "I started getting high at eleven on pot and alcohol. At thirteen, fourteen, I was using hallucinogens. Basically I had a need to fit into the crowd. I fed into negativity. I loved negative attention. There were a lot of broken promises in my family, divorce, death. I found what a good patch it is, drugs. I was asked to move out. I was kicked out. I was robbing my house a lot and stuff. It was very obvious. My family knew about it for years. I was dysfunctional." In the silence of the room he dropped his voice. "My mom is disabled from a stroke. I used to tease my mother. I slapped her a few times and stuff."

Barbara stiffened. A druggie who beat up his crippled mother. Terrific. She was always learning something new.

His visiting older brother nodded agreement. "He was always saying, 'Hit me, hit me,' the brother recalled. "He asked for it. I'd say, 'It's not worth it.' "

"It bothers me too, man," the younger boy agreed.

"Now you two," Bobby Jo commanded, "get up and hug each other."

Hesitantly, the two brothers navigated separate paths to the center of the room and embraced self-consciously.

"Things do get better," Bobby Jo said, to whoops of approval from the others. Barbara felt like cheering too.

"Now, Mary Anne," Bobby Jo said unexpectedly, "is there anything you want to say to your stepmother?"

The question caught Barbara off balance. She watched the circle of faces in the room swivel to Mary Anne, then turn to her.

"No," Mary Anne mumbled.

There was an expectant silence. Bobby Jo waited. No one spoke.

"Well, there's something I want to say to you." Barbara surprised herself by speaking. The words just popped out, and suddenly every eye was riveted on her. This was the first time, Barbara realized, that she had said anything in family group. Patty had always told her that she didn't have to come every time, that he could do it. She always came, but she never wanted to say anything. Until now.

She stared hard-eyed at Mary Anne. Only a slight quaver in her voice betrayed her emotion. "You never talk to me," Barbara complained. "Every time I come here I'm pissed off because you never talk to me. You talk to your father as if I'm not here. I know there's a lot of bad stuff between us, but how come you never talk to me?

You treat me like a dummy." She paused. Mary Anne looked shocked, Barbara thought. The room was completely still.

"I don't know how to act around you," Barbara continued. "I don't even know you. You're a stranger to me. I'm going to have to try to get to know you as a person. I can't think of you as my daughter." Then she stopped as suddenly as she'd started. She had said what she had to say. There wasn't anything more.

The eyes shifted to Mary Anne. "I . . . I feel uncomfortable," she said, "because you're not . . . my real mother."

She went mute.

"Mary Anne," Bobby Jo said quietly, "go over there and hug Barbara."

"No!" Mary Anne shouted.

"Go ahead," Bobby Jo urged. "Act as if."

Bobby Jo turned to Barbara. "Stand up and hug Mary Anne."

Slowly, Barbara got up and walked to the middle of the room. Mary Anne walked toward her, and then they met. Barbara put her arms around Mary Anne and felt Mary Anne embrace her mechanically. There was no warmth.

Barbara leaned back and looked at her. Her face was stony. It seemed to say that she was being forced, that this wasn't her idea. Barbara let go and walked self-consciously back to her seat. Not one of Bobby Jo's wiser moves, she thought.

She was having a tough time there, Barbara knew. She and Patty had had talks with Lisa Leshaw, Lisa with her tangled mass of blue-black ringlets, a girlish hairstyle that along with her hip wire-rimmed glasses made her look more like one of the kids in her program than director of the new adolescent facility that would be opening in November.

Although Lisa sometimes was mistaken for a resident because of her youthful looks, she didn't delude herself. She wasn't one of them, and she wasn't their friend. They didn't need her for a buddy. They needed somebody bigger and smarter and older to look up to, to set the standards, to show them that they were accountable for their behavior. That was Lisa. And, she said, the sooner Mary Anne got it, the better it would be for her.

Barbara liked Lisa, who seemed to know what she was doing with the kids. Lisa said she wanted to keep the program humanistic, get away from humiliation. The kids had already humiliated themselves enough living on the street, eating from garbage pails, selling their bodies for dope. They didn't need lessons in humiliation, they didn't need to be shamed more. They could learn to break dependencies by recognizing and avoiding destructive patterns of behavior. It had been shown to work. No one had any sure-fire cures, but this, she believed, was as good as any.

There were no easy answers, Lisa said, nothing to easily explain why one kid fell victim to drugs and another didn't. A million different variables applied. Some children of alcoholics turned to drugs, others didn't, and she didn't know why. What about the addicts she saw who came from normal, happy homes? There was no standard progression either. Some kids started with drinking, others went straight to crack. She had no idea why. She knew that the country was in massive denial, refusing to face the huge dimensions of the problem. Every community had a drug problem, but how many treatment places did you see? The country was prepared for a nuclear war but vulnerable to drugs. Every kindergartener, she thought, should be warned about drugs; it was never too early.

Lisa said she had a good idea where Mary Anne's troubles lay, somewhere in the relationship with her father. She was a typical adolescent, Lisa said, trying to separate from the outside world. In this case, Mary Anne was deeply attached to her father. She had to learn to let go. She wasn't letting anyone else get close to her. Lisa thought of Mary Anne as the Dear Abby of Apple, always listening to everyone else's troubles, commenting on their lives but rarely opening up or imparting much of her own story. That would have to change if she was going to recover.

Mary Anne struck a responsive chord in Lisa; she knew something of what Mary Anne was going through, she said. While she had never been an addict, had never even fooled around with drugs—one of the few among the Apple staff whose knowledge of drugs was academic—had come from a stable home, and had no kids of her own, she, too, had been extremely close to her father. She'd been working at Apple more than a year when her father was stricken with leukemia and lymphoma. She quit Apple to nurse him, going to the hospital every day for seven months, and then the doctors detected a remission. Elated, she bought her father a new apartment, furnished it, stocked the refrigerator with food for his homecoming, and then he died. Lisa returned to Apple.

Mary Anne had accumulated a thick file of contracts, Lisa told them. Some of them were routine, infractions that couldn't go unanswered but didn't amount to much. Still, she said, it wasn't hard to decipher the pattern. Mary Anne had a ways to go. She still wasn't getting it. She had worked her way up several levels, reaching as high as coordinator, but then she always got knocked down. She was seething with resentments. She was a crimey, both she and Chrissy, and they were tight.

Chrissy had come back after her split and then nearly split a second time. Mary Anne had seen her heading for the road and started to run after her, but fell down the steps of the porch and sprained her ankle, putting her on crutches for several weeks. Her pain hadn't improved Mary Anne's mood. Because she couldn't do much else, she'd been given light duty. One of her jobs was to go to the pay phone by the lake and call in orders of garbage bags for the house. She sneaked in calls to her friends. She had even tried to hobble off the property on her crutches. An upper-level caught her. "Who's going to pick you up, you idiot?" he said.

Lisa said she detected a deterioration every time Mary Anne came back from a home visit. She said she had talked to Mary Anne about it. Was Mary Anne trying to tell her that she wanted to lose her home visits? She could always tell when something was wrong with Mary Anne by her face and the way she talked, Lisa said. Mary Anne had to think about what was going on in her life. In the meantime, her home visits were discontinued.

In the eight months that Mary Anne had been at Apple, Barbara never wrote to her, although she accompanied Patty on visits and diligently attended all the family group sessions. Since Mary Anne's departure Patty had been asking her to write, at least a few lines, but writing, as Barbara saw it, was different from visiting. There was something sacred about the written word. Letters had to come from the heart; otherwise, they were penmanship exercises, hypocritical lies, meaningless. Barbara never bowed to convention. Why would she write a letter she didn't feel like writing?

Patty's prodding only strengthened her resistance. She was stubborn that way. The more he urged her to write, the more distasteful the task became. She would do it, she told him, when the time came.

"The time for what?" he pressed.

"When I'm ready," she said.

Finally he stopped asking.

She had been angry at Mary Anne for a long time, angry at the way she had lied to them, manipulated her father, and nearly broken up their marriage. But with time her resentment gave way to glimmers of pity and compassion. She had never quite understood what drugs did to people. As a cop she had worked the other end and saw them as perps, lowlifes, targets to be busted. But at Apple she'd had a chance to hear their stories, see them as human beings. And Mary Anne was one of them. Barbara began to realize how difficult it must have been for her to surrender to treatment and how hard it must be for her now in there day in and day out. She was a stubborn girl, Barbara reflected, but now for the first time she thought maybe that was good. Barbara was stubborn too. It was good to be stubborn if it gave you strength to change your life and endure hardship.

Barbara always loved the change of seasons, particularly the stirrings of spring. It was something deep-seated in her, something intuitive. Nature was reawakening, and she also felt a flush of optimism, a promise that the world would be renewed. They had made it through another winter and into a new season of warmth and sunlight. Hope was alive. And so one lovely May afternoon, without Patty's pushing her, she selected a few sheets of her stationery and a pen, settled herself in a chair by the pool, and began writing.

May 21, 1989

Dear Mary Anne,

Hi, I hope this letter finds you well. Ever since you went to Apple, your father has asked me to write to you, and I always said no. I said I will write when I feel in my heart that it's the right time. That's what I feel now. I went to the cemetery with Daddy yesterday, and of course I cannot feel what you and him feel, but I have pain for both of you, and for Tommy too. People say that time heals all wounds, but I think this is a wound of the soul that you will all carry all of your life. I was sorry you lost your visit, because I know you really wanted to be home yesterday.

I'm sitting out in the back yard. Its a really nice day today. I just gave Buddy a bath and he's lying next to me, drying in the sun. We cleaned all the back yard furniture and Daddy planted tons of flowers in the barrels. We may go for a walk on the beach later when the sun goes down.

Mary Anne, there are so many things I want to say to you but I never know where to start. I am just beginning to see the fine person that was buried under all your confusion, and I am proud to know you. I feel a trust in you that I never felt before and I feel easy being with you. I am twenty years older than you, but you know, I am learning things from you. Maybe in some ways we can benefit from each other's experiences.

I really hope that you will have longer visits when Aunt Luisa is here. Your cousins are growing up so fast, and I know you want to spend some time with them.

My mother gave me some money to buy you a birthday present. She asks about you all the time, so maybe when you get another visit you can get another outfit at the flea market.

Please find a little time to write to your father. He misses you a lot, and a letter from you is more important than you know. You are the light of his life.

Well, I'll see you Wednesday.

Love you & miss you

Barbara

29

THERE was her name! It was written on a tag and inserted high up on a wall chart in the Apple corridor, at the coordinator level. DeGregorio had been used to seeing her name at the bottom, at level one. Now she was even above supervisor. He reached a finger up to touch it, to make sure it was real.

He joined Barbara outside, and they wandered around looking for Mary Anne before family group started. She was freer now as an upper-level. Her time was pretty much her own. They found her in the parking lot. In a sweatshirt and jeans, she looked relaxed, even radiant, he thought. She threw her arms around his neck for a big hug and kiss. She turned to Barbara and, barely hesitating, embraced her too.

"Congratulations, coordinator," DeGregorio said, grabbing and squeezing her arm. "Ready for family group?"

"Dad," Mary Anne whispered urgently, "you know who's here? Joanne!"

Yeah, he had heard she was coming, he said. He wasn't sure if she was there yet. Amazing, wasn't it? His cousin, daughter of his late uncle Mimi, in the same place with her? Joanne was twenty-eight, twelve years older than Mary Anne. "Did you meet her yet?"

"Yeah," Mary Anne said. "I wasn't really supposed to talk to her, but Londi said I could. I didn't even know her, Dad. She knew all about me, she said, like DeGregorios should stick together. I felt weird, like bad for her."

It was funny, he said, the way things worked sometimes.

They walked arm in arm to the TV room and took seats together on the couch where a few months before, he remembered, Mary Anne had resisted Bobby Jo's order to hug Barbara. Now, he realized happily, they were sitting side by side, and Mary Anne wasn't a lower-level anymore. Having been there a year, she was a veteran, a coordinator, and soon she might even graduate.

When the meeting ended, they drifted out with the other family members and found themselves squeezing through a doorway with Alex's grandparents. In all the groups, it seemed, they and the Strazzantis were somehow always together. They were sweet people, DeGregorio thought, very decent, and like them—and like all parents there—were without a clue as to why life had taken them on this sad path. DeGregorio didn't know exactly why Alex's parents weren't there, but he knew enough to figure out that must be part of the problem. The grandfather was gentle and courtly. His name was Alex too. He reminded DeGregorio of his father. His wife was called Princess. DeGregorio didn't know if that was her name, nickname, or title, but it suited her, he thought. She was Greek and also quiet but genuinely warm. Barbara had been particularly drawn to her, maybe because they were both reserved.

In family group DeGregorio had learned something of their grandson's story, dribbled out in somewhat shy, self-conscious narrations. It wasn't so different from Mary Anne's. His parents had separated when he was twelve. An only child, he had stayed with his mother. They lived in Brentwood, not ten minutes from Kings Park. Like Mary Anne, he smoked pot in junior high but then dropped out in ninth grade and started doing mescaline and coke and then crack. Thank God that Mary Anne never got on crack. Alex had been at Apple before, DeGregorio remembered. He'd split just about the time Mary Anne arrived and returned after she'd been there awhile. He knew they'd gotten to know each other there. He kind of liked Alex, although his story of living on the street, selling drugs, and stealing painted an ugly picture. But after listening to dozens of such stories, each one worse than the last, DeGregorio had stopped dwelling on the details. They were all basically the same anyway. What was important was that these kids were turning their lives around, or trying to.

Alex's grandparents also seemed to like Mary Anne. They always asked about her when they ran into him and Barbara at Apple. Once Princess said with a smile, "Let's hope she doesn't wind up with him."

As her father and Barbara got ready to leave, Mary Anne kissed them good-bye. She had to go boss people around, she joked, that's what coordinators did. Actually, she said, after the families left she had to help run a house meet for rap, then get everyone cleaned up and ready for bed.

Rain was pelting down. Mary Anne walked them to the porch and stood chatting with Barbara. He went back to take another look at the wall chart. Yep, her name was still there, way up near the top.

"Hi, Mr. DeGregorio!"

He turned, surprised. He had been so engrossed that he hadn't seen anyone behind him.

"Brad?" DeGregorio said distractedly, recognizing the polite, sandy-haired young man from previous visits. He dropped his arm for a handshake. "I was just admiring Mary Anne's name up there."

"Yeah, she got moved up to coordinator. She deserves it."

"She sure does," DeGregorio said. He stepped back to make a better appraisal of Brad. His hair was cropped short and neatly combed, and he wore a pale blue sweater under a tan windbreaker. "Looking good, Brad," he said. Brad beamed. DeGregorio liked the young man's forthright manner, his poise and willingness to confront some bad mistakes—the heavy drinking that had led him to pot and then a coke habit he'd bankrolled by stealing his father's insurance check and running away to Florida.

"When are you moving to Ronkonkoma?"

"I'm not going, Mr. DeGregorio. I'm staying at Apple One. But rap's moving out in November."

"Oh, yeah," DeGregorio remembered, "that's what I heard too." Brad was a little older. It was the teen group that would be moving out to separate quarters in a newly renovated old hotel on the lake about fifteen minutes' drive away. He and Barbara, along with other parents, had toured the new place a few weeks before, during the final stages of renovation. They'd found something eerily antiseptic about the glowing powder blue walls, sparkling gray tiles, grainy wood bunk beds, and blinding fluorescent lights, all so silent, bright, clean, and cheerful, as if awaiting something other than a houseful of drug-addicted children.

"Uh, you know . . ." Brad seemed reluctant to say good-bye. He seemed to have something else on his mind.

DeGregorio turned to him quizzically.

Brad shuffled his feet. "Uh . . . I like your daughter."

DeGregorio looked at him blankly. What was he trying to say? Was he asking for permission for a hookup with Mary Anne? What was he, crazy? He knew the rules. They had to learn to live like brothers and sisters, watch out for one another. They weren't there for a good time, they were wounded people who had to heal. That was what Apple's ban on physical or emotional relationships was all about. You couldn't help anyone else until you could help yourself. Romance could come later. They'd have a lifetime ahead of them for that. Now if Brad even laid a finger on her . . . DeGregorio tried to smile coolly. "That's nice, Brad. I like her too. Show her you like her by going through the program." He patted Brad patronizingly on the shoulder and walked off to join Barbara.

He was half asleep already, imagining Maine. They owed themselves a little vacation, they'd decided. They hadn't gone anywhere except that quick trip to Florida since Mary Anne had started Apple. They'd take a week and drive up to Maine. It would be chilly there, but so what? They'd bring warm clothes. It would be cozy. With luck they'd still catch some of the fall colors. They needed time alone, and it would be good to get away.

They'd both been working hard. DeGregorio was marking his first year in Queens Robbery after three years in Manhattan Robbery. He hadn't had a breather. It was the nature of police work: one crisis after another, crime being perhaps the city's last growth industry. He'd no sooner finished the Ridgenarc case and made detective than he was moved out of narcotics to robbery where his first big case was to flush out some modern-day urban highwaymen who were holding up horse-and-buggy passengers in Central Park. He and a partner had just collared that gang when he was called to dust off his old Pasquale Greco identity and go back undercover to meet two Rockland County neo-Nazis who were peddling guns and pipe bombs to blow up Jews. He didn't know anything about bombs, he told them. He dealt in whatever could be marketed— guns, drugs; he was a middleman. He first met them near the heliport at Thirty-fourth Street and the East River. He bought two of the eight-inch-long pipe bombs for $200 each. He arranged to meet them again a few weeks later in the Shea Stadium parking field where he bought five more. The last time he met them in the parking lot of the LaGuardia Sheraton near the airport, where shotgun-toting federal agents burst out to make the arrests.

Queens Robbery had meant another change of pace. Suddenly he was back at the one-oh-nine in Flushing where he'd started out in uniform in 1973. But now he roamed all over Queens tracking robbery teams. Whatever you called it, though, it was still about drugs. They needed money for drugs, which was why they did the robberies.

About the time he started at Queens Robbery, Barbara was moved to Queens sex crimes, based at borough headquarters in the one-twelve in Forest Hills. She was working with little kids who had been abused, raped, or beaten. Here, too, he knew from Barbara's stories, it often came down to drugs. Parents on a downer, babies born addicted who couldn't stop crying. Where did it ever end?

Their schedules kept them busy. They didn't have as much time for each other as they would have liked, but the time they did spend together was all the more precious. After all they had been through, they'd grown closer than ever, he thought. They didn't dwell on the past. Maybe that was the key to their happiness. There was no need to rake it all up again. She never said, "I told you so," and for that he was grateful. They picked up their lives, and their love had sprung up, renewed. It had never gone away.

He heard Barbara pad into the bedroom. He was waiting for the weight of her body to sink down familiarly on the opposite side of the bed when she spoke instead, a rushed jumble of words he had trouble understanding.

"Patty, I found a lump under my arm."

He stirred awake. "Huh?" he said foggily. "What does that mean?"

"I'm going to have to see a doctor," she said.

He was trying to focus his thoughts. Something was telling him this was alarming. He felt his heart starting to race. He was suddenly wide awake. Don't panic, he told himself, don't worry her. "It's probably nothing," he said. "It could be lots of different things." He soothed her into sleep; they would see about it in the morning.

He woke up nervous, tense, and preoccupied, remembering what it was that was gnawing at him. She told him how she found it. She had been in the bathroom drying her hair; her right arm was up, and she was reaching for a towel when she saw the lump under her right arm. She felt it, and it was definitely a lump.

He thought maybe she should call the doctor and take the day off, but she said no, she had to go in. She'd call from the office.

She needed a biopsy. He took the next day off and drove her to the Surgery Center in Smithtown. She was taken into a doctor's office, while he was stuck in the waiting room. He had that dizzy feeling—what did they call it?—when you thought you'd been there before. He realized he was thinking about Tommy. It was like this with Tommy. But then he told himself this wasn't like Tommy, this was completely different. Barbara was going to be all right. He read some magazines, went outside for a smoke, and made himself talk to the receptionist, just to have someone to talk to. It seemed to take forever.

Finally the surgeon came out. "I don't like what I found," he said simply.

"Is . . . is it cancer?"

"Let's wait," he said noncommittally, "until the lab results come back." They'd have the results soon, maybe in an hour, he said.

DeGregorio tried to go in to see her, but the nurse said she was sleeping. Barbara didn't do well under anesthesia, he knew. When she'd had appendicitis years ago, before he knew her, she'd been anesthetized and sick for a while.

He was at her bedside in recovery. She was still asleep when the surgeon phoned him there with the results. "It's malignant," he said.

DeGregorio swayed. He felt like punching the wall, kicking and screaming. "Are you sure?" he bellowed into the phone. *"Are you sure?"* Barbara stirred; his yelling had woken her. A nurse stepped quickly between him and the bed, maybe to distract Barbara, he thought, or else to deaden his voice so that she couldn't hear what he was saying and be upset.

"Do you want me to tell her?" the surgeon asked.

"I'll tell her," he said. He didn't know how, but he'd think of a way.

She slept during most of the ride home. She was still drugged and nauseous. He was glad she wasn't asking him any questions. Let her sleep. It was hard enough to keep control of his own savage thoughts. He couldn't face having to put on a calm appearance for her. My God, he thought, what was it with everyone close to him? Did it ever end? When they got home, he carried her to bed, and she moaned and collapsed into a deep sleep.

He went to sit at the kitchen table. He just wanted to sit quietly and think—no, *not* think, just sit there and not think. He was still in the kitchen a few hours later when he heard her coming down the stairs. He jumped up to see if she needed help.

She was walking slowly but in control. "What did the doctor tell you?" she asked.

He struggled to neutralize his expression, to figure out how to tell her, but he realized immediately that it was useless, that she could read everything in his face.

"He . . . he wants to have more tests," he said.

"Tests?" she asked. "Tests for what?" Then she said, "I know, it's cancer." She had heard him in the recovery room, she'd figured it out.

He didn't answer. She was crying. He just stood there with a dumb, blank expression on his face and started crying too.

"That's all he does, breast surgery?" DeGregorio asked. "Unbelievable."

Barbara had called Mike's wife, Francine, a nurse at a leading hospital in Manhattan. Barbara had been ready to go ahead with the surgeon who performed the biopsy, let him do the mastectomy, but Francine urged her to get a second opinion. She had a lot of good contacts and came up with a popular specialist at her hospital, a surgeon who operated only on breast cancers. She made an appointment for Barbara. DeGregorio was surprised. He didn't realize it had become that big a specialty.

He took the day off and drove Barbara in for a diagnosis. He waited outside the office. When she came out she said she was impressed. He'd felt the lump and knew just what to do; she had complete confidence in him. She made an appointment for the surgery; there was no time to waste.

DeGregorio was eager to meet the doctor and was also impressed. He sounded as if he knew what he was doing. He was a short man, maybe only five feet, no bigger than the cardiac surgeon who had operated on Tommy.

It was moving along quickly now, he felt. There seemed to be no time to mope, just to act. Barbara had a healthy, positive attitude and wanted to get it over with. That was Barbara's way, he realized proudly. She didn't like to hash over things but was strongly practical and unsentimental when she had to be. Once she made up her mind, that was it. Her optimism was catching, and he felt hopeful too.

They had to tell Mary Anne, he thought. He called Apple and arranged to come by with Barbara to give her the news. It was no problem setting up an unscheduled visit because she was now a coordinator.

Tony Cicerani met them in in Bobby Alberti's office. Tony, a tall, mellow, soulful staff counselor, was going to be Lisa Leshaw's deputy at the new adolescent facility set to open in a couple of weeks. Mary Anne, who must have been taken out of class, was there when they walked in. She looked confused, DeGregorio thought. "Your father and Barbara have something to tell you," Tony said and left them alone.

She looked at them searchingly. "What's going on?" she asked.

He was thinking of a way to ease into it. "Uh, we have something to tell you," he began haltingly. "I have cancer," Barbara said. "I'm going to be going to the hospital."

Barbara looked as if she was struggling to keep control. He saw Mary Anne's face contort. She was crying.

"Dad, is she going to be all right?" He had picked Mary Anne up at Apple to drive her to the hospital to visit Barbara. Tony said that it would be no problem, that she could take the day. She was a coordinator and would soon be considered for reentry.

"I don't know, sweetheart," he said. "We have to hear what the doctor says."

Barbara had had the operation two days before. He had driven her in, stopping to pick up Grace on the way to the city. Barbara didn't talk much. He knew she didn't want chatter at a time like this; she just wanted him there as a strong presence. Francine, who met them at the hospital, was a lifesaver; they'd never forget what she did for them. She was working that day, along with Barbara's cousin's wife Adrienne, who was a nurse in the Bronx and had volunteered to spend the night at her bedside. He needed their support; he was worried about the anesthesia, the operation, everything.

They prepared her for surgery and put them in a special waiting area. He'd never seen a waiting room so well equipped: There were magazines, newspapers, a TV, a coffee machine, and a phone. He was glad that Grace was there, someone to talk to. It made the time go faster.

Suddenly the doctor was there saying it went well, that she'd done fine. He had removed the breast and nine lymph nodes. "Did you get it all?" he asked. The doctor said he thought so. It went very well, but they'd have to see, one step at a time. Could he see her? he asked. He wanted to see her right away.

He had to wait until they brought her to recovery. She was sleeping when he came in. He wanted to wait for her to waken, but she kept sleeping. Finally Adrienne said it would be a while and he should go home. Barbara would call him when she woke up. He drove Grace back and then drove home.

The phone rang a few hours later.

"Hi, Patty?" She sounded muffled, out of it.

"How are you doing?" he asked. "How do you feel?"

"Okay," she said dully. "I'm tired."

"Does it hurt?" he asked.

"A little sore," she said.

"I love you," he said. "Get some sleep. I'll see you tomorrow."

"Okay," she said. "Love you."

"Dad," Mary Anne asked, "remember Joanne?" They were driving to the hospital to see Barbara, getting closer to the city, and the morning traffic was backing up.

He nodded, relieved to break the chain of his grim thoughts. "She split."

He knew that, he told her. In the middle of everything, Joanne had called him from a phone booth outside Apple. He had picked her up, drove her to the house, and they talked. She didn't want to go back. She wanted to go home. He put her on the train back to Brooklyn.

She nodded thoughtfully. "It happens," she said. Then she said, "Can I tell you something? You remember Brad?"

Sure he remembered Brad. They'd just seen him there. What about him?

"We hooked up."

Oh, my God, he thought! *Did she . . . did they . . .* He was afraid to ask. What if they got caught?

"But where do you . . ."

"We find places to, like, talk, be alone, in the van."

"In the van!"

"We don't go all the way, Dad," she said. "We just like to, you know, be together." Then she said, "You're not going to say anything? Please, Dad."

He was shocked. This was going on there, and nobody knew about it?

Other kids were also hooking up and not giving up their guilt, she said. "You want to know something else?"

He wasn't sure he did. "What?" he asked cautiously.

"You know Ray? He's a chief now."

DeGregorio knit his brow trying to think. There was a Ray, an ex-junkie he had met at an Apple softball game in the summer. He had pointed out Mary Anne and said, "Take care of my little girl."

"Yeah. He, like, kissed me."

"He *like* kissed you? Did he kiss you, or didn't he kiss you?" He was nearly yelling now, he couldn't help it.

"He kissed me, but he didn't really kiss me." She must have seen his puzzled face. "He tried to kiss me, but I wouldn't let him."

Oh, my God! What the fuck was going on there? Had Ray misinterpreted him? *Take care of my little girl?* Oh, Jesus Christ! "Where was this?" he demanded. "When?"

"In the coordinator's office," she said, "a few days ago." She'd been in there doing some paperwork. He must have seen her through the window, she said. He came in, closed the door, and tried to kiss her.

"Just like that? Did you encourage him? You must have encouraged him."

"No, Dad. I thought he was my friend. He always said he liked me. I was a little afraid of him. We had guilt together, like he knew some of the stuff I was doing. He let me get over, he let me slide."

"So he knows about Brad?"

"That's another thing," she said. "He knows. He's hassling Brad, loading him down with contracts."

Unbelievable, he thought. His daughter is having a thing with this guy, another guy who is after her is practically blackmailing her over it, and this is happening in the middle of a treatment center where all they talk about is honesty.

"Did you tell anyone?" he asked.

"No."

"Not Bobby, not Logan?"

"No. I'm not going to get in trouble. Just don't say anything."

"Did you and Ray ever . . ." He was getting afraid to ask anything.

"No, Dad," she said. "He never talks dirty, nothing about sex or anything."

"Well," he muttered, "that's something."

"He wants to marry me."

"He wants to marry you?"

"Calm down, will you, Dad. I said I didn't like him."

"Yeah, but you also said he tried to kiss you."

"You said you wouldn't say anything," she said. "You promised."

He grunted.

"What do you mean, she's not down for a visit?"

He heard Barbara on the phone and looked up surprised. She was home now, recuperating, and was doing well. Mary Anne was due for a regular home visit the following weekend. It would be nice for her to see Barbara at home, but it sounded as if they were telling Barbara that she wasn't coming. Why not, he wondered. Barbara hung up and said she didn't know. The kid she spoke to at the desk didn't know. All he saw was that she wasn't down for a weekend visit. DeGregorio was disappointed. As a coordinator she was coming home just about every other weekend. He would ask her when he saw her at the next family group.

On the following Wednesday, leaving Barbara home, he drove to his first group session in the new adolescent quarters. In contrasst to their pre-opening visit, the place was pulsing with life. Kids crowded the porch, and the driveway was thronged with milling family members and staff.

When he found Mary Anne, he hugged her tightly.

"Are you mad at me?" she asked.

"I'm not mad at you, sweetheart," he said. "What happened with your visit?"

"I have to work on several things," she said. "I have to work on my temper. I have to learn how to control it. I have to work on my ties with you. They're too strong. We should be close, but in a different way."

"That's okay," he said, comforting her. "I've been your mother and father for a long time. We have this closeness that is okay but not necessarily normal."

"It's just coming out now," she said. "They're telling me I have to associate with other people in the human race. I can't just have one person to confide in."

"You can't put me on a pedestal," DeGregorio agreed. Then he asked, "How's Brad?" He didn't go with her to the new adolescent house, he remembered.

She paused. "Brad split," she said. He'd had it with Ray; he couldn't take it anymore.

"You feel bad?" he asked her.

"Yeah, a little." Then she said, "You know, Mom came to get screened."

"She did?" He was surprised. Mary going to see Mary Anne at Apple? "So, did you see her?"

"No," Mary Anne said. "She came here, but I told them I didn't want to see her."

He was silent a moment. He thought he could understand her anger. "So," he said, "what happened last week?"

"I was talking to my therapist—you know, Jennifer. I had to sign this form. I used Jennifer's pen to sign the form, and I wasn't thinking. I walked off with the pen. I didn't steal it, it was a mistake."

"So?"

"Jennifer came out, 'I misplaced my pen,' she said. 'Maybe one of you kids took it.' I panicked. I didn't confess. I thought I'd get consequences. Then one of the other kids said, 'Mary Anne, didn't you have a pen?' 'Yeah, here's the pen! I didn't steal it!' 'Nobody said you did.' I went to Jennifer's office and blew up. I lost my visit. When I found out I lost my visit, I went into Lisa's office and cursed her out. Lisa said, 'Now you're going back to level one.' "

"You're back to level one?"

She nodded. DeGregorio was stunned.

He tried to put it in perspective. "In the real world if you walk into your boss's office and curse him, you're out of a job."

"I failed to apply the tool of truth," Mary Anne agreed. "For a while, Dad, we're not going to see each other. We're just going to write."

DeGregorio tried to mask his disappointment. "Whatever's best, sweetheart," he said, turning away and blinking fast.

Another Christmas was coming, her second at Apple, he reflected gloomily. Every time things got better they got worse. He was worried about Barbara too. She'd started chemotherapy. She went in on alternating weeks for big doses and small doses, injections of cancer-killing poison that left her wrung-out and retching with nausea. Something in the drug stimulated her appetite, made her hungry, like marijuana. She felt like eating, but then her body couldn't digest the food and she threw up. The doctors were satisfied, but they wanted to make sure the cancer wouldn't spread. Grimly, week after week, he nursed her through it. She was starting to lose her hair.

One day, recovering from another treatment, she felt better, so he drove her to her parents'. It was her sister Kathy's birthday, and they were having a little family celebration. He dropped her off and made a run over to his robbery squad in Flushing. On his phone was a taped message: Call Gina at Apple.

Puzzled, he called.

"Oh, Mr. DeGregorio," she said, "I'm glad we got you. Mary Anne split."

30

"GET in the chair! Get—in—the—chair!" Bobby Jo was bearing down the corridor, walking past the office, yelling. Mary Anne turned around and looked behind her. Who was she yelling at? They locked eyes. *She was yelling at her!* "Why?" she stammered. "What happened?"

"You know why!" Bobby Jo shouted. "Give up your guilt! Now!" Jimmy, a chief, was right behind her. "Right! Sit in the chair!" he echoed. She panicked. She could blow, she could get the hell out of there. Shooed upstairs, she dropped into a chair in a deserted corridor by the girls' rooms and took the paper and pen he thrust at her. What was she supposed to write? Everything?

Shaken, she looked around. No one. That's what they did, put you in an empty corridor where you couldn't see anybody or talk to anybody. They really made you sweat. But why? Did somebody give her up? Who? She had no one to ask. It suddenly hit her: *Fran!* It could have been Fran. It probably wasn't Bill or Gary. Fran knew about Brad. She was one of the crimeys. Although she didn't have a hookup, she did other shit. She could have given her up. She'd bet it was Fran. She sat there wondering what was next. Would they have a big house meeting? She'd pull a heavy contract for sure. She couldn't be dropped any lower; she was already back to level one. She toyed with the pen and wondered how much to admit.

Suddenly there was a deafening clang near her, and she jumped out of the chair. Clang! Clang! Clang! The fire gong! Was it a fire? No, probably just a drill. She'd heard they were going to have a drill.

Glad for the excuse to leave her chair, she took the stairs down. On the boys' floor she saw Bill and Gary. Them too! They must have gotten all the crimeys. She wasn't supposed to talk to anyone, but it was a fire drill. She asked Bill, "Who told?"

"I think Fran," he whispered. *Shit!* So it was Fran! Fran knew everything. She was really fucked.

Outside she lined up on the lawn with the others. It was a nasty December afternoon, and a frigid drizzle had swept in from Lake Ronkonkoma. Shivering in her sweatshirt, she thought of what awaited her after the fire drill and made up her mind in an instant. *Fuck this!* She was getting out of there. She wasn't going to put up with this. When the safety bell rang, she didn't go back to the chair but went straight to her room, threw a few things into her big black pocketbook, and walked out quickly. She wanted to get off the property before anyone saw her or could stop her. Once she was off the property she was safe. They couldn't force her back. She knew there was a pay phone at the lake, and she knew who to call.

DeGregorio heard the words, but they didn't immediately register. *Split!* He was crushed. What did he do now?

There was an embarrassed silence on the line. Gina probably didn't know what to say, he realized. She had just gone through the program herself and was working in the office now. "Tell you what, Gina," he said, nervously rummaging for a cigarette, "I'm going home. I'll talk to you later."

Who was around? The sergeant. "Sarge," he said, "I really have to go." He said it was a problem with his daughter.

The sergeant waved him out.

Before leaving he called Barbara at Grace and Joe's. "Mary Anne split," he said huskily. "I'm heading home."

"I'll meet you there," Barbara said.

He barely got in the door when the phone rang. He snatched it up. "Yeah."

"Dad?"

"Mary Anne! Where are you?"

She ignored the question. "I split," she said. "I don't know . . . what—"

"Mary Anne," he broke in, "I want to speak to you in person. You have to give me that."

She was quiet on the line. Then she said, "I'll call you back."

"Mary Anne, don't play little bullshit games with me. I'm not going to wait here forever. You know what I expect from you."

She said nothing. He hung up angrily and paced the house furiously until Barbara came home.

They sat down at the kitchen table. "Okay, Patty," Barbara said, "this is the plan. Very simple. Mary Anne has to go back to Apple. It has to be our mutual decision, and we have to stick to it."

"Yeah," he said, "I guess so." He had been thinking that Mary Anne had been at Apple nearly fifteen months. Wasn't that enough? Was she supposed to stay there forever?

Barbara seemed to sense that he was wavering. "Patty, listen," she said slowly, as if he were a child and she had to explain it very carefully or he wouldn't understand. "I've had two chemotherapy treatments so far. My hair is starting to fall out. I'm going to get a lot sicker and weaker as time goes on. I do not have the strength to deal with the problem of Mary Anne at home. It's taking everything I have to face my own problem. I have nothing left to spare for anyone else."

Before he could answer, the phone rang. With one eye on Barbara, he reached behind him on the kitchen wall and picked it up. "Mary Anne?" he said hopefully.

"Dad? Somebody's going to take me home."

"Where are you?" he demanded. Then he said, "I guess I know where you are."

"Where?" She sounded curious.

"You're with . . . Brad," he said. She didn't say anything. He knew he had hit home.

"How did you know?" she asked.

Despite himself, he almost started to smile. He knew her, he knew her better than she imagined. "I just figured you were," he said.

"I'll be home later," she said.

"When?" he demanded. But she had hung up.

She walked in at five; he had left the door open for her. She had on a blue jogging outfit. She looked flustered, a little disheveled.

Automatically he stole a glance at Barbara, who looked pale and grim. Probably this was bringing back a lot of bad memories. And then he had a bad thought. He was surprised that it hadn't occurred to him before, it seemed so obvious. Barbara's cancer—had it come from this, this *strain?* He had heard that stress played a part in disease, and he didn't doubt it. Barbara had been under terrible pressure. But would they ever know? Probably not, he thought. He tried to shake off the nagging doubts. They had a lot to deal with here.

He motioned Mary Anne into the kitchen and to a chair at the table. Above her on a ledge along the wall sat two toy Hess oil trucks, still in their boxes. He had bought them the previous Christmas at Hess stations. Cops at the precinct had told him they made good collectibles, they'd be worth something someday. He thought he'd save them for Mary Anne's kids. Would she ever have kids? he wondered.

"What happened?" DeGregorio asked.

She told him about her accumulated guilt, the chair, how Fran probably gave her up, her and Brad and all the other crimeys, about the fire drill that gave her a chance to split. She'd walked to Caldor's and called Brad. He picked her up with his friend Steve, who had also split Apple.

He nodded. They'd discovered her hookup. He'd been afraid of that.

"And you remember about the pen? By mistake I took the pen?" Mary Anne said. "Someone else saw it. I should have given it up then, but for some reason I didn't admit it."

Yeah, he said, he remembered. "It became a symbol of something," he ventured. "That's what came out, dealing with all this guilt. The pen was the straw that broke the camel's back."

Mary Anne nodded vigorously. She seemed to be encouraging him to go on, he thought, as if he alone understood her. They had something going here, she and he. "They said, 'You're on contract— no visit,' " she continued. "That's when I barged into Lisa's office and yelled at her. I got knocked down to level one."

"We know all that," Barbara said dryly. He could see that Barbara was looking at them suspiciously.

Mary Anne shifted slightly in her seat and continued to address him, ignoring Barbara. "I've been there fifteen months," Mary Anne said. "I'm okay now."

He could see that she was focusing on him. Barbara was watching her stonily.

Mary Anne started to cry. "I've been there fifteen months already," she sniffled. "I learned a lot. I'm not going to take drugs again."

"I believe that," DeGregorio said.

"My teachers believe I can stay straight," she continued, blowing her nose in a napkin from the table.

"Mary Anne, I know you're not going to take drugs again," he said. "You're not there now to learn not to take drugs. You're there to learn everything else so you'll never be set up again."

The ringing phone distracted them.

It was someone from Apple for Mary Anne. He handed her the phone. She stretched the cord around the door frame to talk privately in the dining room.

He saw Barbara's eyes rake him with fury. "You're blind," she whispered angrily. "You're being stroked. You know what's going on? She knows how to push your buttons. She's got you believing she can stay home now."

He recoiled under her onslaught. She was relentless. "We all made an agreement when Mary Anne went in to Apple not to lie to each other again because when Mary Anne was here we were all lying to each other. When you're living with a person who is using drugs and you're trying to protect her, you're lying to her. You were hiding things from me. I wasn't telling you certain things not to aggravate you. And Mary Anne was lying to both of us."

Barbara, looking to make sure that Mary Anne was still on the phone, said, "We told her the day we took her to Apple, 'You don't come home till you finish Apple.' That still stands."

"No," DeGregorio said, confusingly, "You're right."

Mary Anne hung up the phone and sat down again.

"Mary Anne," he said pleadingly, with a glance at Barbara, "I know you're not going to take drugs again, but you have to go back to Apple."

Mary Anne put her head down on the table and whimpered. She didn't want to go back.

Barbara motioned to him to be silent. "Mary Anne," she said quietly, "if you decide not to go back to Apple, what's the rest of your life going to be? What are you going to do tomorrow?"

DeGregorio chimed in, "You have no job, no skills. You can't hang around with your friends at Kings Park if you're going to be straight."

Mary Anne picked her head up. "I'm going to try to get my high school diploma," she said.

He snorted. "Where are you going to get that?" At Apple they didn't let you leave until you had your diploma, a waiting job, a car, and $1,500 in the bank. That gave you a running start. You at least had a shot, he thought. She probably needed another six months there to graduate. If she landed on the street now, she'd be right back where she started.

He looked at Barbara and drew strength. "Remember, Mary Anne," he said, "at the last family group Lisa said, 'Listen, kid. Someday you're going to have a spot in the staff parking lot here.' Do you think she says that to everyone? Can't you read between the lines? They like you. You're likable. You have a good personality, and it's easy for people to like you. They want you out of the dark side. You could be a great force . . ."

The phone rang again. It was Lisa. Mary Anne talked to her quietly awhile. As soon as she hung up, it rang again. It was Londi. Then Lisa called again. Mary Anne was crying on the phone. When she came back she said, "They want me to give up my guilt. They want a meeting in the office tomorrow. They said I could stay here tonight."

It was already nearly ten. "Well," he said, "as long as you're here, you might as well see Grandma and Grandpa."

Next door, Anne took one look at Mary Anne and broke down, hugging and kissing her. Kathy and Ralph came over from their house. "Why not let her stay home awhile?" Kathy asked.

"No," Ralph disputed her. "Take her back to Apple immediately."

Going back seemed to terrify her, DeGregorio saw. "Do you know what's going to happen to me when I go back?" she said tearfully.

"They're not going to shoot you, Mary Anne," DeGregorio said. "They're not going to hang you in the basement. Do you think they do that much when you split? You think they want you to stay there forever? They want you to graduate from there. They want you to make it. These people like you. You're going to deal with it."

"I want to call Brad," she said.

They returned home to call. Mary Anne was on the phone for a few minutes.

Barbara put her hand to her head. "I'm going upstairs," she said.

He told Barbara he'd be up later. He'd talk to Mary Anne awhile. "Look at Chrissy," he said when they were alone, "and other friends your age. They split several times. They're coordinators now. Do you mean to say they can do it and you can't?" He had had his second wind, and Barbara had given him strength. "You know, Mary Anne," he said, "in life there are consequences. The only way you can handle something you're afraid of is to face up to it and fight it because one of these days you're going to run into something you can't run away from. You won't have a choice but to face it. This is how you learn to face things you fear."

Mary Anne seemed to go slack, and suddenly she looked drained. "I'm tired," she said. "I'm going to bed."

He followed her up the stairs and waited on the dark landing. When he heard her come out of the bathroom, get into her bed, and click off the light, he walked into her room and sat down on the bed. He could see her outline against the window.

She looked up from the covers, surprised and a little embarrassed. "What are you doing?" she asked.

"I'm tucking you in," he said.

"Get out of here, Daddy!" she said, gigglingly swinging the pillow at him and missing.

He bent down and tucked the covers under her chin, as he remembered doing when she was little. He kissed her and got up to go.

"Dad?"

"Yeah, sweetheart?"

"I missed out on a lot in my childhood."

He moved back to the bed and sat down. "I know you did, sweetheart. We both missed out on a lot. But does that mean we should miss out on the rest of our lives? I told you before, this has to stop with you. You can't dwell on the past. All this addictive personality stuff has to stop. Whatever we lost in the past, we're going to make up."

He fell silent a moment. "You know those Hess trucks downstairs, the fire engine and the gas truck? They're for my grandchildren. That's what I'm looking forward to. We're going to make up for all that lost time, but you have to get your head together."

Then he changed his mind. "We'll never make up for anything," he said. "We'll just go on with our lives, and we'll be normal again. You have a big family here if you want to come back into it."

31

"How's this?"

DeGregorio came downstairs in a powder blue tweed jacket over tan chinos, a blue shirt, and unknotted navy-striped tie. He didn't know what to wear for the graduation. He guessed he should wear a jacket and tie, but it could get warm in the auditorium. He turned around slowly for Barbara.

She made a face. "Awful," she said. "Lose the pants."

He went back upstairs and changed into a pair of gray dress slacks.

"That's better," Barbara said. She was wearing a gray silk suit, her one outfit for all good occasions. Her red wig looked just like her own hair. It was starting to grow back since she had finished her chemo in April.

He nodded and tried to jam his hands into his jacket pockets. They didn't open. Didn't they give you real pockets anymore? "Damn," he said. "No pockets."

Barbara looked at him. "How long have you had that jacket?"

"I don't know, a couple of years." He didn't remember when he bought it.

She got scissors and snipped the pockets open.

"Do we have time for a glass of wine?" he said. "They won't have any wine there."

"We have time," she said. "Kathy will probably be late anyway."

Joe dropped by. "Well, he said, "is she going to be all right?"

"She'll be all right," Barbara said. "I just have a good feeling about that."

"You're confident?"

"I don't know," Barbara said. "It's an instinct I have being around her and talking to her. There's no feeling of sneakiness about her. There's a feeling of honesty. She's trying. There's nothing you can put your finger on. Her goals are normal. She's eighteen. She wants to go to cosmetology school and eventually own her own shop and have her own apartment."

"Her mother was a hairdresser," Joe remembered.

"It's a field that interests her," Barbara said. "Her cousin Annie is so vivacious and glamorous, and Mary Anne emulates that. She's more family-oriented now."

Joe chuckled. "I hope she meets the right guy."

"That's a normal worry," Barbara said, "instead of worrying whether we'll get a phone call one night that she's dead. That's not a normal thing to be worried about."

The phone rang. "Kathy's ready," DeGregorio shouted.

"Tell her we'll come by," Barbara said.

The vast Smithtown High School parking field was already three-quarters full when they joined a long file of cars fanning into spots. They parked and began trudging to the school building in the distance. A soft spring breeze ruffled the trees. Barbara buttoned her jacket.

In the auditorium they slid into a forward row of plush orange seats facing the stage and a curtain of midnight blue. Ushers, kids with scrubbed faces and slicked-down hair, handed out programs.

apple

Institute

A Program Planned for Life Enrichment

proudly presents its

18th Annual Commencement

featuring

APPLE'S GRADUATES FOR 1990

Wednesday, June 6, 1990

The lights dimmed, and Roberto Tirado, Long Island's favorite Channel Twelve television weatherman, bounded out, adjusting his tie mike. "In about four minutes we're going to be on the air!" he announced with breathless excitement. "You're all going to be on TV! As we do the weather, the curtain opens and all of Long Island can see the graduates. Okay, Logan?"

Throughout the theater a low roar of cheers and applause began building to a crescendo, crashing like a wave when Roberto Tirado intoned: "Ladies and Gentlemen, the Apple graduating class of 1990! Let's open the curtain and look at them! Boy oh boy oh boy!"

DeGregorio squinted, searching the ranks of kids who were sitting on folding chairs facing out. The boys were in white tuxedo suits. He skipped over them.

"There she is!" He gripped Barbara's arm. He could feel his eyes watering. In the glow of the stagelights, Barbara's eyes seemed to glisten too.

"I see her!" Barbara whispered back.

She was in the front row near the middle, in a pink gown, her light brown hair frosted, styled, and sprayed. She sat stiffly, with both feet planted on the stage, staring out with an expression of faint bemusement mixed with boredom.

"Oh, she looks beautiful," Barbara said.

DeGregorio nodded, dumbstruck.

"I knew one day I would play the Palace," Roberto Tirado announced.

DeGregorio only half-followed the welcoming remarks of Muriel Farkas, Apple's earthy and yet elegant executive vice president, and her introduction of the first guest speaker, New York State's Lieutenant Governor Stan Lundine, a folksy-looking politician whom she, in her excitement, inadvertently identified as the Attorney General.

DeGregorio, distracted, was thinking about the December day they had brought Mary Anne back to Apple after her split. They met in Bobby Alberti's office with Bobby, Londi, Brad, and the other crimeys, Fran, Bill, and Gary. DeGregorio felt ashamed. He had enabled her, he realized; he had kept her guilty secret. After everything, had he learned anything? But what was he supposed to do, give her up? What would any father do?

Bobby knew about everything—Brad, the hookup, even Ray.

But he wanted to hear about Ray directly from Mary Anne. She told the story—how he had tried to kiss her, how he had said he wanted to marry her, how he had jealously piled contracts on Brad until Brad split. Bobby just listened. When she finished, he said, "Did Ray tell you he had AIDS?"

"AIDS!" DeGregorio was repulsed. The one who had kissed his daughter said he had *AIDS?* What if he'd . . . *Ugh!*

"I heard that," Mary Anne said calmly, "but he said he didn't." She paused.

"He also said he shot dope at Apple," she said quietly.

"What?" Bobby said.

"Heroin," Mary Anne said. "He told me he did."

They all fell silent. "He's history," Bobby said. "He's out of here."

DeGregorio was amazed. All this went on just like that? "How can something like this happen?" he asked.

"That's why we have guilt meetings," Bobby said. "They look trivial, but they're a big deal in the house."

Bobby didn't say much more. He told Londi to drive Mary Anne back to the adolescent house and to talk to Lisa. Lisa would write Mary Anne a contract. It was heavy, Mary Anne told her father later, but not as bad as it could have been. Three eighteen-hour work details, three weeks' loss of privileges, a seminar, and two compositions, one to be read in group.

But it had turned out well, DeGregorio thought. Whatever she had had to go through to get it all out of her system, she seemed to have done it. Maybe she had needed the split to test her limits, to show herself how far she could fall before finally pulling herself up. But was it her last fall? Would it be? After what they had been through, he was almost afraid to hope. She had learned a lot, he was sure of that and could see it in her. She had learned to minimize her emotions, to stop *awfulizing*, as he had heard them say so often at family group. It wasn't *events* that caused suffering, it was how you reacted to the events. If you didn't think something was so terrible, then it wasn't.

You had to learn, train yourself, to deal rationally with irrational fears. Mary Anne had gotten that now. What he still didn't understand was why Mary Anne? Other kids' parents separated. Other kids came from homes with alcoholism and had people in the family die, and they turned out okay. Why not Mary Anne? He drank.

Why didn't he become an alcoholic? That part he didn't understand at all. But he did know that what had helped her was the family's sticking together. All those visits, all those letters. Mary Anne had to realize how many people loved her, how much she meant to them. Sometimes he thought she was pulled through by the sheer power of all their love. Joe had set the tone for the family from the beginning, but in the end they didn't do it. She did it for herself. And she was going to have to keep doing it. He wasn't going to be around forever. She'd be on her own one day.

DeGregorio shook off his thoughts and focused on Lundine, whose boyish face beamed with determination and hope as he denounced the drug scourge, citing his work as head of Governor Mario Cuomo's drug abuse council. "We face a hard struggle," Lundine affirmed, his Buffalo-region accent ringing quaintly foreign. "Drug abuse has taken a terrible toll in New York. How many lives have been destroyed by heroin? How many brilliant futures cut short by crack? How many communities suffered devastating effects because of drug-related crime and disease?" It was a rhetorical question, but he answered it anyway. "Too many families—far too many."

DeGregorio didn't have to be told. But he listened as Lundine hit an upbeat note: "Today we have reason for hope. Today we have reason to celebrate. Today we are honoring Apple and its graduates who are winning their personal war with drugs. Today, the sixth day of June, happens to be a famous day of history. It happens to be an important day. You know why?"

DeGregorio tried to remember what had happened on June 6. The rest of the auditorium was mum.

"This is a young audience," Lundine observed. "It is D-Day! Forty-six years ago, Allied armies landed on the coast of France against Adolf Hitler. We won that war, and I say we can win this war on drugs too!"

Cheers erupted from the back, and DeGregorio found himself clapping with the rest.

"We can put an end to death and destruction," Lundine continued. "Let's declare June sixth, 1990, as the new D-Day. We can call it Drug Day. We can renew our commitment to freeing people from the slavery of drug addiction. We know that treatment works. Sometimes it takes more than one try before a drug-addicted person is able to overcome drug addiction, but we know that treatment works."

DeGregorio searched out Mary Anne on stage. She was still impassive, her gaze fixed on the middle distance. Did she see them there? He wondered what was going through her mind.

Lundine seemed to be winding down now. "I know that each of you has faced personal challenges during your time at Apple. Some of you have suffered setbacks. But even if it seemed sometimes to be impossible, you have reached inside yourselves. You've discovered your strengths. You stuck to it one day at a time. And now you have won! I know it took a difficult struggle to win your battle with drugs, but your victory gives hope to society that each of you has done it and that we can do it as a society. We can and will rid our society of drugs! Remember, today is D-Day. Today is Apple Day. Today we join hands in the battle against drugs!"

The room erupted again into cheers, and once again DeGregorio found himself clapping.

". . . and don't they look beautiful dressed up like that?" Roberto Tirado had bounded onstage again.

DeGregorio was focusing so intently on Mary Anne that he didn't see the next speaker mount the podium. When he looked up, Joe Morris of the New York Giants, his bulging frame stuffed into a dark suit, was responding to the loudest cheering of the afternoon.

Modestly, the star halfback tried to contain the uproar. "The people you should be clapping for are the people on stage now," he said in a low, authoritative voice. He waited for the tumult to subside and displayed an upraised hand to the audience. "In my sport," he said, "the achievement of everything is this little ring I wear on my finger. It's a Super Bowl ring. That's what you achieve." The crowd stirred with admiration, but he didn't pause to acknowledge it. "Super Bowls fade and they don't last. Other people win these things." His hands swept the stage. "But what these people up here achieve will be with them the rest of their life. They have enhanced their lives."

The crowd was cheering again, and this time Joe Morris joined in, clapping. "I applaud them for being the true athlete—someone who works toward a prize. It is greater than any goal, any cup, any medals they ever receive." Once again bedlam erupted, subsiding only when Joe Morris held up a hand for quiet. He dropped his voice for emphasis. "But life is the most important test you ever face. Being a football player is simple, but going through life is a very difficult thing, and being affected by drugs or alcohol is an even greater challenge." Now he raised his voice dramatically. "I'm proud to share the stage with them, and I'd like to give *them* a round of applause!" The crowd was on its feet, stamping, cheering, and whistling. Joe Morris raised his fists in a victory salute and strode briskly offstage.

"Are we ready for the graduation now?" Roberto Tirado was back at the rostrum, introducing Londi, who was beaming as the greeting of the house shook the walls: *Huh-huh-huh-huh-huh-huh-huh!* The uproar drowned out all but the end of her salute. ". . . all the love in the world, especially my aftercare graduates. I love you."

Bobby, a head shorter but resplendent in a tuxedo, joined his wife at the mike, inciting a new outburst of cheering. "This is a special night," he began, "because it shows that drug treatment with a lot of care can work." DeGregorio automatically thought of the red Porsche. "It's special to the young kids up there"—Bobby pointed to the right rear section of nongraduating residents, who whooped in response—"because it gives you some hope this is not just a dream. It's a reality. You just have to put in hard work." He now turned his impish face to the graduates. "You found the courage to confront your problems and eliminate fears, and you end up on stage," he said. "You managed to make it here. I got to give you my respect and another round of applause." Once again he led the clapping.

Lisa, her tangled black locks glistening in the spotlight, now took over the mike, as bubbly as a graduate herself, calling names. And soon they were standing up, one after the other, swaggering or mincing self-consciously to the podium, each offering a little verbal snapshot of their journey:

I REMEMBER THE SIGN IN THE RIC AREA THAT STATES, YOU ALONE MUST DO IT, BUT YOU CAN'T DO IT ALONE. . . .

I DIDN'T BELIEVE IN MYSELF AND THEY TAUGHT ME HOW. . . .

ME BEING UP HERE IS AN AMAZEMENT. . . .

EVEN WHEN I GAVE UP ON MYSELF, THEY DIDN'T GIVE UP ON ME. . . .

MY FATHER DIED OF CANCER LAST YEAR WHEN I WAS IN THE PRO-GRAM, AND I KNOW HE'S LOOKING DOWN ON ME AND SMILING. . . .

I FEEL LIKE I'M HIGH AND I DIDN'T EVEN TAKE ANYTHING. . . .

THEY SHOWED ME EVEN IF I MAKE MISTAKES, I'M NOT A BAD PERSON. . . .

DeGregorio scanned the ranks of graduates for other faces he knew, looking automatically for Chrissy's golden mane and then remembering why she was not there. One day at Apple she had cut her wrists. She had recovered but was ejected from the program. He remembered what Mary Anne had found out when she returned to Apple after her split: Chrissy had been at an upstairs window in the house and saw Mary Anne walking off the property. She'd gone tearing down the fire escape, running to the edge of the property, screaming, "Mary Anne! Mary Anne! Come back!" But the wind was blowing the wrong way, and Mary Anne had too big a head start. She never heard Chrissy, not that she would have turned back anyway. When he heard the story it touched DeGregorio. In their way, these kids knew what love was.

Lisa paused in the roll call.

"Before I introduce this young lady," she said, "I'd just like to say to her father, Pat: Thanks for trusting us."

DeGregorio stiffened in his seat, gripping the velvet armrest to steady himself. He felt tears welling. He swiped his eyes with a tweedy sleeve.

"Mary Anne DeGregorio!"

She got up, wobbled for a moment on her high heels, and stepped to the mike next to Lisa. "Uh . . . when I . . ."

"Yay, Mary Anne!" came a raucous cheer from the back, echoed by other yells of triumph. They built to a roar—yaaaAAAAYYYYY!

Flustered, she waited for them to subside. "When I first came to Apple," she began in a timid monotone, "I was a scared little girl who was trying to find my identity. I fought for things I believed in and I didn't let anyone in. With the help of my peers and the staff I learned how to find out what I was looking for. That was almost two years ago. Now I can proudly say I made it."

In the darkness, DeGregorio felt Barbara grip his hand and squeeze it.

"I would like to thank Lisa Leshaw for helping me when I was going through my hard times and for caring and being a true friend, Londi Alberti, Bobby Jo, Jennifer Eldridge, Tony Cicerani. . . . I would also like to thank the rest of the staff and my peers for all their support, and most important, my father. I love you, Dad."

32

"WHO needs? C'mon, I have some well done here. Folks, please. Patty, another?"

DeGregorio smiled. Everyone had already turned down fifth and sixth helpings. Still, his father wasn't giving up. Screened behind clouds of sizzling meat smoke, a red barbecue apron stretched over his impressive girth, Joe was juggling burgers and franks flaming on the grill.

Labor Day, 1990, had united the family as usual at Joe and Anne's for a traditional barbecue. He and Mary Anne were over from next door and Ralph and Kathy were there from the other side with Joey, Chris, and Jimmy. Their brother Louis was there, even their brother Joey was up from Florida with his girlfriend. Luisa couldn't make it, and Barbara begged off because she had to work a three-to-eleven.

Despite everything, DeGregorio thought, they had a lot to be thankful for. Mary Anne was doing fine. After being graduated from Apple, she was even on the outdoor stage for the June graduation from Kings Park High School. They had all gone to see her. She was doing so well that they felt comfortable leaving her home in August while they took a two-week vacation on their own, down to the Bahamas with a side trip to Disney World where they linked up with Mike and Michelle. Joe and Anne could keep an eye on Mary Anne; this time they weren't worried.

Now Mary Anne was halfway through her training at Wilfred Academy. When she finished in February, she'd look for a job in a hair salon. Her cousin Annie said they'd probably be glad to take

Mary Anne in the shop where she worked in Bensonhurst if Mary Anne didn't mind commuting. Barbara had completed her chemotherapy. Next month she'd start reconstructive surgery. She'd need a couple of operations, but the doctors were optimistic. DeGregorio knew now what he didn't know before: She'd been terrified about the surgery. She had put on a front for him, letting him believe she was stoic and confident. That was ridiculous. Of course she'd been panicked. What woman wouldn't have been? But he didn't realize that at the time. He thought she was being brave. He was always surprised by what he didn't know.

Like the business with Jimmy.

They had bought Mary Anne a car, a used 1985 white Buick. She needed wheels, some means of transportation, to complete the program. If she was going to stay straight, Apple figured, she needed a job, and she couldn't get and keep a job without a way to get to it. So a car was part of the graduation requirement, and that's what many of the kids saved for. He had made it easier for her by picking one out and surprising her with it. Someday she could pay them back. She had taken driver's ed at Apple, and with a good word from the counselors, the state had dropped the old hit-and-run charges. Mary Anne would start off with a clean record.

She was excited to have her own car and spent the first weeks driving around to all her friends. One Sunday, she said, she was going to see Chrissy, who was home now. She had never gone back to Apple but had stayed off drugs. They were still friends, but they were growing apart. Mary Anne had different interests now.

She called him from the road. The car had broken down. "Where are you, sweetheart?" he said, "I'll pick you up." He cursed the used car, he thought angrily, already breaking down. Later, DeGregorio visited the car in the shop. "I hope you can fix it quick," he told the headless body poking under the hood. "I just got it for my daughter for graduation. She needs it to get to beauty school."

"Workin' on it," the mechanic grunted. He pulled his head out to wipe his grimy hands.

"Hey," DeGregorio said, looking at him for the first time. "Jimmy!" He'd been at Apple with Mary Anne; he'd been a chief at one point, DeGregorio remembered. He thought Mary Anne had told him Jimmy was going out with Chrissy.

"Oh, hello, Mr. DeGregorio," he said, recognizing him. He looked away, maybe embarrassed.

DeGregorio suddenly remembered. "You split, didn't you?"

"Guess so," he mumbled.

DeGregorio felt a stirring of compassion. "How's it going?"

"Okay. I got thrown out of my house."

"You did? Where are you living?"

"In my car."

He and Barbara talked about it at dinner, while Mary Anne was out visiting friends. Barbara said she thought it was pathetic, a kid living in his car. "How can we know a homeless person?" she asked. Homeless people were winos in the city, not kids Mary Anne's age on the island. "You want to let him stay here?" she asked. "He can sleep in the basement."

He went back to the garage and invited Jimmy over. He moved in with a few paper bags of belongings after work the next day. "If you can take care of lawns," DeGregorio said, "I can get you some work, sixty dollars a day." Between Joe and Ralph and the neighbors, they'd find Jimmy plenty to do.

He was scooping his wallet and keys off the bureau a few days later when he remembered that he ought to leave Barbara some cash. He started to take out some bills, then stopped, confused. He had only $19 there, and he thought he had about $70. He shrugged. He must have spent it somewhere.

That night, undressing for bed, Barbara went into the closet and gasped. "Some of my jewelry is missing," she said.

DeGregorio felt a stab of panic. "Are you sure?"

"I don't know," she said. "I can't find it."

"Maybe Mary Anne . . ." He was going to say "borrowed it," but the words stuck in his throat as a sickening thought hit him. *O God, no, please no, don't tell me it's starting again!*

"I don't think Mary Anne stole it to get high, if that's what you're thinking," Barbara said.

"No," he rushed to agree, shamed by his immediate suspicions. "But then what?"

The ringing phone interrupted them.

"Oh, Mr. DeGregorio . . ." He recognized Chrissy's high trill.

"Mary Anne's not here, Chrissy."

"We got burglarized today. You know what they took? They took . . ."

He figured it out. DeGregorio took the stairs two at a time down to the basement. He wasn't there. He raced back up and ran outside. Jimmy's car was in front of the house. A dark form was curled up in the backseat.

DeGregorio wrenched open the door. "Get out of the fucking car!" he shouted. "I know what you've been up to. You went down the fucking sewer."

Jimmy struggled blearily awake. "Yeah, I fucked up everything," he mumbled.

"Damn straight! Now get your shit and get the fuck out of here! You did steal Chrissy's two VCRs, didn't you?"

"Yeah."

"And you hocked them. Where'd you hock them, Lindenhurst?"

"No."

"No?"

"Amityville."

"What are you on?"

"Crack."

"You piece of shit. Everything was offered to you. Nothing was asked of you. Now you're going to jail."

He went back inside the house and called Chrissy's mother. "Call the detectives," he said. "Yeah, have them call me. . . . Yeah, I have him here. . . . Yeah, they can come and take him."

Jimmy went off to jail. DeGregorio felt like a jerk. He thought that after everything he had learned something. Could anybody just get over on him? Maybe you never learned, maybe you had to figure out each situation as it came. He didn't know what to think anymore.

"Last call!" His father was pointing the barbecue fork at them one by one, trying to drum up customers for a final incinerated frank. He was in great spirits, DeGregorio thought. He made the rounds of the grandchildren, stopping to talk and kid around with each one. When he got to Mary Anne, he hugged her and said, "I'm very proud of you. You're great. I love you, I love you a lot."

The sun was getting low. DeGregorio said good-bye and crossed the backyard to go home. Mary Anne said she'd stay a little while.

They were in the house a few minutes when Chris came running over, breathless. "Something's wrong with Grandpa," he said.

DeGregorio, alarmed, dropped some old mail he was leafing through and sprinted back next door.

He found Joe in the den lying on the loveseat. On the bookshelves over his head were rows of photo albums, every trip Joe and Anne had ever taken, marked with the dates.

"Dad!"

There was no response. Mary Anne looked ashen. "He said he had a little gas," she said. "Me and Grandma said, 'Take an Alka-Seltzer.'"

"Take care of Grandma. Keep her out of here," DeGregorio commanded. He eased his father onto the floor, rolled him on his back, and began CPR, the way he remembered it from his police training: *Open the airway, tilt head, lift chin, look at the chest for movement, listen for breathing, feel for breathing. No breathing! Clear the airway, two quick breaths, feel for the pulse. Quick, find the carotid artery, feel for the pulse. No pulse!* "Joey!" he called his brother, "call nine-one-one!" *Circulation! Chest compressions!* He found the sternum and locked his fingers, pressing the heel of his hand on his father's large chest. *One-and-two-and-three-and-four* . . . He did ten compressions and two rescue breaths, ten compressions and two more rescue breaths.

Joe stirred and opened his eyes. He tried to say something, slurring his words. It's a heart attack, DeGregorio thought. It's a stroke! The ambulance wailed up, and the crew bundled Joe into a stretcher and lifted him out. DeGregorio jumped into the ambulance, shouting for Joey to follow with Ma in the car. They were going to St. John's Hospital in Smithtown.

Kathy yelled that she'd call ahead. She was a nurse at St. John's and knew all the doctors. She'd see who was on and get the best one. Mary Anne said she'd pick up her cousin Joey at Romeo's Pizzeria where he worked and meet them at the hospital. She'd call Barbara at sex crimes and tell her to meet them at the hospital.

They paced outside the emergency room, jumping each time the door flapped open. Finally the doctor came out. It was an aneurysm, he said, a ballooning of an artery carrying blood to the stomach. He would need an operation quickly. After they stabilized him, the doctor said, they'd operate that night or the next day.

Anne started crying. DeGregorio clutched her. "He'll be all right, Ma," he said soothingly. "Dad's tough."

They took turns standing vigil. When they heard the operation had gone all right, they said they'd see him in the morning.

The next day they regrouped in the waiting room. The doctor came over, somber. He needed a second operation, the doctor said. He was bleeding into his liver. They'd have to do it right away.

DeGregorio and Anne waited nine hours, joined by Barbara, Mary Anne, and other grandchildren, Ralph and Kathy, and shifting groups of Joe's brothers, sisters, and cousins who had been rallied by phone from around the country. Luisa had flown up from Florida.

Finally he was wheeled out. They ran to the gurney. He looked ghostly. His eyes were flat and dull, and his large nose, which had always given his face a jolly, robust animation, now poked ominously from sunken cheeks. He seemed to recognize Anne and tried to smile. "I love you," he rasped. "Thanks for everything."

Trailed by relatives, they wheeled him into intensive care while DeGregorio went to talk to the doctor. "We have to wait and see," the doctor said. "The blood has stopped leaking into the liver, but there may have been damage. It might be too late." DeGregorio nodded grimly. What he had expected.

They had to take turns going in, two by two. DeGregorio and Anne went in first. Joe was on a respirator. His color was awful, DeGregorio thought, yellow. The liver had to be failing.

DeGregorio didn't know what to say and was afraid he'd break down. His father had always been there for him, the strength of the family. "I'm not ready for this, Dad," he said.

Joe moved his head slightly and seemed to wink. DeGregorio wondered, did he understand? What was he trying to say?

Mary Anne went in and came out red-eyed. "I told him, 'We love you,'" she said. "He didn't move, he didn't say anything." DeGregorio hugged her. "I thought he was going to be all right," she whimpered, "I feel so bad. He helped me a lot." She started bawling. "I was gone for two years, and then I get home and this happens."

He hung on for nearly two weeks, comatose. A doctor who had treated Joe for many years told DeGregorio, "There's nothing more to do, Pat. He's not going to get well."

What was he saying? DeGregorio thought he knew, but he wanted it spelled out.

"I know your father a long time," the doctor said. "This is not him. It's not human to keep him alive like this. He's dead already. It's only the machine. You have to make a decision."

He told his mother and Luisa. They were horrified. *They* were supposed to turn off life support? What if he rallied? What about a miracle? There could be a miracle. Miracles happened.

No, he argued. The doctor was right, it wasn't fair to Pop. He wouldn't want to be this way. He was always so full of life. How could they let him lie there like that? Pop was always practical. He'd be the first to agree.

Luisa said she wanted to go in one last time. When she came out, she was resigned. "It's okay," she said, wiping away tears. "It's okay, he gave me a sign." She said she had stood by the bed saying, "Dad, tell me anything. Tell me if we're doing the right thing. Give me a sign." He opened his eyes then, she said. "I feel at peace now," she said.

They signed the papers and drove home, gathering at Joe and Anne's house. DeGregorio made coffee. The phone rang. He answered and listened a minute. Then he said for all to hear. "He's gone."

"Good of you to come. . . . So good of you to come." DeGregorio stood in the vestibule of the Clayton Funeral Home clasping the hands of a steady strem of mourners who filed out of cars in the parking lot off Indian Head Road and snaked up the porch steps of the comfortingly small town mortuary. Joe had lots of friends in Kings Park, he thought. Some of the old Bensonhurst crowd was there too.

In the back, in a carpeted room filled with flowers, Joe was laid out in an open coffin. He wore a dark suit and a serene expression. He seemed, DeGregorio thought, simply at peace.

Mary Anne in a white blouse and black skirt that Barbara had bought for her greeted mourners politely, thanking them for coming. DeGregorio was proud when they said to him afterward how mature she was, what a fine young lady she'd become. She had been out of the house when the call from the hospital came. Her cousin Annie was getting married, and her friends had arranged a shower. Mary Anne had said she didn't feel like going, that she would spend all her time at the hospital. She wanted to be thinking of Grandpa, not parties, but Anne insisted. Grandpa would have wanted her to go. Her aunt Connie showed up unexpectedly at the shower. "Come," she said to Mary Anne, "we have to go." Mary Anne was surprised because the party wasn't half over yet. Grandpa died, Connie said. Mary Anne was so upset, she couldn't drive. Her uncle had to drive her car home, and she rode home with Connie.

DeGregorio comforted mourners at the wake, recalling Joe's words in June at Mary Anne's graduation from Kings Park High School. "If the Good Lord took me tomorrow, I'd say it's time to go," he'd said. "Everything looks beautiful."

"You know," DeGregorio said, "in the last days we all got a little signal from him. As if he touched everyone before he died. He told Mary Anne he was proud of her, he loved her. He told my mother, thanks for everything. He opened his eyes for Luisa. I was looking at him when he winked at me and smiled and shook his head. I think he always prepared me to be in charge of the family."

Epilogue

THERE are many more chapters in the lives of Pat De-Gregorio, Mary Anne and Barbara—they are writing new ones every day. Where their story may take them tomorrow is impossible to predict, but it can be said that nearly two years after finishing her drug treatment program, four years after reluctantly entering Apple, eight years after her first experiments with whiskey and marijuana as a sixth and seventh grader, Mary Anne remained clean: recovering or recovered—take your pick. In that sense Mary Anne beat the odds. She was the one out of four who successfully made it through the Apple program and aftercare. And on a hot June afternoon in 1990, two weeks after graduating from Apple, Mary Anne joined Chrissy and 269 other teenagers who mounted an outdoor stage to accept their diplomas on the ball field of Kings Park High School. She has since taken some big steps on her own. In December 1990 she picked up her ringing phone to hear a familiar voice she couldn't immediately place. It was Alex. She hadn't seen or talked to him for more than half a year, since she'd left Apple. He had split a few months after she had. He'd made coordinator but then worried he wouldn't be moved up. He came back just before she graduated. He graduated four months later, in September, and was working with his uncle building hydraulic car lifts while living with his grandparents, Alex and Princess, in Brentwood. Now he wanted to get together. They met at a restaurant on Lake Ronkonkoma then drove to Mary Anne's house to watch TV and drink Cokes. He asked her if she was free the next day. Tomorrow became tomorrow and the day after that. In April

1992, Mary Anne moved out of her house to take an apartment with Alex on the ground floor of a private house near Kings Park, sharing the $625-a-month rent. They were inseparable and planned a future together.

Mary Anne was graduated from the Wilfred Beauty Academy, but after working for nearly a year as a shampoo and perm assistant in a Long Island hair salon while waiting for certification as a hairdresser, she decided to switch careers and enrolled in a training program at a nursing home near Smithtown to become a nurse's aide. She later passed the state certification test and was planning further studies to become a licensed practical nurse or health technician.

As for her mother, Mary Anne called her once a month or so and saw her for brief visits several times a year, but otherwise there was little contact. Through therapy Mary Anne had worked out much of her anger; what was left was mainly sadness for her mother.

Two and a half years after her cancer was discovered, two years after she finished her chemotherapy, a year after her last reconstructive surgery, Barbara was continuing her strong recovery. In July 1991 she went back on full duty at the Queens Sex Crimes squad in borough headquarters at the One Hundred and Twelfth, where she'd been posted three years earlier when things were at their worst at home, a few months before Mary Anne had been caught holding the bag by the 7-Eleven. At sex crimes, where detectives had various specialties, Barbara's was children under eleven. With babies who'd been raped or beaten, it was easy to stay motivated. She and Mary Anne had grown close, as close in some ways as mother and daughter. They shared confidences, went out together, shopped together, and like all mothers and daughters, sometimes squabbled. On days off, Barbara often drove in to Whitestone to visit Grace, now a widow; Joe Adametz had died of a heart attack on December 26, 1990, Barbara's thirty-eighth birthday.

And what of DeGregorio? In November 1990, the fall after Mary Anne's graduation from Apple, he was transferred to the Hundred and Thirteenth's robbery investigation program. He accepted the transfer to the bustling eastern Queens precinct as he accepted so much in his life, with a willing shrug. Everything you did in life, he figured, prepared you for the next thing. At Queens robbery in the One Hundred and Ninth, he had worked on the big picture. Now he was working with local people, victims. A consoling and supportive boss, Detective Sergeant Gerard Cassagne, helped him over the blow of Joe's death and the aftermath of the long trauma with Mary Anne. By October 1993 he would be on the job twenty years and could retire at half-pay. But he figured he might wait and put in twenty-five. Barbara would have her twenty in 1999. Maybe he'd wait and they'd retire together. Or maybe not? Who knew?

When Mary Anne said, as he had long known she would someday, that she wanted to move out to a place of her own, he accepted that too, as he had to, but with the pangs of any father. He was proud that she had reached the point where she could leave *for* something, on her own terms, with an apartment, a job, and some savings in the bank. But he was fearful of letting go. And to live with a boy, to move in with Alex? He shrugged. What could he do? It was a sign of the times. He had gone down that path himself, he remembered. He no longer feared for her future. She—they, if that's what she wanted—would make it, he felt sure. One thing he told Mary Anne: when you're in love with somebody, don't just look at the person, look at the whole family. The apple doesn't fall far from the tree, he told her; you're not just marrying a person, you're marrying a family. Alex, he noted, was from a big, loving family, not unlike the DeGregorios.

Despite everything, DeGregorio felt blessed. It could have been a lot worse. They had gone through it all, and they were still together. He and Barbara were closer than ever. She had stayed with him through everything. He could never forget that. They were stronger than other families who hadn't been through what they had. He knew now what was important. If the car didn't start on a cold winter morning it didn't start. It didn't matter. He could take one through the heart and survive.

AUTHOR'S NOTE

This book grew out of a story I wrote for *The New York Times* in September 1989. I had been introduced to Pat DeGregorio a few years earlier while writing a book on the Pizza Connection drug case. As the undercover in Ridgenarc, I found, DeGregorio knew a lot about the street workings of the Sicilian and American Mafia drug trade. I reached out for DeGregorio again in the summer of 1989 when I wanted to know something about police undercover work for a news story I was writing.

We agreed to meet at a restaurant in Flushing, near his station house. Cautiously at first, and then movingly, DeGregorio talked about life undercover, what it was like to live a lie, a life in fear. At one point he mentioned his daughter who was in drug treatment. I stopped him: He had a daughter in drug treatment? After what he had done to expose drug traffickers, a daughter turned to drugs? He said he never thought it was so strange. Lots of kids turn to drugs, and it didn't matter who their parents are. As it turned out, he himself had caught her selling drugs. Suddenly the undercover story didn't seem so important. What I wanted was the story of the narcotics cop and his daughter who sold drugs.

This book would not have been possible without, first and foremost, the participation and cooperation of the DeGregorio family—not just Pat, Mary Anne, and Barbara but Joe, Anne, Ralph, and Louis DeGregorio, Luisa Fiebe, and Antoinette and Al Venditti, who shared their insights so this story could be told. Joe and Grace

Adametz were similarly forthcoming, as were Pat and Barbara's many friends in and out of the Police Department.

I was also fortunate enough to talk to Mary, Pat's first wife. Mary admitted that she had had a drinking problem from which she says she has recovered. She also shared with me the hardship of having grown up in a family of alcoholics and the pain of losing a child and coping with her other troubles. In a few instances, people recalled vividly certain incidents involving Mary, such as Mary's hitting or threatening Mary Anne, that Mary either denies having happened or does not recall.

I am grateful to Logan Lewis, Bobby Alberti, Mark Howard, and Lisa Leshaw, among many other administrators, counselors, and residents of Apple, who told me their stories and let me see how a drug treatment program really works. I have guarded the identity of residents and their families by not using their last names and, in some instances, changing their first names. I have also changed the names of some of Pat's and Mary Anne's friends.

But everyone is a real person. There are no composite characters. Quotes are either each person's best reconstructions of what he or she said at the time or the best reconstructions of others who were present. In latter stages of the story, after Mary Anne entered Apple, I myself was present for some of the events. In the Ridgenarc case, government tape recordings provide verbatim transcripts.

Greg O'Connell, the Ridgenarc prosecutor in the United States Attorney's office in Brooklyn, helped me retrieve the trial transcript and other public records of the case, as did Joel M. Lutwin, the lawyer who successfully defended Calogero (Charlie) Davi. The Police Department answered many questions about day-to-day police operations.

Fred Hills, my editor at Simon & Schuster, provided shrewd counsel and unfailing encouragement at all stages, as did his able associates, Burton Beals, Daphne Bien, Rose Ann Ferrick, and Jennifer Weidman. Gloria Loomis, my agent, was, as always, a powerful advocate and trusted friend. And at the *Times,* metropolitan editor Gerald M. Boyd let me accumulate some blocks of time to write the book.

I have left my greatest debt for last. There are no words to adequately thank my family—my wife, Deborah, our girls, Anna and Sophie, and my late father-in-law, Herb Danto—for their unstinting love and support. I hope this book is in some way a repayment for all their sacrifices.

Ralph Blumenthal
New York, April 1992